The Converts

The Converts

Tereska Torres

Rupert Hart-Davis London 1970

First published in Great Britain 1970 by
Rupert Hart-Davis Ltd
3 Upper James Street
Golden Square
London W1R 4BP

ISBN: 0 2466440 20

Printed in Great Britain by
Compton Printing Ltd London and Aylesbury

To Marek's grandchildren

I would like to thank Lillian and Gerold Frank,

without whose encouragement

this book would not have been written.

Contents

"Most of us live by our group loyalties,

but we have to rise above them,

above our competitive and overlapping loyalties

to the values of humanity which should transcend them

so that we can cooperate and coexist

lest we don't exist at all."

NORMAN THOMAS

in a speech at a college graduation

❦ *Prologue*

I always hate to read about people's dreams in books. Other people's dreams seem boring or irrelevant, but I feel this dream is of such importance for this story that I must not only tell it, it must be put here as a prologue.

. . . Last night I dreamed . . .

I am in a Gothic cathedral in Paris, but the religious ceremony is Jewish, the assembled congregation is composed of Jews, and the prayers are conducted by a rabbi.

Suddenly a group of people enter the cathedral; I recognize them: they are all Jews converted to Catholicism; I know all of them. They form a procession and start singing Christian hymns. I am shocked by this. I feel it is wrong of them to interrupt a Jewish service, even if this service is taking place in a cathedral, but they beckon to me to join them and I know that I have to; I can't abandon them, I belong with them even if I disapprove of this particular action. I mingle with the group, hoping to escape attention among them; instead I find myself pushed to the front line and marching at their head, feeling both ashamed and afraid lest my husband see me there.

On either side of our procession stand rows of Jewish women screaming at us and throwing stones at us. The cathedral-synagogue is filled with angry cries. We make one complete circuit before I manage to escape and rush away. I run as fast as I can to a one-room apartment where I hope to find my husband, but the flat is empty. I sit down and wait.

The door opens. Meyer enters. His face is ghastly and livid, as if he were dead; his eyes are closed. A man supports him on either side. My first thought is that it is all my fault. He must have seen me in the cathedral at the head of the converted Jews and gotten into a fight. He is wounded; if he dies, it will be my fault. I run to him. I cry: "Darling are you hurt? Tell me please, what happened to you? Are you in pain? Please speak to me."

I am struck with horror and I sob, my arms wound around his neck.

At this moment I awake . . .

I dreamed this one night in Israel in the nineteen-sixties. In this dream I stand between two identities, the Catholic and the Jewish, as all my life I have been standing between countries and religions and allegiances. . . .

Part I 🌷 The First Years

I was in kindergarten. It had a beautiful singing name: Montessori. I liked that name—Montessori. My mother told her friends: "Tereska has started school this year; she goes to a Montessori kindergarten."

I was five years old. I lived in Paris. I had been in another school before for a while—I don't remember it clearly, only that I cried and that the teacher sat me on her lap until I stopped.

This new kindergarten was part of a big school called the Collège Sévigné standing in a narrow little street off the Boulevard de Port-Royal. There were many rooms and many floors and children of all sizes going to all these other rooms.

But very soon I knew my room. It was large and quiet and light. I liked it there. It was full of nice things to do: playing with shapes, with colors, touching, dancing, singing. You touched each letter cut out from sandpaper and then the tickling feeling at the tip of your fingers reminded you of the name of the letter. You were blindfolded and the teacher gave you samples of materials to feel: velvet—you recognized it with your fingers, soft purry velvet; silk—liquid, cool silk; cotton—wholesome, neat cotton. When you touched things you found their names. Through physical contact you learned to know. Other games: walking slowly, slowly, holding a cup filled to the brim with water; I didn't spill it, and I was proud.

In that kindergarten I didn't cry, I had a good time, and they called me Thérèse, not like at home: Tereska. I liked the sound of Thérèse. It sounded French. Tereska sounded foreign—and I was not foreign. My father told me I was French. I was born here in Paris after a war people called "the last war," and I had my own passport, a French passport my father used for me each year when we went to Poland to visit my grandparents. My parents had Polish passports, but I had my own French passport. Last summer we had been in Poland; that's why I was late for kindergarten. When we arrived back in Paris, it had already started. All the children were very busy and I didn't know anyone, but the teacher took my hand and went around the room with me, telling my name to everyone and telling me their names.

It had already been snowing in Lodz when we left. But my father had had an exhibition of his sculptures and we had to stay for the exhibition. My mother had put me in my nicest dress to go to the *vernissage*. She called it the *vernissage* even when she spoke Polish, but I knew it was a French word. I always spoke Polish with my grandparents because they didn't know any French. My grandfather Ludovic, my mother's father, was very, very tall and he wore a beard and he smoked cigars and he collected stamps. He was a furrier. In my grandparents' large apartment overlooking Lodz's main street was also the fur store: a room full of closets. When you opened them the smell of furs attacked you like so many wild animals—bears and leopards and beavers and seals.

I didn't usually go there in the daytime, when customers were coming, but in the evenings I would play in the large empty room that smelled of wild animals. Or I would look out the double windows at the street below, at the barefooted little boys running in the rain calling out the headlines from their newspapers: "Pilsudski—Pilsudski." They were always calling that name. My grandparents talked about him too, but I had no idea who he was. I looked down at the old women covered in shawls selling things out of baskets. My aunt Yadja lived across the street and I would wave to her from the windows and she would wave back, but I couldn't hear her voice because the street was very wide.

This aunt was my grandmother's sister; I liked her. She worked in a school for deaf-mute children and she took me there sometimes to play with her charges.

My grandmother Sofia was as small as her husband was tall. Walking together on the street they looked funny, one so tall and the other so small and plump.

My grandmother was always screaming at her poor maids, who were always doing everything wrong. I didn't like her to scream at them like that.

And I didn't like her to kill the flies with the long yellow ribbons of gluey paper that hung in the kitchen. I used to sneak into the kitchen when no one was there, climb on a chair, and unglue the flies one by one. But even then they didn't seem able to fly again, and my grandmother would come back into the kitchen and start screaming at me: "Tereska, get down, you'll fall and break a leg; what are you doing! It's disgusting, how can you touch those dirty things! Go wash your hands! Kácia, Kácia, where are you? Why aren't you watching this child? Come here and clean up this mess."

The only place my grandmother never screamed was at the synagogue. At the end of each summer there were religious holidays and my grandmother and her sister and all her lady friends spent days at the big synagogue. My mother would dress me in my nicest dress again, buy flowers, and take me to the synagogue to bring the flowers to my grandmother. All the ladies sat upstairs, talking to each other in whispers, and they would beam at me and kiss me, and say I was so pretty and looked so French. They said I didn't act so spoiled as their own grandchildren. My aunt would say: "Pani Pinkus, this child is raised in France, you know." I felt that it must be something very special to be raised in France.

I would look at the men's section downstairs where all the men wore white shawls and undulated like waves in the sea as they chanted and prayed.

My grandfather Ludovic was not there because my grandmother said he didn't believe in all that.

🌷 In Paris I had no friends my age. In Poland there were always cousins—but in Paris there were only grownups, until I entered the Montessori kindergarten.

After I had been in school a few days, the teacher came in, holding a new girl by the hand; she had arrived even later than I.

She looked about my age, had very dark hair cut in straight bangs across her forehead, dark eyes, and an extremely serious expression. I didn't pay too much attention to the new girl until the teacher took her hand and pulled her toward me, saying: "Thérèse, here is another little Polish girl; her name is Sonia."

Another little Polish girl! I looked at her, she looked at me— and we instantly hated each other for the same reason. She didn't want to be called "Polish" any more than I did. So I avoided her, I never talked to her, and the pleasures of the beautiful room full of things to touch and smell were spoiled for me. I was still there every day and I could tell velvet from silk with my eyes closed and I could carry a full cup of water without spilling a drop; I now knew the names of all the letters just by looking at them, but always there was that mirror of myself, that Sonia, with her foreign name, who stole quick glances at me, glances also full of reproaches. Why should I be there to spoil things for her?

One day I was walking along a windowless corridor in the school, going on some errand. Suddenly, there was Sonia coming toward me. We were alone in the rather dark corridor—and, without a word, we jumped at each other, hands raised, fingers spread, hissing, scratching, biting. It lasted maybe two minutes. Then we stopped and, without looking at each other, continued in our different directions. After that I remember hating her a little less.

The other big event of that year was that we moved into our first real apartment. Until then we had lived sometimes in my father's studio, where I slept on two chairs tied together, but mostly in one room in a boarding house on Boulevard Raspail.

Now my father was becoming better known. He had more or less stopped painting to work almost exclusively on sculptures. He had started doing bas-reliefs in copper and brass of biblical stories with patriarchs and angels who all looked and dressed like Polish Jews, and these bas-reliefs were selling well. When we three went out together and sat on the terrace of the Dôme, where I had a *baba-au-rhum* while my parents drank *café filtre,* many artists came up to shake hands with my father. He had started having exhibitions of his works in Germany and Paris as well as in Poland.

We could afford to live in an apartment now. It was a six-story walk-up, but it had five large rooms. I had a room all to myself, where I spent hours reading. One of my first books was a large Bible bought for me by my father, illustrated with the *images of d'Epinal.* Each story fascinated me and reminded me of my father's bas-reliefs. I too painted and drew— Bible stories, patriarchs and angels, Jacob and Abraham, Isaac and Sarah. My father admired my paintings and kept each one. Every Sunday we took long walks through the Louvre, where I was bored to death always looking at the same rooms—the rooms my father loved and where he returned again and again—

until I knew each sculpture, each painting, by heart—the Egyptian rooms, the Italian and Flewish primitives. I could recognize each painting by its name and the name of the artist, and before I could read I knew every nail on every toe of every Egyptian pharaoh.

For Easter, during the spring, we went to Lectoure. I had always known this little town in the south, not far from the Pyrénées. There we stayed with two ladies—Mme Dalie, a painter, and her daughter, Mya. They lived in a house half suspended in midair above a vast orchard full of fig and persimmon trees, rows of lettuce and strawberries, flowers and bushes. This garden, the *enclos,* looked like a Bonnard painting.

How I loved Lectoure! It was always warm and full of cats and dogs, chickens and snails, bees and flies; I went everywhere with Mya. She spoke with the singing accent of Gascogne and told me about plants and animals. She loved animals passionately and every stray in Lectoure found refuge in her vast half-suspended house.

The house had many rooms, all standing one after another in a long row. An outdoor corridor ran parallel to these rooms and ended in a sort of round balcony high above the *enclos.* For hours I stood on that balcony, as in the basket of a Montgolfier, feeling the wind pushing me forward toward unknown places.

That year I had my sixth birthday in Poland and at the end of the summer it was time to go back to Paris again. Lots of aunts and uncles and cousins took us to the station. I knew the train so well. For two days and two nights we lived in a compartment; at night, if there was enough room, I would stretch out on its wooden bench and my mother would cover me with a blanket. She and my father sat on the opposite bench. Often it was snowing outside. The train would mutter to itself—takatoum, takatoum, takatoum—and I would listen to its voice until I fell asleep. It was wonderful to be nowhere for two days—between worlds—unbelonging to anything, unburdened. The life on the train was all freedom, with no hours, no duties, only one long dream.

All day I looked out the windows at the running fields and the flying trees. Or I walked all along the train, down endless corridors. There were some very elegant compartments with stuffed seats covered at the head with lace doilies, but they were mostly empty. In our part of the train there were more people and they were eating and sleeping, like us, on the seats of the compartment; each year the train would stop in a town called Frankfurt where, in the station, we would buy a delicious-tasting warm red sausage with mustard on the side, which my father would take in through the window on a paper plate. That warm sausage at Frankfurt was a tradition for us.

My father, my mother, and I were, the three of us—in some way I couldn't explain—alone and separate from the large Polish family—from the grandparents in Lodz with all the furs and the big up-to-the-ceiling white porcelain stoves, the grandparents with the big house with a courtyard in the little village of Zgierz, and all the cousins, so many cousins of all ages. I knew we were different because we lived in Paris and because my father was an artist, had much longer hair than his brothers and brothers-in-law, and wore corduroy suits, not dark wool suits and ties like theirs. And my mother didn't dress like other ladies, but wore those long purple-and-black dresses with wide sleeves.

We three stood together and everyone was very nice to us and kissed us and welcomed us each year, but I knew we were apart.

Part II ❧ The Secret

Among my parents' friends there was one who didn't paint or sculpt or write or play any instrument; he was a student of Hinduism. His name was Olivier. He was a young man, tall, very slim, very blond, very gentle. He always carried his head slightly bent to one side and he always talked to us about India, about Gandhi—whom he had met in India—and about Buddhism.

My father chose Olivier to teach me my religion.

One day my father said he had to have a talk with me because I was now six years old and I had to learn something important about us three. He explained that while most Jews belonged also to the Jewish religion, we three were Jewish but belonged to the Catholic religion. It was really very simple: we were Jewish, said my father, but religious Jews were awaiting the arrival of the Messiah, while he and my mother believed that there was nothing to wait for, because the Messiah had already come—that he was Jesus, the little Jewish baby born in Palestine two thousand years ago, whom I had seen so often, as an infant or crucified, in the Italian and Flemish primitive paintings in the Louvre.

My father told me that when he had first come to Paris from Poland when he was sixteen he had started visiting the cathedrals, Notre Dame, Chartres, Reims, looking at the sculptures, listening to masses, and wondering about Jesus in whose honor the cathedrals had been built. He thought too about that Messiah for whom the religious Jews of Poland were waiting, singing the old song "Ani Ma'amin" ("I believe, I believe the Messiah will come"). My father kept thinking and reading about Christianity for nearly ten years.

When he met my mother after the First World War, in Poland, and they had gotten married three weeks after their first meeting, they had gone to live in the country near Cracow, and when my mother was five months pregnant, they had decided to be baptized. That was the reason, my mother then said, that my parents had left Poland right after being baptized. They couldn't keep their religion secret there because everyone knew them—and they had to keep it secret so as not to inflict a terrible pain on my grandparents. My grandparents could not understand this conversion, my father said, because for hundreds of years, whenever Jews had converted it had always been to escape being Jewish, so they were considered traitors by other Jews. Jews had been terribly persecuted for centuries by Christians, because for centuries primitive and intolerant people couldn't understand that others should have freedom of thought. Belief in freedom of thought was a relatively new idea in the world, my father said; in the past people burned and killed others who didn't conform, who had different faiths.

In those days Jews had sometimes been forced to convert, and conversion for them was tantamount to treason. My grandparents would never be able to see how my parents could remain loyal Jews and also believe in and practice another religion.

It's like being French, said my father; you can be French and at the same time you can be a Catholic or a Protestant or a Jew. A religion doesn't change your national or ethnic group. You can also be Jewish and not have any religion at all, like your grandfather Ludovic in Lodz, who is an atheist but still a Jew.

It all seemed very simple to me. I couldn't understand why my grandparents should be so upset. What did it matter to them if we believed Jesus was the Messiah?

Then my father told me how I had been baptized when I was a year old. It had been in Lectoure and Mya had been my godmother.

One day my parents told Mya that they had converted to Catholicism in Poland before my birth, but that they had half forgotten this impulsive conversion. My mother had converted to please my father, as all her life she followed him in everything without hesitation. As for my father, he had only wanted to be baptized to show faith in the Messiah, Jesus, but he had never thought about conforming to formal Catholicism.

Now they started long discussions with Mya. They told her that it had never even occurred to them to baptize their baby and Mya said I should be baptized—I was nearly a year old. For the first and only time in her life, my mother opposed my father. She didn't want me baptized. She felt that what they had done was their own responsibility, but that I should be left to decide for myself. By then my father felt he wanted me to be raised in the Catholic religion. Mya's mother, Mme Dalie, was mixing everyone up with her anti-religious speeches. For a Catholic-born provincial lady, she was a formidable atheist.

Finally, my mother agreed to my baptism, on the condition that my father would write her a signed letter that he took all responsibility for this baptism on himself and that he was doing it against her wishes.

At last the agitated household quieted down. Over Mme Dalie's last protests I was dressed in a white lace dress which had been Mya's, and Mya carried me to the cathedral, where *l'Abbé* Moussaron performed the ceremony.

Now I was six and was to be prepared for my first communion.

"Olivier will do this," said my mother. "You can't go to catechism classes with other children, because nobody knows, even here in Paris, that we are Catholics. It is a secret."

"Tereska," said my father, "now you must keep this secret with us. You will know what you are, you are big enough, but no one else must ever know. So be very careful. You don't want to hurt your grandparents—and not only would it hurt them deeply, but everyone around them would suffer too. All their friends and all the family would be shaken by something that would be viewed as a scandal."

I said, "All right, don't worry. I won't tell anyone; I understand." And I went back to play. I was not terribly impressed by their big secret. It seemed to me that grownups were always attaching importance to things that were not very important. So I was Jewish and Catholic too; so what? I was French and somehow Polish too. But I was proud to have been given a secret. A secret was a nice gift.

Nobody knew, my father had said, but of course Olivier knew. Now he came twice a week to our house and taught me New Testament stories and all I had to know for my first communion.

He also spoke to me of Gandhi and of India. The language they wrote was called Sanskrit and their God was Buddha. Olivier gave me a ring, a precious ring he had brought back from India. An Indian princess had given it to him. It was made of rubies and emeralds and I believed it was magical. Whenever I wore it I turned it around my finger and made wishes, the way they did in fairy tales I had read.

I had it for forty years: through a world war, the London blitz, two marriages and three children, an illegal boat trip across the Mediterranean, and a stay in jail; I had it through the first six-day war and a trip around the world, and I lost it in New York City. The day I lost it I felt none of my wishes would ever come true again.

While I was being prepared for my first communion, my favorite uncle came to visit us in Paris, as he often did. He was my father's oldest brother, Samuel. My father had nine brothers and sisters who lived all over the world: in Palestine, Uncle Samuel in Portugal, one had lived in Russia, my father was in France, and some were in Lodz or in Zgierz with my grandfather Isucher, who wore a little black cap on his head and had a cabin called a *sukkah* built each year in his courtyard for a special holiday. As many as thirty people could sit inside it. There was a large table there with lots of food and my grandfather sat at the head of the table and sang songs in Yiddish and told stories.

My uncle Samuel was about twenty years older than my father. He had studied in Paris to become a mining engineer; he had married a Russian girl, the daughter of a banker from Odessa, had settled in Portugal, and had become a Portuguese citizen. Once, on a trip to visit his family in Zgierz, he had seen my father's drawings all over the house and had heard my grandparents complain that Marek didn't do anything but draw. Marek was a terrible student in school, they told Samuel; he was a daydreamer. Once when he was ten or eleven, the teacher had asked all the boys in his class what would they like to become one day and they had all said "doctors, lawyers, bankers, and such things, but do you know what Marek answered?" said my grandparents to Samuel. "Marek said he wanted to become a prophet." It had been Samuel who had paid all the expenses to send my father to Paris to study sculpture in 1910 or 1912.

Samuel told me many stories—one was about how my father had run away from home when he was six years old. He wanted to go to America, but he only got as far as Lodz—about an hour away—and was taken back home, crying and hungry.

"And once," said my father, "when I was three years old, I was walking at the edge of the forest with my brothers and sisters. There was a sunset, the sky was full of red and orange clouds, and I saw an angel in one cloud, a large, reclining, beautiful angel waving at me."

How I wished I could see an angel in a cloud, too. I looked at the sky over Paris, but I never saw one.

My uncle Samuel was very tall. He would take me in his arms and hug me and kiss me with very loud kisses. He looked very South American. Maybe it was the way he dressed, like the South Americans around the Opéra and the boulevards. He was very rich and stayed in a luxurious hotel whenever he was in Paris, and bought me beautiful toys and dresses.

He had traveled all over, and once in the north of Portugal he had discovered, in some tiny mountain village, the first known *marranos*—those hidden Jews who had been forced to convert during the Inquisition but who still kept some Jewish holidays, customs, and Hebrew words. Samuel had written several books about them, and he felt very fatherly toward them—as if they were his own children. He wanted to help them back to Judaism. "Think," he would tell my father, "all those lost Jews keeping alive this thread of Judaism." "Our family came from Spain, or Portugal too, I think," he would tell me. "We must be Sephardim. We escaped to Poland rather than convert during the Inquisition. Our name was Suarez then, but the Poles couldn't pronounce it, so they called us 'Schwarz,' meaning 'black,' because we were all dark people—even today all our family is very dark." It was true; my father and his parents and all his sisters and brothers looked very Oriental. They all had dark eyes, black hair, and, compared to other Polish Jews, they had very dark skins. Only I was fair and had light eyes. My mother always reminded me that I had had blue, very blue eyes. Everyone spoke about it, because I was the only blue-eyed child among all my cousins and because my father and my mother had brown eyes—my father's almost black.

My mother said that one summer when I was three or four those eyes started turning green and the green turned to yellow and the yellow turned to a sort of hazel. No one spoke of my blue eyes any more; instead they talked of my cat's eyes.

Samuel was very proud to be a Sephardic Jew and I, even without dark eyes, felt proud too. So I was a Sephardic, Jewish, Polish, Catholic, French girl! I felt much richer than those other children who were only one thing, "Jewish," or at most two things, "French and Catholic."

My uncle's hotel in Paris was enormous, full of red carpets, gilded furniture and palms in pots. On this particular day, I remember he gave me candies to eat, and I sat near the window and watched the children playing in the Tuileries. Samuel was talking to my father and I was listening. "You remember that rabbi who was considered such a *tzaddik* in Zgierz," my uncle was saying, "and who was such a close friend of our father? I had a very unpleasant experience because of him; I must tell you. It was long ago, when you were little, maybe eight or nine. I was already in Paris, studying at the École des Mines. One day our father went to see his friend, as he always did—each week. When he arrived the servant who opened the door went to announce him, but when she came back she said that the rabbi did not wish to see him. That was very strange. Our father was upset and thought the servant didn't understand and started arguing at the door. Then the rabbi appeared and he looked very angry and called our father into his study.

The rabbi was considered a sort of saint in Zgierz and everyone was very much in awe of him. But our father was the chief of the Jewish community and he also was used to being treated with respect. The rabbi asked our father to be seated and he said to excuse him but that he had been terribly upset. He told our father that he had first been deep in prayer and he had had a revelation. He suddenly knew for certain that one of my grandfather's sons had converted to Christianity, and it was such a painful revelation that at first he hadn't even wanted to see our father.

"So," said Samuel, laughing, "of course our father went home thinking that as I was studying in Paris then, I must be the traitor son. He wrote me a very angry letter—I still have it, I must show it to you some day—accusing me of having converted in Paris! What do you think of that, isn't it incredible? I had a hard time proving to him that the rabbi had been all wrong."

That had happened years and years before my father had converted. He had been a little boy then, eight or nine years old, Samuel said.

I didn't dare turn my head to look at my parents. I couldn't very well imagine what my uncle would have said if he had known our secret, but I was scared anyway by the idea that he might guess it. My father was asking Samuel for more details, and Samuel was very indignant at the rabbi.

Sitting there listening I told myself it was all part of the miracles. I lived in a world of miracles, so much so that they seemed normal occurrences. There were all the Bible miracles my father was always telling me: the burning bush, Sarah and the three angels, Eli taken alive to heaven, Jesus rising from the dead, Daniel in the lion's den; all the prophecies too—the angel announcing to Miriam the birth of her God-child and Joseph's dream before he fled to Egypt. The New Testament was one long story of miracles, and it was for me so completely a part of the Old Testament, just a few more chapters, that I never felt any interruption. The Jewish baby born in Bethlehem was so much like that other Jewish baby, Moses. And the angels were the same ones, the ones who came to Sarah and the ones who came to Miriam in Nazareth. It was not unbelievable then that a Jewish saint in a small Polish village could predict, years in advance, my father's conversion.

Very soon after telling us this story Uncle Samuel returned to Portugal and I went back to my catechism lessons. Olivier explained that in a few days I would go to confession for the first

time. He told me what to do: what prayers to say in the confessional, how to cross myself, to tell the priest this was my first
confession, and how to say "Forgive me, Father, for I have
sinned."

"You must think about it," said Olivier. "Whatever you remember having done that you feel bad about, tell it to the
priest—any little lie or anger in your heart, any time you were
lazy or greedy or mean to someone. Because if you feel you were
wrong those times, if you feel that you shouldn't have lied or
been mean or angry or anything else, and if you intend seriously
to try to improve yourself, if you are really sorry for anything
wrong you may have done, then God will forgive you and
you'll receive Him on the day of your first communion with a
clean soul. When God comes into you, you must receive Him
with your soul all pure and clean."

I listened very attentively. I wanted so much to receive God
with a pure soul. I certainly could think of many things I had
said or done that were wrong—such as the many times I had
been impolite or disobedient to my mother. I always had fights
with my mother. She would get on my nerves and I would not
listen to her at all, while if my father only looked at me in a
certain way with his dark eyes, I wouldn't dare to move a
finger. My mother always complained about me to my father
when he came home from his studio, and my father would
listen to her. But always before scolding me he would first ask
me what I had to say about it.

I remember when we lived on Boulevard Raspail—I was no
more than three years old—I had gone to an umbrella store
with my mother and I had seen a tiny toy umbrella. I had
quietly taken it with me when we left, but my mother had
noticed it in the street and had made me take it
back.

Then there was something else I remembered with shame,

something that had happened in Poland about two years before. I had a girl cousin who was my age, and we sometimes played together. I don't know how it happened, but suddenly I was lying on my stomach and she was pulling down my panties and giving me very pleasurable little slaps on my bottom. Maybe we had been playing mother and child. Anyway, it was such a nice game that we repeated it several times with many variations; the next thing I remember I was sitting on a table in the dining room while a governess I had then was putting on my shoes to go out. I was crying and my governess and my grandmother were scolding me about these games with Ianka and my grandmother was repeating: "Don't ever do that again, it's very bad; nice girls don't play like that." I had never again played in such a way with Ianka and I felt we must have done something really terrible because my grandmother had never scolded me before.

So should I now tell this to the priest too, so that my soul could be quite clean? Was that also a sin?

For a few days I kept thinking of everything that bothered me, all the things I felt guilty about, and I was glad that I remembered them so that I could unburden myself and know that they would all be forgiven and gone.

But I knew I had to tell the priest my worst sin—my hatred of Sonia. Olivier had said that meanness to other people, anger, and hatred were the worst sins. He had said that when Jesus' disciples had asked him what was the most important commandment, Jesus had said: "You must love the Lord your God with all your heart . . . and you must love your neighbor as yourself." And here I had been so mean to another little girl who had not done a thing to me, whose only fault was that her parents were foreigners, Polish Jews like mine.

I felt terribly repentant when I thought how I had attacked her in that corridor and how I had always refused to play with her or talk to her in class. But I knew, too, that even before going to confession I had to go and ask her to forgive me so that God would know I was really repentant.

I waited for an occasion to be alone with Sonia. We were now both in first grade, and at one recess I found myself next to her at the end of the courtyard, while all the other children were playing farther away. Sonia never stood near me alone, because she knew I hated her, and she was just going to move away when I quickly got up my courage. I said to her, "Sonia, let's be friends; I am sorry I have been so mean. I don't want to be mean to you again. Let's be friends instead."

Sonia always looked sad, or very serious, I couldn't tell which. Now her face lighted up with the first smile I had seen on it, and she threw her arms around my neck and hugged me.

Of course I couldn't tell her how it happened that I had asked her to forgive me.

Each spring in the streets of Paris I had seen little girls on their first-communion day. I knew there were two communion days—one when children were six or seven, the private first communion; the other when they were twelve or thirteen, the solemn communion day. The six-year-old girls wore short white dresses and short veils on their heads. The twelve-year-olds were dressed as brides, in beautiful long dresses and long veils.

All day they paraded in their white dresses, short or long, and everyone who passed looked at them and the grownups would smile and exclaim at how pretty they looked. I had visions of myself under the chestnut trees in the white dress my mother would buy me and of everyone looking at me and smiling and saying how nice I looked.

But these visions were soon shattered. A few days before my communion day I asked about my dress. My father said: "But you are not going to have your first communion in a group with other children, darling; you knew that? You didn't go to catechism with them; you know why. That would be impossible.

You are going to go to mass with Mamy, Olivier, and me; but you can't walk in the streets in a communion costume, someone might recognize us."

I don't think that my father had any idea how heartbroken I was. For him, communion was something private anyway. He had never been a little six-year-old girl. He couldn't understand the importance of wearing a white dress and walking in the streets to be admired. For him, the only important thing was the act of taking communion itself—and I was going to do this. The rest was unimportant trimming.

I finally prevailed on my mother to let me at least wear a short white dress, but over the dress I had to put my regular everyday coat. My mother said we were going to take a taxi to the church, and when the taxi was almost there my father told the driver to stop at the corner near the church, but not in front of it. We got out, my father paid the driver, my mother looked all around nervously, but we didn't see anyone who knew us, except for Olivier, who had been waiting for us in front of the church but not looking at us.

Finally, we all went in. The mass was just starting. Mya had sent me my first prayer book from Lectoure, a big missal bound in soft leather, the pages as thin as breath and the edges gilded. Olivier had taught me how to follow the mass in it and I read the prayers and turned the pages carefully. I felt happy and light and clean. I didn't mind anymore about wearing my everyday coat and kneeling between my parents in a crowd of people who didn't pay any attention to me. But it did seem somehow strange that no one here knew that this was such a big day—my first-communion day!

The little altar boy dressed in a red robe with a white cassock over it rang his bell, the priest bent his head over the chalice. Candles were burning on the altar and there were flowers and stained-glass windows. An organ was playing softly. It was very, very quiet and I knew that I had been forgiven everything I had done wrong up to then and that I was as clean as the second after my baptism. If only I could always keep my soul so clean forever—how wonderful it would be! Everyone got up and people started walking toward the altar where the priest stood at the railing with the chalice in his hand, holding the Eucharist above the chalice. We got up, too, and walked to the railing. We knelt, and I thought: "God is going to enter my soul. My soul is like a clean little room, all white. God is certainly going to be pleased in there. God is one; He is the God of Moses and He is the God of Jesus, the same and one God as in the prayer my father taught me to say in Hebrew: 'Sh'ma Yisrael, Adonai Elohajnu—Adonai éhad.' "

I opened my mouth and felt the light, light host which dissolved on my tongue almost instantly. It had no real taste; it just touched my tongue and was gone.

I walked back to my seat. I had taken my first communion. We left the church in the large crowd of Sunday worshippers. My parents must have felt hidden and safe in the crowd. We walked along Avenue d'Alésia toward the Place. My mother said she wanted to stop at the bakery to buy a cake for lunch; Olivier was having lunch with us. He and my father walked on to our house on rue de l'Amiral Mouchez and I waited for my mother outside the bakery.

A little girl was playing hopscotch on squares she had drawn with chalk on the street pavement. She didn't know what a big day this was—she didn't know I had a secret. She didn't know I had just had my first communion.

Slowly I unbuttoned my coat, let it fall open on my white dress and looked at her. Maybe this way, seeing my white dress, she would realize that today I was not an ordinary little girl in ordinary clothes.

Now I had a friend. Now I had Sonia.

We became as passionate friends as we had been enemies. Like me, Sonia had been born in France and her parents were Polish and Jewish. Like me, she was an only child. Like me, she loved France with the adoration which can only come to those who are unsure of their adoration.

Under Sonia's influence I hung two French flags above my bed while my mother said that I certainly was the only seven-year-old French girl who slept under two tricolors.

In school we sat next to each other in the last row of the classroom, and while the second-grade teacher made boring speeches about boring subjects we talked and no one seemed to pay any attention to us.

Sonia didn't live with her parents; she lived with her grand-mother and her uncle. If I asked about that, she always changed the subject.

Every Thursday, when school was closed, and every Sunday, we visited at each other's houses to play. We disguised ourselves in my mother's or her grandmother's clothes and acted out all the books we read.

We read every book written by the Countess de Ségur who had lived in the nineteenth century and had dozens of grand-children to whom she was always telling stories. These stories were published in a collection of red-bound books called *La bibliothèque rose*. Each volume was beautifully illustrated with nineteenth-century engravings of the heroes and heroines of these novels. They were all children of the aristocracy, as the grandchildren of the countess were. Little Camille and Made-leine de Fleurville, and their cousins Paul, Henri, and Georges and their friends lived in nearby châteaux with their maids and governesses, drove in horse-drawn carts, went for picnics on their estates, had donkey races, and fished for prawns.

For hours we played at being Camille and Sophie and Madeleine; we dreamed of white ponies and of large family affairs.

❧ In school one day Sonia whispered to me: "You know, I have found out that I am an aristocrat too, something like a princess."

I looked at her in astonishment. "Yes," she said, "my uncle told me that the Levys are descendants of high priests, from the time there were kings in Palestine. High priests were just like dukes and counts, so I am like a princess."

That night I asked my father about the Levys and he confirmed it. Yes, the Levys were the high priests of Israel. So, now I knew it was true.

"What about us?" I asked my father, "aren't we descendants of high priests too?"

"No," said my father, "I don't think so. But I think we come from the tribe of Benjamin."

I didn't know how he came to that conclusion and I didn't care. At least it was better to be of the tribe of Benjamin than to be nothing at all.

At night in bed, I thought of the kingdom of Israel and I repeated to myself: "Yeroushalaim, Yeroushalaim," a word so beautiful, so musical.

So Benjamin was my great-great-great-grandfather. Did Jesus's family come from the tribe of Benjamin? He was a descendant of King David. Were we descendants of King David, too? If so, then I would be a cousin of Jesus.

Sonia talked and acted like a little grownup. Sometimes it embarrassed even me. She made long speeches the way grownups did, and my parents kept saying that she read books which were way beyond a girl of her age. On the other hand, she didn't even know how babies were born and I, who had had it all explained by my parents a long time before, had to tell her about it.

It was a Thursday afternoon and we were at Sonia's grandmother's, dressing up in her dresses and shawls. We had been playing all afternoon, concentrating so deeply on our parts that we were far away, in another country, in another world, when suddenly Sonia's eyes filled with tears and I knew at once that she was not playing any more, that her tears were real. She was lying on the couch in a long dress, hitched up with her uncle's tie, her hair covered with a tablecloth, crying. She said, "I must tell you because you are the only one who can know. You are like my sister."

That was the way she talked, not like a seven-year-old girl, but like some lady in a book.

"I couldn't tell this to anyone else, only to you. Yesterday, yesterday . . ." She cried more and bitterly. ". . . yesterday I was crossing the street, here downstairs, Boulevard St.-Marcel, and a car was coming toward me, and I tried to get it to run me over. But the car avoided me, it nearly crashed into a tree. I wanted to die."

I was so shocked I couldn't find any words. But I knew that Sonia was different from other little girls and that if she told me this it must be true. Still, the idea of trying to kill oneself was terrifying, incomprehensible. Finally I asked, "Why did you do that?"

She didn't want to answer at first and cried more and said she was too ashamed to tell me. But in the end she said, "You see, Thérèse, I live with my grandmother; I didn't know why. My parents always told me that it was because they had to work and couldn't take care of me, and because they had no apartment. My father has only a room in the hotel and my mother—I don't know where she lives. I thought she lived with my father in that hotel . . . but it is not so. Now I know." She cried again.

I asked, "So what, Sonia? What happened? Why are you crying?"

And she said: "Because I found out my parents are divorced.

That's why I don't live with them. That's why I wanted that car to run me over yesterday!"

I was overwhelmed by this revelation. I felt so sorry for Sonia. It was terrible—as if I now knew that her whole world was rotten and broken. How can a little girl of seven live if she has no parents? I thought, too, that having divorced parents was like having no parents. You had a mother and a father, yes, but you didn't have the unity called "parents." I put my arms around Sonia and hugged her, and said, "I understand, it is terrible, I didn't know. But you have me, you have a sister, don't you?"

Because neither of us had any brother or sister, because we each had a father and a mother who were foreigners, because we each had no friend before we became friends, the idea that we were sisters was something important. We built on it and it consolidated our world. I knew that if anything could console Sonia it would be my being her sister.

All year we were together; we told each other our most precious secrets. We read the same books, and we wrote each other long letters whenever we were separated, such as when I went to Lectoure or to Poland during vacations.

🌷 During the winter I had pains under my knees. I had had these pains several times before, even when I was very small. I had heard something said about rheumatic fever and heart palpitations, but I never knew what it meant. Once I had gone with my grandmother to a special resort in the Tatra mountains and every day there I had had to take special baths. Now my mother had to take me out of school again to go to a town called Salies-de-Béarn for those same salt baths. During those few weeks, we wrote each other, Sonia and I, almost every day. Her letters were full of big words and passionate emotions. She was slightly older than I—already eight years old while I was still seven. She had more to say and sometimes I felt that I was not up to Sonia in knowledge of things and people.

But most of all, what bothered me was that my best friend, my sister, didn't know the most important thing about me. It was as if I were lying to her. I swore to her in those passionate letters that she knew all my thoughts—she told me all of hers, but I lied because she didn't know my secret.

We came back to Paris. I felt better and was glad to be back, although I hated school. It had been pleasant in kindergarten, but since then school had become nothing but a place where I had to present myself at nine in the morning and was allowed to leave at three. It had no other meaning—I sat in school in total boredom. I never listened to the teacher, I never did homework. I just sat there. Fortunately, there was Sonia to talk to most of the time—but not always, because she missed school often. Those days I sat frozen and only tried to make sure that the teacher didn't notice me.

And she didn't. She must have given up on Sonia and me long before. Not only did I come to school each year at least a month later than anyone else, but I also left a month earlier. Our trips to Poland didn't coincide with the school year. In school all I did was daydream or whisper all day with that other little girl who didn't do her homework or pay any attention either.

At home my parents never asked me about homework. They must have felt that I received enough artistic and intellectual stimulation from them. I spoke two languages fluently, and read and wrote well for my age. I knew about Fra Angelico, and many other painters. So my parents didn't worry about my homework, or take school too seriously.

Once again Sonia had a secret to tell me.

We were sitting in the Parc Montsouris, which was near my house. It was spring and the swans had babies. The mother swan glided across the lake with all her babies following her. I had bought a circle of licorice at the old lady's booth. The licorice was sold in long strings wound round and round on themselves. I chewed on mine and Sonia ate a *petit pain au chocolat,* a soft bun filled with chocolate cream. In the last weeks Sonia had spoken a lot about religion. She discussed God and whether He existed and whether people lived after death. Her ideas on this subject were confused, while mine were straight, thanks to my catechism lessons with Olivier. Sonia felt I knew more about religion. I had more answers. We sat on a bench and watched the swans, then a family of ducks, and Sonia threw some of her bun to them.

Children played all around us in the alley. No one was allowed on the grass. All over the immense expanse of beautiful grass were signs: "Forbidden to walk."

Children skipped rope and played ball on the narrow walks under the watchful eyes of maids or mothers, intent above all that they not dirty their clothes. Nobody worried about Sonia's clothes. Her dresses were always too long for her, because she chose them herself and her tastes ran toward dresses which looked as adult as possible. That's why she always seemed slightly in disguise. My mother had even made some remarks about that, which I knew had hurt Sonia.

Now Sonia had started discussing Catholicism and I shut up, knowing it was a dangerous subject. I might say something that would make her guess.

Sonia said: "I have been in a church a few times, you know. Have you ever been in one?"

Prudently, I answered, "Yes, a few times."

She said, "How did you like it?" and I said, "Heu, heu," not daring to venture more. But she didn't notice, and said, "You remember that maid, Germaine, who worked at my grandmother's last year? I'll tell you something, but you must swear not to tell it to anyone."

I swore.

She said, "Germaine took me to church with her. If my father knew he would be mad, so don't ever tell your parents; they might repeat it to my grandmother. Germaine was very religious, you know. She told me all about Jesus Christ and the Holy Virgin. She showed me the manger last Christmas; I should have told you, but I didn't dare—and there is something else. . . ."

I waited.

She said: "When I am grown up, I want to become a Catholic; I like their churches, I like their religion, I like the story of Jesus. I have thought about it and I've read the Gospels. I found a Bible at my grandmother's which had the New Testament too. I read it. I loved it. Are you mad? Are you shocked? Tell me."

She looked at me with dark, sad eyes, and I was dying to cry out, "How can I be shocked, you idiot! I am a Catholic myself!" but I couldn't say that. So, my face all red, I just mumbled something like, "No, no, of course I am not mad; it's all right with me." My heart was breaking, I wanted so much to tell her, but I couldn't.

We got up from the bench. We were wearing light-colored cotton dresses and were in sandals. It was hot that spring day. At the entrance to the Parc Montsouris a photographer was waiting next to his old-fashioned wooden camera and tripod. He smiled at us and Sonia, who always had money from her father or her uncle, said, "Let's have our photo taken."

So we stood there next to one another. The photographer put his head inside the black sleeve. I put my arm protectively around her shoulder. She looked very seriously at the camera while I smiled. . . . I have the picture. There we are: one smiling blonde girl with wavy hair and long skinny legs and one dark-haired girl, very grave, with bangs falling down to her eyes.

Sonia took the bus and I walked home. I lived only a few
minutes from the park so my mother let me walk alone from
there, but I could never have taken a bus or the metro alone
all over Paris the way Sonia did.

Children didn't go anywhere alone, especially girls, but Sonia
was not brought up like other girls. She was free to choose her
own dresses, to read any book she wanted, even to go to the
movies as often as once a week. The idea was incredible to me.
I went to films two or three times a year, and then to very carefully chosen films, so Sonia used to tell me every detail of every
film she saw. For me going to a film was as tremendous an
experience as going to the season's ball would be for a debutante.
For days in advance I couldn't eat; food would not pass through
my throat, it was so contracted by emotion. When the day
finally arrived, my heart would beat madly until the moment I
was in the dark movie house and the film started.

In Poland I had seen a few Tom Mix movies and a few of
Laurel and Hardy's. In Paris I had seen *The Kid* and some
Buster Keaton films. But of all the films I had seen, only one
really had an enormous impact. It was *Uncle Tom's Cabin.* I
saw it five times—each time it played I begged my parents to
let me see it again, and each time I cried and cried until I
couldn't see the screen any more. I felt the suffering of the
black people who were sold and humiliated as much as if they
had been my own father, mother, sisters, and brothers. Then
someone gave me the book and I cried so much I couldn't continue reading because I couldn't see the lines on the page. How
could people act this way toward other people? I, who had
never experienced anything but kindness, couldn't understand
it at all. But I identified completely with Topsy, Tom, and the
other black people. From the day I saw that film and read that
book, I hated man's injustice toward man; I hated it with a
vengeance that I didn't know a small child could feel.

I knew one thing: that somehow, although in the grown-up world everyone seemed so nice and friendly to me, I could not really be myself—openly—because of some incomprehensible intolerance. It was as if under my white skin there was also a black skin. People only knew of my white skin; that's why they were so good to me. But if they found out our secret, they would discover the real skin, under the other one, the black skin—the skin which would make my grandparents, uncles, aunts, cousins, all our friends turn away from us, chase us, disown us.

I was growing up. I rarely talked about my parents' conversion with them; I accepted having to go to mass in secret, looking left and right before entering a church and never mentioning religion to anyone, not even to my best and only friend. But I knew that if the secret had to be so well guarded it meant that if we were found out the consequences would be very tragic, and I was deeply hurt and angry that I was not allowed to be what I was, openly and freely.

To get home, I took the shortcut—between the park and my street there were stairs going down to my street, which was on a lower level than the park. I loved those stairs, which were like the stairs in Montmartre. I skipped down, jumping from step to step, holding the iron rail with my hand.

I came home that day in a great state of agitation. My father was still at his studio and only my mother was home. I would never have told my mother why I was upset. She was not that kind of mother. If she had known I was unhappy she would have been the one to cry and I would have ended up consoling her.

Once, when I was younger, I had been walking to school with my mother. She was a little behind me and I ran ahead in the spring sun on the Boulevard de Port Royal, under the blooming chestnut trees. Suddenly I tripped and fell on my knee—maybe it bled a little. I started to cry and turned toward my mother, but she had stopped where she was. She hid her face with her hands and it was she who screamed without looking: "Are you hurt? *Mon Dieu!* Are you hurt?"

So I got up, brushed my knee and limped back to my mother to console her. "No, I am all right; it's nothing; you can look, really—"

My mother was wonderful to play with. She could read books to me and tell me stories. I could also dictate stories I invented to her which I didn't feel like writing myself. In a way she was like a sister. She couldn't cook at all and she was quite useless at housekeeping. But we had a solid, pleasant woman who came every day and cleaned and cooked, so it didn't matter.

The day of Sonia's outburst I went to my room and tried to concentrate on a book. It was a book I had read many times, and I loved it. I had already reread this book so many times that I knew some passages by heart. It was called *The Little Silver Slipper* and was the story of a girl from the Caucasus, stolen and sold into a Turkish harem in Constantinople, and how she was rescued by a young shepherd from her village.

When my father finally came home we had dinner. After dinner I sat for awhile at the table listening once more to my father's tales of his adventures in Russia during the Revolution. My mother and I could sit every night for hours listening to my father's stories.

But later when I went to bed my unhappiness all came back. I was tired, my head was full of red flags and revolution, black slaves and secrets. I wanted Sonia to know all about me. I wanted her to love me as I was—me—real me—Jewish and Catholic as I was, not with a mask, not with a secret.

When my father came to kiss me good night, he sat on my bed, as always, and asked me if I had said my evening prayer. I nodded, but I had tears in my eyes, and he put his hands on my head with that gentleness he had in all his movements. He had beautiful hands, with long slim fingers. He said, "What is it, Tereska? Why are you crying?" And I told him what Sonia had said to me in the Parc Montsouris that day, and cried some more. "And, Papa, I couldn't even tell her—I wanted so much and I couldn't tell her the truth about us. She is my best friend, I tell her everything and she tells me everything, but I have to lie to her about that."

For a long while my father didn't say anything. He just sat there, his hand gently caressing my head. But when I looked at him, his face was so sad. "All right, my darling," he said, "you can tell her. You can tell her the truth—I will trust her. Tell her she must never repeat it to anyone. I don't want you to feel that you can't speak openly to your best friend. But you are still two very small girls and I am entrusting this secret to you both."

I laughed with joy and hugged him. I was so happy and I told him, "She will never tell it to anyone, Papa. I swear to you. I know her; I am sure of her."

So Sonia found out.

I whispered to her in school the next day, "I have something *very* important to tell you after school," and she looked at me and raised her eyebrows and whispered back, "What is it?" But I shook my head and said, "Later, not now!" My mother was waiting for me at the school door at three o'clock so I couldn't speak to Sonia then either, and she was getting really curious.

She came to my house that day, as her grandmother had to go shopping at *Bon Marché*. And as soon as we got home we ran to my room and I closed the door mysteriously. "So what is it? Tell me now!" I could see she was intrigued and I enjoyed it.

Finally I said, "Sonia, what I must tell you is a big secret. Not only mine but my parents' too, so before I tell you anything you have to swear that you will never, never repeat a word to anyone."

She swore. She seemed very impressed by my speech and sat on my bed while I told her.

Her eyes were wide open and she kept asking questions I couldn't answer, because they had never occurred to me, such as: if my grandparents found out would they take me away from my parents. In any case, she was astonished, and she swore she would rather die than reveal a word of this conversation.

Now it was much easier for me. I could discuss everything with Sonia and since she kept telling me that she wanted to be Catholic too, I started instructing her in everything I knew of religion. We had a common passion that we kept to ourselves. We would stop in a church on our way to the park and kneel until our knees hurt, in imitation of the saints' mortifications. One day Sonia arrived at my house limping. She had put a pebble in her shoe because she had heard that some mystic had been in the habit of doing it. We prayed together in my room or hers. We lighted candles and collected holy images which we hid in our desks.

My parents didn't know about all this and, of course, Sonia's father, with whom she was living again, didn't know either. From time to time her mother also appeared in her life, but I had seen her only once and Sonia rarely spoke of her.

Once, in our intense devotion, we stood in a garden outside a monastery near the Parc Montsouris, and when we saw a priest coming out we both knelt in front of him and asked him to bless us.

The priest was old. He looked very surprised. He put his hands on both our heads for a second, then smiled and said, "Little girls should play and not wait here to be blessed; go on, get up, go and play!"

✿ In early June my family left for Poland again. Sonia was going to spend the summer in Brittany and we were going to write to each other every day.

A letter from Sonia:

> *Thérèse, oh Thérèse, little loved sister of my heart and of my soul. Two days ago I got your letter. I shivered with pleasure, seeing it so heavy, so full. The longer your letter, the greater my joy. I thank you because I know you will pray for me whether it be in a little chapel lost in a forest or in a big cathedral known not only by God and His angels but by men and centuries. . . .*
>
> *It is extremely hot here and we fan ourselves all the time. There is not one shop here, not even a bakery. Thank you very much for your cards; they are very pretty.*
>
> *I, too, my Thérèse, love you more and more. Often I feel that an invisible cord binds our two hearts together.*

In another letter, Sonia wrote: "In my prayers today, I asked God that we live very long lives but that when the hour of dying arrives I wish we could die in each other's arms and that our souls fly together to Heaven."

In Poland my grandmother had hired a governess who would take me for walks every afternoon and speak French with me, so that I wouldn't forget French during the four months I was in Lodz. My father was organizing an exhibition of all the bas-reliefs he had done that winter in Paris and my mother was busy because her only brother, Henio, was very sick and she was spending her days at the clinic where he was. I heard that he had cancer of the brain and that we might have to go with him to a place called Baden in Austria, where he could be operated on.

My governess dressed in black; she may have been in mourning. I remember her as a blonde young Polish girl who spoke French well. On our walks together, she asked me nearly every day if I would mind if she stopped in church and I always said no, I didn't mind. Then we would go in and she would cross herself and pray and sometimes cry. I waited for her and tried not to look as if I knew all about churches. To my governess I was a normal little Jewish girl, and so sometimes she would ask me if I would like her to explain to me what was going on. I would politely say yes, and she would explain everything I knew very well already.

It rather amused me—it was like a game. I didn't mind her not knowing the truth, because she was not my best friend the way Sonia was. I would even push the game by asking her many questions and trying to confuse her in her answers. When she came back home, she would always tell my grandmother that I was very intelligent and that I was so curious about things. She even told my grandmother that she had taken me to church with her as I had expressed an interest in seeing what was inside. My grandmother didn't care. She was not very religious herself, except when she went to synagogue on the high holidays. Her husband was an atheist and she thought that my parents wouldn't mind, that they would say it was part of my education to know about other people's religions. As long as we were Jewish she didn't mind.

That summer I spent a month in a children's camp, because my uncle was getting sicker and my mother and grandmother were with him most of the time.

When I came back to Lodz, my parents said that we might go to Austria straight from Poland, instead of going back to Paris. I was going to be eight years old in September and I had grown. I was suntanned and a little fatter, although not much. I was still a very skinny little girl.

One evening I was alone with my grandmother at home; my parents and grandfather were at the clinic. My grandmother ran a bath for me. I sat in the warm water and my grandmother sat on a chair next to the bathtub and told me about her childhood and how she had gotten engaged to my grandfather. My grandmother was small and round and fat. She had kinky hair and a small fat nose and very thick lips. I couldn't imagine her as a beautiful young girl getting engaged.

My grandmother soaped my back and told me to wash my ears. She described her own father, who had had stables and horses in Poland, and who had taken the horses across Europe to sell them in Lyon. That must have been in Napoleon's time. She also told me how handsome my grandfather had been when he came courting her. That I could well imagine; my grandfather was still so handsome. She told me about my mother and my uncle Henio when they were small and she described how long my mother's hair was: "So long she could sit on it," she said proudly, and brought a photo glued onto a hard piece of cardboard to show me. I saw my mother and her brother holding hands. They both wore astrakhan hats and winter coats; they were beautiful, pale-looking, old-fashioned children. My mother was sitting on her black hair next to Henio on a sort of marble bench with a background of painted trees and flowers like scenery in a play. Then my grandmother brought another photo. She said, "Careful, don't touch it with your wet hands." It was my grandfather, but looking younger, with a black beard, a bowler hat, and a high collar. He was seated in a cardboard cart holding the reins of a cardboard horse in front of more of the theatrical painted scenery. He was so funny sitting there in his bowler hat, looking so solemn in the make-believe carriage with the toy horse. I laughed and felt so good, the water was so warm, the house was so quiet.

I loved my grandmother's house; it was big and it had such

heavy furniture and so many drapes and carpets and plush covers. I loved the gleaming white porcelain stoves up to the ceilings. There were big cupboards full of sheets and tablecloths and blankets. It was a house full of things: pictures and vases and potted palms—you could imagine so many stories in such a house.

I sat in the warm water feeling good and friendly toward my round, small, plump grandmother and I loved her very much. Suddenly, I said: "*Babćia,* Grandmother, I have a secret." I heard my voice saying it and I couldn't believe it. It wasn't me. I hadn't said it, someone else must have spoken.

But my grandmother said, "The water is getting cold, come out quickly, you'll catch cold."

I was rather offended that she didn't pay any attention to what I had said—because now I knew I had said it—and here she was acting as though she hadn't heard me. So this time it really was I who said: "I have a secret, *Babćia;* don't you want me to tell you?" She pulled me out of the bath, threw a long terry cloth bathrobe over me and started rubbing my back. "All right, you have a secret; so what's your big secret?" she said.

My heart beat; I was very hot. I knew that in a second I could break the trust my father put in me. I could be a traitor to my father and give away his secret. Maybe my grandmother would be glad to know the truth and would be thankful to me. Then I would be on the other side, with all of them—the big family of aunts, uncles, cousins—they would all be thankful to me. But I would have abandoned my parents then.

My grandmother dropped the terry cloth bathrobe to the floor and put my nightgown over my head; I raised my arms and disappeared inside the nightgown, only my legs and my hands could be seen. I struggled inside the nightgown and my grandmother said, "So, what were you telling me?" My head appeared, my nightgown fell into place and I sighed and said: "Oh, nothing."

❧ Once more I would not be back in school in time for *La rentrée—*

We were in Austria; my poor uncle Henio was very sick and he had been operated on and might die.

We had already been in Baden three months and I began speaking German with the nurses and with the children at the hotel where we lived.

There were also three American children from Chicago in that hotel. Their father was a surgeon. We played together. They spoke to me in English, which I didn't understand, and I spoke to them in French, which they didn't understand, but we got along very well together.

My father had to go back to Paris to work, but I stayed in Baden with my mother, my grandfather, and my uncle's fiancée, a young girl from Poznan.

My uncle was so sick because during the 1914 war he had served in the army and gotten hit on the head with the cross of a rifle. That blow, the doctors said, had brought on a brain tumor.

We stayed about six months in Baden and then took the Orient Express back to Paris, bringing Henio with us. There was a doctor who might save him, so Henio entered a clinic in Paris.

I went back to the Collège Sévigné, just in time for the Easter vacation and the teacher raised her eyes to heaven when she saw me. But Sonia was there waiting for me and that was all that mattered.

All the children in school wore black smocks, but my mother didn't like a black smock on a child—she thought it was too gloomy-looking—so she bought me a sleeveless flower-printed smock, open at the sides but attached there with two small ribbons. I wanted a black smock like everyone else's—even Sonia wore one—but I had to wear the flower-printed one.

The first and only time I remember the teacher talking to me in that school was the day she called me to her desk. I went, astonished at being called, and she told me to stand on her chair. Then she showed my smock to the class and said: "I want you all to see what apron this pupil is wearing because this is exactly the type of apron I don't want anyone to wear to school. It is all wrong—first, it has no sleeves to protect your arms; then, it is not even closed properly on the sides; and, lastly, it is the wrong color. A school apron must be black or at least a dark shade so as not to get dirty right away." I stood there, a model of everything that shouldn't be. I felt foolish, and grinned. The teacher said, "It's all right, you can come down now. Go back to your seat."

I went and sat next to Sonia, who whispered: "She is an idiot, that teacher; don't pay any attention to her. I wish I had a beautiful apron like yours."

So I felt fine again.

❀ Sonia got a new book and it was more fascinating than anything we had read. It was called *Fabiola* and it was about a Christian slave girl. But no one knew she was Christian because this was at the time the Romans and Christians were meeting in the catacombs in secret.

Our games switched to playing Romans and slaves and we became hidden Christians going furtively to secret masses and finally being eaten by lions rather than abandon our faith.

It didn't occur to me that my life was not so removed from that of those first Jewish Christians in ancient Rome.

❀ Then one day there was a commotion at home. My parents

had to rush to the clinic and my uncle's fiancée, who had been living with us for a while, had to leave too. My parents ran to the corner café to call their friend Stanislas Fumet, a French writer who lived near the Arênes of Lutèce. Aniouta, his white-haired Russian wife, came to take me home with her.

It was while I was at their house that Aniouta told me that my uncle Henio had died.

He has died, he has died, I told myself and I just didn't feel anything. I remember how I cried once when I had a little cat in Poland and it died. Now, my uncle was dead and I didn't feel anything. But Stanislas and Aniouta's daughters looked at me and I could tell that they expected me to cry. I didn't want them to think that I had no heart, so I cried and they asked me, "If our uncle had died would you cry too?" I didn't know what to say to that.

In their house many artists and writers and poets met. Stanislas and Aniouta knew all about us, that we were Jews of Catholic religion. As a matter of fact, Aniouta was also Jewish and Catholic. So in their houses we could always talk and act openly.

The person I liked the most among them was Stanislas's father, because he was so funny and had such a big voice. He was a poet and an organist. I didn't know his real name, because he changed it to Dynam, and my father explained that it was because he was an anarchist and Dynam stood for dynamite. But that didn't prevent Dynam from playing the organ in the church. We went there every Sunday, the church on the Avenue d'Alésia where I had had my first communion.

The Sunday after my uncle's death we went to church. My mother looked very sad and her eyes were red. When we got near the church, just as we were going to turn into the entrance my father noticed a Polish lady whose name I didn't know—a friend of my parents. She saw us and waved and my parents stopped. The lady came up, shook hands with us and said:

"What are you doing out so early on a Sunday?" My mother
motioned to the bus stop at the corner and said, "Oh, we are
waiting for that bus."

The lady smiled and said she had a few minutes; she was going to see her daughter but would walk us to the bus stop.
We all walked to the bus stop and she stood and waited with us,
talking about her daughter who had recently married a painter
and how Mane Katz had come to the wedding and about the
apartment the couple had found just opposite the Dôme; and
wasn't that lucky? And what did my father think of the new
French Cabinet? My father didn't think anything of the new
French Cabinet. He didn't read newspapers; he was not interested in politics.

Finally, the lady remarked that my mother looked sad, and
my mother told her that her only brother had just died of cancer
and started crying. Then the bus arrived and we got on. We
stood on the outside platform and the lady waved at us. We
waved back, the bus left, and the church looked smaller and
smaller until, finally, we couldn't see it any more.

❦ We didn't go to Poland that summer, but to Lectoure. My
godmother Mya, had invited us and we stayed in the little Roman town for two or three weeks.

I asked my mother one day how my parents had ever found
Lectoure and Mya and Mme Dalie. My mother said that when
I was six months old my parents were so poor they couldn't
afford to stay in Paris and my mother was too proud to write to
my grandparents for help. She had married my father against
her family's better judgment.

When she met my father she had been engaged to a successful
lawyer. She saw my father for the first time when he came with
a friend to a party my mother was giving at my grandparents'

house. She had fallen in love at once with that bohemian painter who had lived in Paris, who had just returned from Bolshevik Russia, who wore his hair long, and who was absolutely different from anyone she knew in her very bourgeois, well-to-do circle. My mother broke her engagement and married my father three weeks later.

My grandfather liked my father, but he thought my mother crazy to marry a poor unknown artist. That's why my mother didn't want to write home and say she was starving. When she saw an ad in a Paris newspaper for an apartment in Lectoure, renting at an amazingly low price, she and my father got together all the money they had left, packed a few things, took the baby, and went off by third-class train to Gascogny. There they found Mme Dalie and Mya. Mme Dalie was delighted to have a painter for a tenant, and Mya kept bringing my parents fruits and vegetables from her garden without showing that she knew they had nothing else to eat.

They became very good friends—this fiercely independent free-thinking painter and her very pious spinster daughter, both so French and so provincial, and these young bohemian Polish Jews. My father sold a few paintings of landscapes around Lectoure, very much in the Vlaminck style, so my mother could buy some extra food to go with Mya's free fruits and vegetables.

Mya wore dresses in the style of before the First World War. Her dresses were always black, except when she sometimes wore a black skirt and a white blouse. She had very red, round cheeks and blue eyes and smelled of vegetables—of crisp lettuce and radishes. Mya had "consecrated her life to her mother" said my mother. Her mother "ruined her life" said my father. Mme Dalie was a tyrant. Everyone in Lectoure knew that. She had never allowed her daughter to marry because Mme Dalie was a widow and she didn't want to stay alone. So they lived together and Mme Dalie painted pictures that looked like those of Madame Vigée-Lebrun, in the Louvre, and Mya collected stray cats and dogs.

"When you were baptized," Mya told me, "when the priest put the salt on your tongue, you cried and cried; you were already a big baby, one year old, so you were strong and you really kicked him." I laughed. I knew the priest who had baptized me. He lived in the *presbytère*. He was *l'Abbé* Moussaron, who came every Sunday to Mme Dalie's house after lunch for a glass of Armagnac. I got sugar lumps dipped in Armagnac and *l'Abbé* Moussaron sat and sipped and argued with Mme Dalie about religion. Because Mme Dalie was a confirmed atheist, she hated the church and priests, but she loved *l'Abbé* Moussaron's Sunday visits and wouldn't have missed them for anything.

Mme Dalie said every Sunday: "How can you believe in God? Look at this insane world and all the suffering and injustice. How can a God allow it? If He exists and He allows it, then He is a bad God and I don't want to bow to Him."

Another person who came to Mme Dalie's house not only every Sunday but every other day, too, was Romeck. That was not his real name, but my parents had nicknamed him and everyone in Lectoure called him that. Romeck taught Latin and Greek in the Lycée, and was married but didn't love his wife. He loved Mya in secret. I had heard all about it in the way I had of hearing the adults' conversations, but no one knew that I knew.

Romeck was small and wiry and always very agitated. He couldn't stand to be contradicted and if anyone objected to what he said, even Mya, he went into terrible rages. I was quite scared of Romeck's rages but I loved him too, because he was intelligent and kind and easily hurt.

That summer Mya and Romeck proposed to my parents that they take me with them to Héas. It was a small valley in the

Pyrénées, very high up, two thousand meters above sea level, near the Spanish border. If my parents stayed in Lectoure with Mme Dalie, then Mya could leave, and if I went with them Romeck could come because the conventions would be maintained and they would not be alone. Even Romeck's wife wouldn't mind, as she was going away for the summer to Brittany.

Everyone agreed and I couldn't wait to go with Mya and Romeck. We were going to stop at Lourdes so I could see that miraculous place. Then we would take a bus to Gèdres in the Pyrénées. From Gèdres on, there were no more paved roads. We would ride donkeys to get up the mountain to Héas, where Mya had rented a smuggler's house for a month. There were only about ten families in all who lived in Héas; half of them worked as smugglers and the other half were customs guards. Besides, they were all related by marriage. Our smuggler was away in Spain that summer, so he rented his house to Mya.

We got to Lourdes. It was my first glimpse of the Pyrénées. The town nestled at the foot of the high mountain walls. It was a strange town, completely taken over by religion. Thousands and thousands of sick and crippled people converged upon it from all over the world to get cured before the Grotto where the Holy Virgin had appeared to Bernadette.

We walked the steep narrow streets bordered on both sides by innumerable shops selling horrible-looking statues of the Holy Virgin and of Bernadette. Romeck thought the Basilica was the ugliest in the world but Mya, who was very religious, said that was not important, what mattered was the faith of all those people.

At night there was a candlelight procession over the mountains around Lourdes. It circled the Basilica and ended at the Grotto. Millions of voices sang in the night, "Ave, ave, ave Maria, ave, ave, ave Maria."

The next day we left and arrived in Gèdres, the last "civilized" town. After eleven kilometers of climbing I discovered Héas. Héas has remained for me through my whole life my personal paradise. Maybe there is no heaven after death, but even if there isn't, I will have had Héas, so I can't complain.

We came to Héas on a July day. The donkey I was riding stopped of his own accord at the entrance to the narrow valley and I sat there and looked on in silence.

On both sides were very high mountains, quite bare, mostly rocks. During the French Revolution the peasants had burned all the forests which had belonged to lords. Since then the mountains had been falling down in big chunks and had buried entire villages. At the entrance to Héas there had been an avalanche some years before which nearly completely blocked the entrance by huge rocks. But the donkey passed, and beyond there was the same Gave torrent as in Lourdes, but much narrower, gaily jumping from stone to stone in a froth of foam. On either side of the Gave were fields full of wildflowers, and in the fields stood a few low stone buildings, half barn, half house.

At the other end of the valley I could see the steeple of a small church and high up, near the blue sky, a large open mountain curved round like a Roman circus, patched with large spots of eternal snow.

I filled my lungs; the air smelled like no other air I had ever smelled, the sky was of a clarity such as I have never seen, and in the grass at the donkey's feet grew little dark blue flowers and wild pink carnations.

Mya and Romeck had told me all about Héas for weeks and I knew how it would look, but it was a thousand times more beautiful than anything I had expected.

More than thirty years later, my son came from the United States and happened upon Héas by pure accident. It was the son who was so much like my father Marek, that I knew there was no death, or maybe for some of us there was life again.

What Héas gave me was lightheartedness, lightheadedness, and a total sense of freedom and peace. It was as though I were on some Tibetan mountain far away from the whole world. The mountains belonged to me and I belonged from the first second to those severe and proud mountains.

Our life in Héas was perfect. The house had three or four large, low-ceilinged rooms and a fireplace. It was a peasant house, with a vast kitchen and bare stone floors. At the back of our house lived a flock of sheep. I would hear them bleating every night as I fell asleep in the high, comforter-covered bed where I slept with Mya, and very early each dawn when we got up I would enter the warm barn and give them salt to lick from my palms.

We got up before the sun each day because we climbed the mountains and we had to be high up before the sun came out. Mya and Romeck prepared and packed our food for the day: hard-boiled eggs, salami, sardines, cheese, tomatoes, and bread. Before leaving we each drank a bowl of coffee with milk and ate some bread and butter. Then the picnic food was put in a rucksack on Romeck's back. I wore espadrilles, a cotton dress, and a sweater that I would take off as soon as the sun was out and it got warm.

Each morning we left around four or five o'clock at the latest. The valley was asleep in a blanket of heavy mist. We walked in silence along the mountain paths that Mya knew so well. After a time, the fog would start to lift and light would stretch across the sky, tearing the fog slowly apart. Then suddenly the sun would appear. We would sit and rest. Now we could see the mountains around us, and from somewhere came the tinkling of cowbells and the murmur of a running spring.

I was acutely aware of every sound, every smell, every moment of my happiness. My happiness was not something I remembered later with nostalgia—it was a precious state I lived in and I knew I possessed. I kept thinking, "I am nearly nine years old and I wish I would never, never grow up. I wish I would never be nine because I can't possibly ever be happier than I am now at eight."

After ten o'clock the sun became very hot but the air was so light and cool that we didn't feel too warm. We would walk, then stop to rest or to pick some flowers or berries to eat.

I was perfectly happy with Mya and Romeck, who were like a second set of parents, although totally different from my real parents. Romeck was a tyrant—an adorable, wonderful man, but a tyrant. First of all he tyrannized Mya. As far as I was concerned, I was perfectly willing to do whatever Romeck wanted, but I wished he wouldn't get into such rages all the time. And his rages were always directed toward the most futile things: Romeck got into a fury if we were two minutes late in the morning or if Mya indicated a wrong path while climbing, or if she forgot to bring an extra knife or tried to argue about politics with him. It was all funny because these things were so unimportant, anyway, and because Romeck was such a small man. A big man in a fury doesn't seem as funny as a small man in a rage.

But Romeck forgot his anger at once. His face, after he had been angry, took on a sheepish little boy's expression, full of remorse. He became his real self again, wise and tender and interesting. Mya forgave him right away, I saw it. Maybe because Romeck loved her. She must have been aware that he loved her, as everyone in Lectoure seemed to know it. But their love could only have been spiritual. I slept in the same bed with Mya every night, our house having only two beds. I kicked her every night while I slept, she told me.

. . .

Mya was so religious. In Lectoure, she went to mass every morning. She couldn't possibly have been Romeck's "mistress" as Sonia would have said, because no one who went to mass every day could be. If they loved each other it was more in the manner of an old couple, very used to each other who quarrel a lot, than like a pair of lovers.

Mya was rather husky. She was much bigger than Romeck. We climbed the slopes and I looked at them. Mya walked ahead, wearing a black dress as usual, and black stockings, high shoes, and a straw hat. Wiry Romeck followed behind with his beret on his head. With his cane he pointed to a slope on the opposite mountain, quite far away, and said to Mya and me, "Look there, look at that flock of goats near that big rock, aren't they pretty?" I looked all over the mountain but I couldn't see any goats anywhere.

"Where are they, Romeck?" I asked. "Where are the goats?"

"There, there," Romeck pointed again. "Mya, don't you see them?"

Mya looked here and there and then said, "Ah, yes! Of course, the goats. Black ones. How on earth can they stand on such an incline?" But I didn't see any goats. I looked all over, up and down the slopes. Nothing! No goats. Romeck was starting to fume. "What do you mean, you don't see them? They are right near that big rock. Don't you see a rock?" I hated it when Romeck got angry. Generally it was at Mya, but now it was at me.

"Can't you see the white spot, near a bunch of pink flowers? Now you do see the pink flowers?"

"Yes," I said, "the pink flowers."

"All right," said Romeck, a little more calmly. "Do you see now, one, two, three, four stones in a row?"

"No, I don't see them. I see two stones." But Romeck said it was not those stones. He got mad again. "Mya, show her. This child is doing it on purpose. How can she not see those goats? You see them, don't you? I see them. It's ridiculous. She must have much better eyesight at her age than we have!"

I was ready to cry. I didn't see any goats, maybe because my eyes were full of tears and everything was blurred. Then I said, "Oh, yes, of course, you are right, Romeck. I see those goats, black ones, on such an incline. I see them, I see them."

Romeck sighed with satisfaction. "Finally!" he breathed. "I knew you would see them. Let's keep going, now, we'll never reach the top if we stop like this for hours."

We started climbing again. I had not seen any goats, anywhere, but Romeck was not angry at me anymore and I felt a mixture of pleasure at his good mood, remorse at having lied to him, and a sort of sad wisdom about the adult world. You sometimes had to lie to them to make them happy.

As we were climbing the mountains Romeck would point out special sights to me, like the Brèche de Roland, which I had learned about in French history, the place where Charlemagne's nephew, Roland, had died after losing a long battle; or Mya would tell me about the plants we saw around us, the wild irises and rhododendrons, or about the multicolored butterflies, the tiny deep blue ones and the large white ones with velvety red and blue eyes on their wings. While climbing mountains with Mya and Romeck I learned more about history, geology, and botany than in my years in school.

Often our climbs would end at the deserted Circus, more than two thousand meters above sea level, called the "Cirque de Troumouze." There was no sign of man there, only a freezingly cold lake, eternal snow all around slashed with deep blue-green crevices, the wide expanse of sky, and a sort of majestic silence. Behind Troumouze was Spain—another country.

On Sundays we generally stayed home. Mya washed our

clothes and Romeck gave me some tutoring in spelling and arithmetic and tore his hair at my total ignorance in these subjects. There was one mass on Sundays in the little chapel and we went with all the peasant women who wore long black handwoven capes with hoods lined in bright red. The inside of the chapel was whitewashed and the people sat on old wooden benches, polished like mirrors from use. The Virgin set in an alcove was very old, maybe thirteenth century, carved in oak.

In Héas I didn't have to worry that anyone I knew would recognize me in church!

We went back to Lectoure after a month in Héas—in time for my birthday.

On that day, my ninth birthday, in Lectoure's stationery shop, I bought a notebook with a picture of Joan of Arc on the cover. That day I wrote on the first page:

> Today I am nine years old, this is going to be my diary. Dear Diary, I just came back from Héas. . . .

I have continued this diary over the years, adding more and more notebooks—and over the years I have told this diary everything that has happened to me. I still keep it, and by now it must be the longest diary in history!

🌷 Once again we left Lectoure at the end of that September I was nine. We came back to Paris and for the first time I started school on October third like other children. My mother had begun writing a book with my father's help. It was a story called *The Water Bearer* and took place in a Jewish village in Poland in some vague century. It was about a very poor, half-witted bearer who became a *tzaddik,* a sort of miracle-performing saint. It was a Jewish legend my father had heard in Yiddish—his Yiddish and Hebrew were very good; he spoke and read Yiddish fluently and knew the biblical Hebrew he had learned in the *Cheder,* the Jewish religious school, as a small boy. My father told the story to my mother and explained details about life in a *shtetel,* which my mother, who had been brought up in an assimilated city family, didn't know. My mother was writing the story as a novel.

To give her more time to write, my mother hired a mother's helper that year—a young German woman called Minie who was to help with the housekeeping while she learned French in Paris.

Minie had the longest nose I had ever seen. Not only was her nose out of proportion with normal noses, but the nostrils were as wide open as two dark caves.

I hated her instantly and passionately.

My diary became full of indignant pages about Minie's nose and my fury at having her around.

> Dear Diary, I must tell you that I hate Mademoiselle Minie and I can't wait until she goes back to Germany. Sonia also hates her. She is ugly; she has a nose I must draw here for you. . . .

An enormous nose decorated all of the opposite page.

There was a young man named Jacques, a painter who was also a violinist. He came from Poland and had no money. He came for dinner often and talked about painting. He had red-rimmed eyes and a very round face. Sometimes when my parents had to go out at night Jacques stayed to watch me. He had a room on the first floor of the building where my father's studio occupied the loft. Jacques's room was strewn everywhere with clothes and half-squashed tubes of oil paint and dirty rags, unfinished canvases, and leftover food. On a table in the middle of the food, the paint, the clothes, and the rags was Jacques's violin.

Minie's nose notwithstanding, Jacques suddenly seemed to be

coming every day to our house, helping Minie dry the dishes in the kitchen, then sitting and talking for hours with her. Minie even went to his terrible room in the building where my father's studio was, and my father said that Minie had succeeded in cleaning that room, had positively given it the look of the inside of a Swiss chalet.

I, who had always been extremely fond of Jacques, began disliking him for his visible interest in Mlle Minie.

Before we left for Poland the June I was going to be ten, we found out that Jacques had proposed to Minie and that Minie, who was a Catholic, had answered she couldn't marry him unless Jacques would convert.

I thought that was pretty shocking. How could anyone insist on having someone convert in order to marry! My parents were shocked, too.

When one of our friends heard that Jacques was going to study Catholicism in order to see if he wanted to convert for Minie's sake, she gave him a big speech. She was right, I thought. Besides, how could anyone marry a woman with such a nose? But Jacques was very obstinate and said he didn't care. He was not going to become a Catholic anyway, unless he was really convinced when he studied the religion.

Sonia and I had been reading the books of Alexandre Dumas. As there seemed to be hundreds of them, we had enough reading for several years and I was learning French history as seen by Dumas, maybe not very accurately but certainly romantically.

Our games, in which we disguised ourselves and re-enacted what we had read, continued, and our religious fervor was as strong. After the mood of Alexandre Dumas's novels, Sonia gave me one of a pair of a doll's red leather gloves and she kept the other. It was to be our secret sign. If one of us should ever

have desperate need of the other, we had only to send the little
red glove, and Sonia or I would fly to the rescue. The little gloves
were exquisitely cut and sewn and made of the softest leather,
the size of the hand of a large doll. I kept mine for long years
(I remember coming upon it quite recently), and then it van-
ished mysteriously, as such a glove should.

Sonia's father worked in a bank, which seemed a very strange
kind of work to me. What could anyone do in a bank? She
lived with her father all the time now in that one little room in
a small hotel. And, at the age of ten, Sonia cooked for both of
them in the kitchenette and took care of her father's clothes
and her own.

Our life at home was pleasant and quiet. The same friends
were around, Stanislas, Jacques the painter-violinist, and Jacques
the philosopher, Olivier, my uncle Samuel who would arrive
from Portugal for a few days, and the writer Levin who would
come from Chicago. I remembered having met Levin many
years before, when I was about three or four.

We were living in a boarding house where we ate in a common dining room around a large table with all the guests. One
day there was a young man sitting next to my father who said
that his name was Levin and that he was from America; he was
looking for a painter in Paris, he said, to write about him for an
American magazine. Did my father know this painter?

"Who?" asked my father. "What is his name?"

And this Levin said, "I am looking for a Polish artist called
Marek Szwarc."

So of course my father said he was Marek Szwarc and how
funny it was.

Levin was staying in the same boarding house where the landlady was so stingy "she was counting the matches," my mother
always said. Levin was great fun to have around because he
liked me. He had invented a game for me. He would tell me to

step on his feet and then he would hold my hands and start walking with my feet on his, while I balanced and wavered like a ship on a stormy sea.

Levin had brought a present for me this time. It was a puppet theater. He told me that he had one in Chicago, a real one where he gave shows from plays by famous authors, not for children but for adults. I was enchanted with my small puppet theater. It had everything: scenery and a curtain and half a dozen puppets with strings attached to their heads, arms, and legs.

But after Levin left and I started playing with his puppets, all the strings got tangled. It became a mess and I couldn't disentangle the puppets from one another.

My parents had told Levin that we were Catholics. He was such a close friend that they felt he should know and he didn't mind at all. It had been about ten years that my parents had kept their conversion secret and by now a few people knew it.

My father's work was selling quite well. He was considered one of the leading Jewish artists, and knew Chagall and Mané Katz and most of the figures around Montparnasse in the twenties. Everyone loved him. I had noticed how he could charm them all. But he was a quiet man, didn't talk much or loudly, and never pushed himself forward in any way. What there was about him was an extraordinary gentleness and warmth that would light up his whole face. But under that gentleness, he had great strength, the same solidity as the rocks he carved in his studio or the bronzes he cast. When I was near him he made me feel totally secure because I was aware of his strength, but I never feared this strength because of the tenderness and warmth emanating from him.

It was different with my mother. About her, I always had a feeling of insecurity. She wasn't strong; she was dependent on my father and on me, and she spoke much of how she had suffered when I was born.

Any information my mother gave me about sexual matters was always tied to pain. She told me over and over about how much she suffered giving birth to me—how lonely she was in the Paris hospital, how she could hardly speak French then, how the nurse scolded her because she screamed too much and then how terrible it had been to nurse me because her breasts were small and I had hurt her nipples when the milk wouldn't flow as it should and the nurse had had to press it out with a rubber tube. But what impressed me most was one bit of information she gave me some time later, I think, when I must have been about twelve. It was about the hymen being broken on the wedding night and how painful that was. This came to me as a great shock. I kept repeating "It hurts? It hurts?" I didn't mind the penis business, the place it entered—all that seemed fine; but that it hurt was shocking to me.

Once my father and I were walking near the Hôtel de Ville. It was a Jewish quarter of Paris, but a prostitutes' quarter was next to it. I knew about prostitutes. My parents had always explained to me anything I asked about, and I had asked about those very painted ladies waiting in the streets.

My father had said something about "making love for money." It wasn't very clear, but clear enough for the time being. Sonia, who didn't know how babies were born, but knew all about divorces, adultery, and prostitution, had explained things better.

As my father and I walked, we passed a street where many painted women stood in doorways. One of them came toward us. She smiled at my father and said, *"Tu viens avec moi, chéri?"*

I was horrified. How could such a vulgar-looking person say *tu* to my father and ask him to go with her? As if my father would ever have anything to do with a woman who "made love for money." Couldn't she see that my father was not a man who would accept making love for money? Couldn't she see that my father must have a wife who loved him for love, and a daughter who loved him with all the love there was in the whole world?

But to my great astonishment, my father smiled back, his same kind, gentle smile, and answered: *"Non, merci, madame,"* as if that woman were a friend of his to whom he was very considerate. And after looking at his smile, the same smile he had for me, and hearing the way he answered, so politely, the woman was changed in my eyes too. Suddenly she was no longer a vulgar, painted woman, but some lady working on that street, whom one should respect like anyone else.

My father didn't explain anything, didn't comment, and I didn't ask anything. It wasn't necessary.

My parents had a friend whom I had heard about without having met him. *Père* Lamy had had visions of the Holy Virgin. She would actually come and sit in his room and talk with him.

As I knew of the rabbi in Zgierz who had predicted my father's conversion, and as I had heard so often about miracles in the Bible and visions of angels and of God talking to Noah and Moses, and about the voices of Joan of Arc, and about Bernadette, who saw the Virgin in Lourdes, I saw nothing particularly extraordinary about an old priest in Paris being visited by the Holy Virgin.

One day my parents said that they were going to take me to meet *Père* Lamy. I ran to my room. If I was going to see *Père* Lamy I would ask him to give a letter to the Holy Virgin for me. Not being lucky enough to receive Her visits myself, I would at least use the opportunity of Her visiting him.

So I wrote a letter that was more or less like this:

Dear Holy Virgin,

I am so happy that I can write to you. I hope Père *Lamy will give you this letter when you come to see him. Please, Holy Virgin, I want to ask only one thing of you. It is that my best friend Sonia becomes a Catholic one day. This is the only thing I want. Thank you, dear Holy Virgin.*

Yours,
Tereska

I put my letter in an envelope and sealed it and wrote, "For the Holy Virgin."

Then we went to see *Père* Lamy. A priest took us to his room, the room where the Holy Virgin came to see him, and I saw a very old man with a peasant's face, very white hair, and a warm smile. He spoke with a provincial accent and patted my head and asked me in what class I was and if I was a good pupil. My mother asked him what the Holy Virgin did when she came to his room and *Père* Lamy said: "She sits above that chair, there." He explained that she didn't sit *on* the chair but a few inches above it, and that she seemed quite comfortable. She was a beautiful lady, he said, and she spoke very nicely. She wore a long dress and a veil, as the statues did. She was very kind to him and asked about his health. It was only if she spoke about the sadness of the world that she sometimes cried and two or three tears would roll down her face.

At the end of the visit, I pulled out my letter and I asked *Père* Lamy if he would give it to his illustrious visitor. *Père* Lamy took my letter and said "Of course, if she comes again I certainly will give her your letter."

He never knew if she would come again to see him.

A few years later the old priest died and Jacques Maritain

put all his papers in order. When I heard that, I asked Jacques if among the papers he had seen, by any chance, a letter I had written to the Holy Virgin. But he said, no, there was no such letter among any of *Père* Lamy's papers.

❦ I loved to listen to my father explaining things. He never got angry when he discussed anything, would listen attentively to what the other person had to say, and then, if he was asked directly to explain his own position, only then would he do it—quietly and simply. My mother was not so interesting because she always just agreed completely with my father. He could have said that the night was daytime and she would have been certain that it was so.

Otherwise it was touching, even for me, to watch my parents together. They held hands and kissed in corners like teenagers. My mother would worry if my father was five minutes late coming home and would go up and down the five flights of stairs to watch the street. Living with them was like living with a pair of lovers, forever kissing and looking at each other with adoration. Marriage looked to me like an ideal situation, a long happiness, but when I was thirteen or fourteen I must have asked my mother if I was ever going to have a brother or a sister, because then she said no, she and my father were not going to have another child ever because they had for years now had a "white marriage."

She explained. When I was about seven years old, they had decided to try it for a year. Some friends of theirs had had the same idea; they all wanted to spiritualize their love, they wanted to love on a higher level or something. When they saw that it could be done and that it hadn't hurt them and that, on the contrary, they felt their love for each other was better, purer, and greater, they continued. For years now they had

had no physical relations. That was a "white marriage."

Also, as my mother explained to me then, they wanted in some way to sacrifice their physical love because they were so happy together while so many couples were so unhappy. It was like an offering to God, like Abraham sacrificing his son so that in return other couples might receive from God such happiness as they had.

I was extremely impressed and felt that it was very noble of my parents. It also seemed easier to think of them as brother and sister than lovers, although I could see much tenderness between them.

My father was always so good to my mother: he treated her as someone precious to him and she depended on him totally. However one judged their decision, however strange it might seem, it was the decision of two very unusual people, and in their case it brought them closer together and kept their desire for each other young and intact.

That summer in Poland there was an exhibition of my father's works, and newspapers interviewed him; my mother was busy organizing the interviews and the meetings with art dealers and art collectors. She was still writing her novel and a French publisher was interested in it. My mother had gained some weight in the last years. She had been extremely slim, even ethereal-looking, when she married my father. She had always been very beautiful, and she still was. Just before she had met my father she had even been offered a part in a film, but she had arrived late for the interview and someone else had been chosen. I was always sorry about that as a child. I would have liked my mother to be an actress. She had remained slim until she caught sleeping sickness on the train between Warsaw and Paris. That sleeping sickness was *encéphalite léthargique,* and everyone always said how lucky we were that my mother had come out of it so well.

In Poland we took that same train to go and visit my father's parents in Zgierz. On the outskirts of Lodz the train passed the Jewish streets where all the stores had big paintings hanging outside, advertising what they had to sell. Those paintings always fascinated my father: the ladies in high-heeled shoes and fancy clothes, the bearded gentlemen getting haircuts, the large painting of a very red and blue shoe or an opened umbrella or a gorgeous turkey. My father said Chagall got his inspiration from these store shields and that they were genuine art. As we climbed my grandmother's stairs, we saw the angel my father had drawn on the wall with coal when he had been my age. My grandmother Salomé opened the door. She had such a beautiful name. She was very different from my grandmother Sofia. First of all she was tall and good-looking. She had been married to my grandfather Isucher when she was only fifteen years old, but that had been long ago.

The floors at my Zgierz grandparents' were wood, painted a bright red color, and my grandmother always had things to eat which my mother loved: marinated herrings, sweet carp, sweet carrots, and noodle puddings. My grandfather came out from his study to greet us in his absent-minded way. I always thought that he was never sure which of his grandchildren I was. With my father he spoke mostly in Yiddish or Hebrew. He was a Zionist and a friend of famous early Zionists like Bialik and Ushiskin. One of his daughters and one of his sons lived in Palestine and my grandmother would show me photos of them and of other people in Palestine, working in fields or on horseback, and all the photos had been taken under a strong sun. My uncles and aunts and cousins who lived nearby always came to greet my parents and I could see that everyone was proud of my father. He was the artist, the famous son who lived in Paris and was photographed in the newspapers. "That lazy Marek who would never study in school," my grandmother would say, laughing and putting her arm around my father's shoulders. I had the feeling that he was her favorite son.

My Zgierz grandparents were very different from my Lodz grandparents. There was for me something exotic about them, about their house, about their family. It was exotic the way my grandfather Isucher was a scholar and nothing else. He had never worked for a living. He only studied all day long, closed in his study, surrounded by so many books written in the strangest languages, languages long dead, belonging to civilizations that didn't exist any more. I was very much in awe of him. I would never have dared to sit on his knees and play with his beard as I did with my Lodz grandfather. The Lodz grandfather was a man very much of this earth, smoking cigars, collecting stamps, selling furs, telling jokes, always very well dressed, a very handsome, tall man. On the other hand, the Zgierz grandfather hardly talked or if he did it was with my father in Hebrew or Yiddish and I couldn't understand it. Everyone sort of whispered around him or told stories of how absentminded he always was—forgetting dates, appointments, people's names, even his own ten children's names. Ten children! What a big household that must have been in my father's childhood. I loved to hear him tell of the large table around which they all ate when he was a boy, with a waiter in white gloves serving them ceremoniously.

My Zgierz grandfather had grandchildren born in Palestine who lived among Arabs and orange trees. Somehow I could feel this family movement in the Zgierz house like some powerful underground river. Even then I wondered when I was with that family what had produced such diversity among its children. I looked around me with great curiosity. I liked that house—it was large and full of a feeling of the past which the Lodz apartment did not have. It was at once a Slavic house and a Jewish house. It had Jewish candelabra and very old furniture and those wood floors painted a bright red, in the Polish peasant fashion. And it had my grandfather's books and many green plants in pots and many photos on the walls in ancient carved frames, and sofas covered in green velvet. It smelled of camphor and lemon essence and my grandmother's cooking. Through the open windows voices entered from outside, Polish voices, children's cries, songs, music.

Going there was always an adventure. It was like going to see people on a boat just before sailing time; and as on a boat at those moments there were always people coming and going. One of my father's sisters came, her cheeks as red as the basket of apples she brought. She had very black eyes and very black hair. She laughed and talked loudly. She would take a big apple and say, "Look, Tereska," and split the apple in half with her bare hands.

My grandmother was reading aloud a letter from a son who was away, a neighbor dropped in, another daughter came to say good-bye. I walked out on a long wooden verandah and looked down in the courtyard where many blond Polish children were playing, running, crying, jumping rope. The noises, the movements, were all around me.

Later that summer I went again to the children's camp for a few weeks. I remember the name to this day—*Wisniova Gora* (the mountain of the cherries). At camp I taught the children French and played with them. My stories of life in Paris were something of a sensation at camp. We took long walks through immense Polish forests, looking for mushrooms. We hid in cornfields and in sunflower fields as vast as a sea, we ate blackberries with fresh cream that peasant women would bring to the camp. They were very pleasant, uneventful weeks. But I still remember the smell of the Polish mushrooms and when, years later, I was in Russia and saw some growing in a forest, and the same sunflower fields soaking in the sun, their petals all mussed up by the wind, and peasant women selling the same blackberries as in my childhood, my husband and my children couldn't understand my rapture over some ordinary mushrooms, berries, and sunflowers. But how could I explain to them—born in Chicago, born in New York, born in London, born in Neuilly-sur-Seine—what a little girl had felt, what happiness she had enjoyed, what tied her forever to a Slavic landscape which had no meaning for them.

And I wonder if for my children the landscapes, smells, feelings of their own childhood will remain as vivid in their memories as these remain for me.

That year when we were ready to leave Poland it was, as usual, after my school had begun. It was already snowing in Lodz and long after the High Holidays. I had gone, as I did each year, to the synagogue to bring flowers to my Lodz grandmother.

Wednesday in Poland was my grandmother's day for playing poker or mah-jongg with all her lady friends. They would assemble in her living room and seat me in turn on their knees to bring them luck. These were the same ladies who were with her in the balcony at the synagogue, who smiled and patted my head and kissed my cheeks.

My cousin Ianka, the cousin with whom I had indulged in those "bad" games when we were about four years old, came a few times to play with me. We never mentioned those games. Now we were big girls—almost ten—and we would rather forget such shameful memories. I had confessed all that long ago and been forgiven, but I was sorry that Ianka couldn't wash all guilt away too. I felt sorry for children who could not go to confession and repent and then be forgiven. It must have been so much harder for them, carrying so much guilt and remorse, accumulating it in their hearts.

Of course during the months in Poland I never went to confession or mass, but I was going back to Paris and there we could resume the Catholic side of our lives even if it was in secret.

All the family took us to the train in Warsaw. I had always liked the kissing and the good-byes and the commotion of the departures. Everyone brought us gifts and repeated the same bon voyage wishes and promised to write.

But this year, for the first time, I cried when we left. I looked at my grandparents, my tall, white-bearded Lodz grandfather Ludovic, so aristocratic-looking, and his little plump wife. And the absent-minded grandfather from Zgierz wearing a homburg hat, with his energetic, big-bosomed, wide-hipped wife. And I looked at all my uncles and aunts, the aunt who lived across the street from my grandmother and who always waved to me from her windows, and my cousin Ianka and my cousin Pietrek who was always considered my "fiancé" among the family, maybe because he was blond like me and just the right age, everyone said. I looked at them waving their handkerchiefs and growing smaller as the train picked up speed, and I cried for the first time, so bitterly that my father couldn't console me and kept saying, "We'll be back next summer, darling; don't cry, we'll soon be back again."

But maybe deep inside me I had some inexplicable knowledge that I would not be back for a very long time.

Paris. School again. Sonia was reading Victor Hugo and I too buried myself in *Notre-Dame de Paris* and *Les Misérables*. Some girl had given me a book by the fashionable, saccharine author of the period, Delly, who wrote edifying stories about poor governesses marrying rich heirs. My father found me engrossed in this book and got so angry he pulled the book away from me and threw it out the window. He said in an angry voice, "I won't have you reading this trash. If you have nothing to read come with me to the bookstore." And we went out, I, sniffling back my tears because I wanted to know if the poor governess would marry the son of the industrialist. But I knew better than to argue when my father got mad.

We went to the corner bookstore and my father told me to look around and see what I would like there. Finally we settled on poems by Musset and *The Flowers of Evil* by Baudelaire. The saleslady murmured that those books might not be "for that little girl's age" but my father said that if I wanted poems those were beautiful and if they were beautiful I could read them.

I took them home and I read and read. I loved them, especially Musset. I copied some verses in my diary:

Vous me demandez si j'aime ma patrie?
Oui—j'aime fort aussi l'Espagne et la Turquie.

Une heure est à Venise, heure des sérénades
Lorsqu' autour de St.-Marc, sous les sombres arcades,
Les pieds dans la rosée et son masque à la main,
Une nuit de printemps joue avec le matin.

Au-dessus des étangs, au-dessus des vallées,
Des montagnes, des bois, des nuages, des mers,
Par-delà le soleil, par-delà les éthers,
Par-delà les confins des sphères étoilées. . . .

and this verse:

Ta tête, ton geste, ton air
Sont beaux comme un beau paysage,
Le rire joue en ton visage
Comme un vent frais dans un ciel clair.

My mother found out that there was a studio and an apartment for rent inside an artist's city not far from Montparnasse. We went to see it. It was a dream. Around a courtyard full of flowers, bushes, and trees stood rows of artists' studios, two stories high. There was an entry room, then a very large and very tall studio with a whole roof of glass. Stairs led to a kitchen and cellar; other stairs to another room overlooking the courtyard. That room led in turn to a balcony—a *soupente*—which was suspended over the studio. It was ideal for us. My father would not have to go out to work. My parents would take the balcony as their bedroom and I would have the first-floor room with a small shower room. Downstairs the entrance would be our living quarters and we could eat in the kitchen.

We moved. The whole building, about twenty-five studios, had been built as a model artist's city for the World's Fair in Paris in 1900. The place hadn't been repaired or painted since, and our studio and apartment needed painting badly, but we had no money left once we paid the movers and the rent. Still it was so beautiful I couldn't believe we would live there. I immediately started dreaming of working in the garden and planting flowers as soon as spring came. I could see myself sitting there in warm weather reading a book.

Everyone in the building was an artist—a painter, a sculptor, or musician, even a few architects had sneaked in. But it was a very quiet place to live—no noise, no wild parties. Each tenant lived enclosed in his own house-like apartment. Each one got up early, worked hard, went to bed early. At ten o'clock all the lights were out and all the bohemians were asleep.

We also found out there was an excellent girls' school a five-minute walk away, but it was a convent school so it was impossible for my parents to send me there. How could they explain that I was going to a convent school? I had to stay on at the hated Collège Sévigné.

That spring would have been about the right time for my solemn communion—my long white dress and veil—but all that was out of the question too. It was much too visible.

Maybe as a reaction to all the imposed restrictions, my religious fervor increased, and Sonia was as mystically inclined as I. When we wrote to each other now I signed my letters "Apostle" and she signed hers "Discipulus" because in our religious relationship I was the leader. Sonia's uncle had given her a large box of stationery. The box locked and unlocked by pushing up the front like a garage door. We emptied it and inside, in secret of course, we built a small chapel with holy images, birthday candles, and a rosary. Each time I went to visit Sonia, she unlocked the box, lifted the front and we lighted the candles and knelt and prayed.

Then we played as usual, always the same game of acting out books we had been reading. We were still in our Alexandre Dumas period and so were in turn D'Artagnan, Athos, Portos, Queen Margot, Milady, Anne of Austria, the Count of Monte Cristo, Richelieu. A chapter in one of Dumas's books about a king of England was called "Remember" in English. I looked up the word and liked it. I had likings for certain words, like "Montessori" and "Yerushalaim"—and I decided to write in my diary, under the title "Remember," everything I did remember of my early childhood. I figured out that I was only ten and could remember many things which were still quite near me, while later I would forget them if I didn't write them down.

So I wrote about the image I had of myself walking for the first time in Lectoure, and many other memories.

REMEMBER:

The first thing I remember . . . my first steps. A very long time ago in a fog—a black piano leg. I catch that leg . . . the open door . . . Mommy. A young Mommy with a pink dress and black hair. I see only half of her. I don't know anything, only that I was over there near the door and that I am now alone near that black leg.

Lectoure. My little boyfriend cries. I take him home.

Lectoure—a convent. A nun gives me a not-yet-consecrated host to eat. The sun—the hot sun.

Paris— I go out with Daddy. A car. The car approaches me. Daddy catches me, pushes me behind him. The car passes so near us that I think the wheels must have driven over Daddy's feet.

A kindergarten. The one I went to before the Collège Sévigné. The teacher: "What is the largest animal?" I say, "The elephant." The teacher gives me a *bon point*.

The same school. A big girl pushes me. I cry. The teacher takes me in her arms.

I want more *bons points*. The children are all in the garden. No one is in the building. A classroom . . . the open door . . . a desk. I open the desk. There are *bons points* inside the desk. I take one . . . the largest. I go away. My heart doesn't beat. I feel very calm. I look at the stolen *bon point*. It doesn't have the same color as the ones I get from my teacher. Why? This *bon point* belongs to a higher grade. I can't use it!

The train between Warsaw and Paris. The cook has a tall white hat. Behind the windows it is all white . . . the snow.

Baden—I am lost in the hotel. I don't cry but I feel a tickling in my throat. Everyone is eating in the dining room. The red-carpeted stairs. Where is Mommy? I feel my eyes watering in spite of myself. A lady comes. She takes my hand. I am saved— here is Mommy!

In the children's summer camp in Poland—Little Janek asks me who Moses is. I am astonished that he doesn't know. He even doesn't know who God is. It is summer. The window is open. I look at the starry sky. In one corner the moon shines.

"Look, Janek," I say, "look, God lives there in heaven."

He says, "Where?"

I say, "There—in the moon."

Poland-Summer: All the children are still asleep. I get up. In my nightgown I softly open the door to the garden. I can just see a little corner of the park. There is a quiet sun, an early morning sun, flooding everything. I can see the dark spots made by the leaves of the trees on the ground. Chickens are pecking. There is a bench, a tree, and the sun. Such a quiet sun. Then, this silence . . . this quiet silence . . . this quietness. . . .

That winter we all had a complete surprise—especially Mlle Minie. Jacques had been studying Catholicism for about a year. He had decided that he believed in the religion and wanted to join it. He was baptized with my parents as his godparents. I mustn't have been present at his baptism because I don't remember it at all. Then, after Jacques had had his first communion and confirmation, he announced to all of us, but to Minie first, I imagine, that he had to go further than just becoming a Catholic. He wanted to follow the ideals of Christianity to what was for him their logical consequence. He wanted to become a monk, to dedicate his life completely to God, and so began looking for the right religious order.

Poor Minie! Even I felt sorry for her.

By now there must have been quite a number of people who knew about us. Even in Poland the summer before an artist friend had told my father, but laughingly as if he was repeating a great joke, that some people were gossiping about my parents and saying that they had secretly converted. As he didn't ask my father directly, but only repeated what someone had said, my father's only answer was a dry, "Really?" which didn't mean much. It must have been enough for this friend, because he changed the subject and didn't seem to attach any importance to the gossip. But I knew that my parents lived in fear that one day their secret would be uncovered and that their whole world would collapse. On the other hand, I think that in some ways they, like me, wished that the thing would come out in the open, so that they could face it once and for all and be rid of all the secrecy. More than ten years of it must have been enough for anyone.

That winter I wrote in my diary:

Dear God, please grant me one wish: Let me marry one day a converted Jew and have children who will be at the same time Christian and Jewish and make me that way the mother of a new tribe of Jews of Catholic religion.

We were living in the new studio-house and I was very happy there, but in school I was hopeless. I hated the school more than ever and my parents were seriously thinking of taking me out the next year.

To help me a little with my total confusion about arithmetic they asked a teacher at the Collège Sévigné to give me some tutoring at her house. Once, as I was leaving her apartment, her daughter, who was my age but went to a regular lycée, was talking to me in the doorway as my mother and the teacher were discussing something near us. The other girl said she had to hurry as she had to go to her catechism lesson and she mentioned she was studying the Gospels now. Before I knew what I was doing, I answered: "Oh! I have finished that part already!" The teacher heard me and looked astonished and puzzled and I blushed terribly and said quickly: "I mean I just read them out of curiosity." My mother quickly said good-bye and we left.

Spring came, as it did each year, in an abundance of blossoming chestnut trees. The boulevard where our building stood was lined with rows of tall, old trees. I started digging in the courtyard, turning up the earth and planting hyacinths, tulips, and narcissus which I had bought with my mother at the flower market on the Quai. Next to the *marché aux fleurs* was the bird market, and the scents of thousands of different flowers drifted among the cries of thousands of different birds.

That spring my father went one day, as he often went, to the cathedral of Notre Dame de Paris to look at the carvings, the statues, the stained glass windows. He loved especially the smiling Madonna, Notre Dame herself, standing under a blue velvet canopy holding her baby. There was a low mass in progress and as it was early morning my father decided to stay. He knelt in one of the rows in a side chapel and took communion with other people.

As he was crossing himself and leaving the chapel, a man who had been standing at the entrance to the chapel watching him all through the mass followed my father down the aisle and out of the cathedral.

He was a Polish-Jewish journalist, on a visit to Paris, who had himself come to Notre Dame for sightseeing. He knew my father well. He had heard the gossip about my parents' conversion and had not paid any attention to it, until by accident that morning he had noticed my father enter the side chapel of the cathedral and kneel. He came up to my father on the cathedral's *parvis*, shook hands, and asked if my father would have a cup of coffee with him.

They went to a nearby café and sat down. The journalist was pleasant and quite soon came to the point. He said he had seen my father at mass; had seen him kneeling, praying, crossing himself, and taking communion. My father said that it was all true. He was a Catholic, had been for about eleven years, and had kept it secret because of his and my mother's parents. He spoke quietly and firmly and asked the journalist not to tell anyone. He explained what a shock it would be for the families in Poland, what suffering and shame they would feel, how they couldn't possibly understand. When my father came home he was very calm. He told us what had happened and said that the journalist had sworn he wouldn't say a word about it, that he had been understanding and very friendly.

Three days later every Jewish newspaper in Europe and probably in the United States, too, carried the story of my parents' conversion.

Letters began arriving, from my grandparents, my uncles, my cousins, from my parents' friends—at first letters of disbelief, then letters of anger, then letters of accusations and threats.

My grandfather Isucher in Zgierz sat *shiva.* My father had explained to me what it meant, so I imagined my grandfather with ashes on his head and torn clothes, mourning his son as if he were dead.

My uncle Samuel wrote to my father saying he was a traitor. Another brother said that my grandmother would never write to Marek again—and she didn't. Most people from Poland had stopped writing or wrote only letters of insults, and in Paris the Jewish art colony also stopped seeing my father. When we walked along Boulevard Montparnasse or entered the Dôme, people would turn away, or get up and leave, or make unpleasant remarks. So my father avoided going to Montparnasse. Only a very small number of his old artist friends, painters like Yankel Adler, came directly to my father to ask his reasons for his conversion. These few good friends remained and kept coming back as if nothing had happened.

My grandparents from Lodz were less upset on religious and national grounds, but their social life was being wrecked. My grandfather Ludovic's customers stopped coming; their friends shouted at them; their family was ashamed to be seen with them. What should they do? Perhaps they should sell everything and come and live near us in Paris? They didn't want to lose us, whatever folly my parents committed, and they could see that we would never be able to come to Poland again. They had no one left since Henio's death except my mother and me, so they wanted to leave Poland. Life would be impossible for them now. My mother cried a lot, but she always cried a lot anyway.

I closed myself in my room and wrote a letter to my uncle Samuel. Maybe my uncle sent the letter back to my father, because I still have it.

Dear Uncle Sam,

My dearest daddy has read me your letter. I am writing to you by myself, without anyone, because I want to tell you everything on my mind.

Uncle Sam, you were my dearest uncle, the one I loved the most of all my uncles. But how can I love the slanderer of my father?

Can I love the one who calls my father a madman?

Dear uncle, I certify to you, I swear to you, that Daddy, Mommy and I have been Catholics for the last eleven years and you can see that during all those years my parents have been just as kind and that they loved Grandpa and Grandma just as much although you didn't know that they were Catholics. Me, too, I am a Catholic and I am proud of it. And I love Grandpa and Grandma. I am not Jewish by religion, but I am Jewish by race. I feel like Jews feel. I love the Jewish people.

O! My Uncle Sam, answer me, tell me if I am not right. It is you who are a coward to insult my daddy. You are free to be what you want to be, but if my daddy chooses to believe in Jesus, you have no right to call him a criminal and a madman. You should have regard for his wife and for his daughter.

I kiss you.

Yours,
Tereska

My uncle never answered.

All these events happened at the end of winter, I think. But although they must have been quite upsetting in our lives, I don't remember them well. I can vaguely recall people coming to our house and shouting, people we knew but also people we didn't know.

A knock on the door. My mother opened it. A man I had never seen before stood in the garden screaming in Yiddish the word for traitor—"*Meshumad.*" A knock on the door again. My mother was scared to open it so my father did. Someone else was there, and he yelled in Polish. My father stood still, he didn't answer, he didn't close the door, he waited. When the man had finished yelling, he muttered something and he went away. Then my father closed the door. He was pale, but he looked at me, smiled, and shrugged a shoulder. My mother spoke in Polish, as she always did when she was upset, and she called my father "Maretchku," a nickname she always used when she was very happy or very sad. "Maretchku, why didn't you answer? Maretchku, who was it? Do you know him?" Then in French she moaned, "*Mon Dieu, oh! mon Dieu,*" and she sat down and closed her eyes, a little dramatically, I thought, but I knew that she liked being dramatic.

I felt mostly anger. What right had these strangers to come to our house and insult us? What business was it of theirs?

My father kept saying, "These are sick people—fanatics—disturbed people. Every time something happens which comes out in the papers, there are always fanatics like that who get involved. One bit of news or another unbalances something in their minds and they have to react to it. It is really not even personal."

What about the others, the ones who did know us and who also came and screamed? Perfectly normal people, nice people, who were supposed to be friends, acquaintances, relatives. Those were not sick and they were not fanatics. Still they came, too, and started talking in an agitated way. They said: "Why did you do it? How could you do it?" And then, right away, "You! A Jewish artist, the son of Isucher, the brother of Samuel, such a distinguished Jewish family. Your father the chief of the Jewish Community of Zgierz."

I remember my father sitting, his head a little bent to one side, his eyes half open, his face closed. My father had a way of closing his face. He was sitting there and around his face there was a wall. He didn't speak. How could he? They wouldn't let him say a word. My mother tried to speak, to argue, but my father put his hand on her knee and said, "Let me handle this, Guinusia." To me he said, "Don't stay here, darling, go to your room. I'll come to see you later. There is nothing you can do, it's all right, don't worry."

I went to my room, picked up a book and tried to read. When I saw Sonia I discussed it all with her and described the latest happenings and we both became very indignant at some people's ways.

Sonia had a shock, too. Her father, hearing all the commotion, suddenly got suspicious of our long hours closed in behind locked doors and one day, while we were in school, he went into Sonia's room, forced open the stationery box, and uncovered the hidden chapel.

Sonia's father was totally unreligious but the idea that his daughter might be influenced to join the Catholic religion was abhorrent to him.

He rushed to my parents' house and made a scene, calling them names, screaming that they were trying to convert his child. My poor parents had no idea of my missionary zeal. Sonia's father made my father swear that I would never see Sonia again and my father promised that I wouldn't.

When I came home from school, upset as I already was over

all the letters, the scenes with friends, the threats from strangers who came knocking at my father's studio, I heard about Sonia's father and I was crushed at the idea that I had added to my parents' troubles. But when I heard that I was not to see Sonia again, I was overwhelmed with anguish. This was the first time in my life that I had encountered suffering. I had never been unhappy; I didn't know the feeling. I had been protected and loved by everyone and I had lived in a secure, warm world for eleven years. Now not only had that world become full of hatred and insults but also I was to lose my best friend, my only friend. My feelings for Sonia were much stronger, I think, than regular little girls' friendships. We really had only each other for friends; we shared all our enthusiasm, our loves, our reading, our games, our secrets. We were together every day in school and on every school holiday. We wrote each other long letters. We were as tied to each other as twins. But how could I make things worse for my parents? Didn't they lose their friends, too, their families, their parents? I cried but I agreed. I only asked my father for one favor: I wanted to say good-bye to Sonia. But even this my father refused. He said that Sonia's father had made a point of my never seeing Sonia again, even for a last good-bye.

So I thought of a plan. I asked my father to let me go up to Sonia's hotel and there write my good-bye to her on the pavement. To this my father said yes.

We went hand in hand. I was holding a piece of chalk and tears ran down my face. In front of Sonia's hotel I stooped and wrote in big letters on the pavement: TERESKA CAME HERE TO SAY GOOD-BYE TO YOU, SONIA. Then we left.

Years later in New York Sonia told me she never saw the message.

Part III 🌷 *Convent School*

My parents immediately took me out of the Collège Sévigné and my mother and I went to visit the convent school for girls, around the corner from our boulevard. Now I could go to a convent school, as I had wished.

It was a large white house set in an enormous garden full of flowers. We waited for the Mother Superior in the parlor, which reminded me of living rooms in some of Lectoure's provincial houses.

There was a round table covered with red plush, with palms and green plants in pots. On the walls were pictures of saints and photos of the nun who had founded the order. There were eighteenth-century chairs against the walls, a chaise longue covered in bottle-green velvet, and a Persian carpet. The air smelled of mothballs and ,ax.

It looked comfortable, middle class, and secure, and I liked it. The Mother Superior came in. She explained to my mother about the order, which was a female version of the Jesuits. The school was devoted to the education of girls from well-to-do families and tried to make them future good wives and mothers. By good, the Mother Superior said, was meant well educated, cultured, pleasant, emotionally stable, reliable, responsible women who would have good taste, a serious religious upbringing, would be companions to their husbands, and know how to bring up their children as good Catholics and good French people. In other words, the order was devoted to raising generations of middle-class bourgeois Frenchwomen, in a tradition of rationality and equilibrium.

To achieve this the nuns followed the doctrines of Saint

Ignatius Loyola and, of course, most girls' brothers were being brought up at the corresponding Jesuit schools. My mother explained that we were Jewish as well as Catholic and that she and my father were Polish and artists, and that up to now I had done very little studying in school and was probably very ignorant compared to the rest of the pupils.

The Mother Superior smiled and asked me a few questions, and told my mother that my dress was much too short. I would have to wear the school uniform and it had to cover at least my knees. Otherwise all was well and I could start the next Monday. The hours were from eight thirty to three thirty, and I could go home for lunch as I lived so near. I would have to take Latin. My mother shouldn't worry about my spelling and arithmetic, the nuns would give me any extra help I would need. And now she would show us around.

I had never seen such a beautiful school. The floors shone like mirrors. All the windows had long, immaculately white, hand-crocheted curtains. There were green plants everywhere. Whenever we entered a classroom all the girls, in light blue smocks over navy blue uniforms, would rise and look at us with interest.

The Mother Superior told my mother what the class was. A nun stood at her desk and smiled at us. When the Mother Superior started to leave, a girl walked to the door, held it open, and curtsied.

If we met a child in one of the long corridors she would stop and curtsy too. I was duly impressed and looked forward to the navy blue dress and the curtsying and the large classrooms with windows opening on the garden full of flowers.

At one end of the garden there was a tennis court and at the other a small grotto imitating the Grotto of Lourdes—with the Lourdes Madonna in her white dress and blue sash, and a veil on her head, her hands joined.

The Mother Superior took us to the chapel which was decorated in what my father called "the St.-Sulpice style," meaning plaster saints with red lips and blue eyes and pinkish complexions, raising convulsed stares to heaven.

But I didn't care. I wanted to go to this school even if its taste in art wasn't perfect. Now that I was completely free to be a Catholic, I wanted to be in a really Catholic school. I brushed aside any idea of studying spelling and arithmetic. Here I would spend my days praying in that lovely chapel.

When I got to school the next Monday I was shown a desk and introduced to the seven or eight girls who were in the same class. Classes were small, because the nuns had not been officially allowed to teach since a law had separated Church and State and done away with most teaching orders. It was explained immediately that if I heard a certain bell ring all the teaching nuns would disappear, the few civilian teachers would gather some classes together and various older pupils would take over the rest. The bell meant the visit of a state inspector coming to make sure that the nuns didn't do any teaching. So I was back in a state of secrecy.

But it didn't bother me. It added to the fun. I sat at my desk for half an hour impatiently, listening out of politeness to the nun who was giving us a *dictée*. Then I thought that was enough academic effort for the day, and raised my hand to ask if I could now go to the chapel and pray.

The amazed silence in the class quickly gave way to a peal of laughter. The nun rang a little bell to re-establish order and told me sternly that I was not to joke but to concentrate on my spelling.

I felt mortified and considerably cooled in my enthusiasm for the school.

The nuns seemed extraordinary creatures to me. I had never seen so many at such close range. I had imagined them as ethereal souls praying and mortifying themselves all day. But these nuns were young and old, some of the young ones quite pretty. They laughed and jumped rope at recess, played a quite rough ball game and seemed very much made of flesh and blood. The old nuns were full of funny little habits which the girls knew well and exploited. There was a nun who was always too hot and who had to have all the windows open in her class and one who was an ardent royalist and would talk for hours about the pretender to the throne, the Comte de Paris, and forget all about the lesson she was supposed to teach.

The nuns lived in a separate house, an annex to the school, which could be reached by a long, glass-walled corridor. There they slept and gathered for their own recesses; we could hear them then, laughing like ordinary people. The nuns' dining room was next to ours and sometimes I would see a nun coming out of it still chewing on some food. I couldn't believe that they actually ate food like all of us.

There were sister-nuns and mother-nuns. The sisters were all uneducated countrywomen who had joined the Order to perform domestic tasks. They cooked and cleaned and gardened. They were mostly old and very friendly, and the mother-nuns always spoke extremely respectfully to them, to show us, I guess, that they were in no way inferior.

In class the mother-nuns were quite stern; I could never escape a nun's gaze. If I didn't pay attention for a minute and looked out the window at the garden, *Mère* Anne-Marie would tap her desk with her ruler and call me: "Thérèse, don't dream. What did I just say to the class? Repeat it."

Mère Anne-Marie was young and pretty. She wore her order's habit—a little round bonnet with a white ruffle framing her face, a long black dress, and a black shawl.

After I had been in school about two weeks she called to me after class one day and asked me to wait. When the other girls had left, she took me to my desk and asked me to open it. Inside was my usual mess. Nobody had ever taught me to keep things in order, so my desk was a hodgepodge of books and notebooks, pencils, paints, rulers, my knitting all tangled, the remains of my ten o'clock snack, and a half-open, almost spilled bottle of ink.

Mère Anne-Marie showed me how to arrange all my books neatly in a row on one side, then how to pile all the notebooks one on the other; how to put the pens and pencils in a leather pouch I had, and how to close the ink bottle securely. She untangled the knitting and threw away the crumbs of bread and the sticky, melting lollipop. Then she said: "Thérèse, you are a new girl so I don't want to ask you to do too many things at once. But I am going to ask of you only one thing. Will you do that one thing for me?"

I said yes enthusiastically. I already loved that nun and I was sure she would ask me to spend more time in prayer.

Mère Anne-Marie said, "I want you to keep your desk in perfect order, the way it is now. That's all I ask of you. Because once your desk is in order, it will be easier for you to learn. You'll see."

I have been orderly ever since.

On the whole I was getting along well with the nuns, old and young. But not with the children.

When I arrived at the school I had been very eager to make friends. I wanted so much to find a new friend, someone like Sonia. I was suffering very much from the loss of Sonia's friendship. I had never seen nor heard from her again, and although I knew that she had been under great pressure from her family not to see me, I had hoped that with all the liberty she had to move around she would manage to sneak in to visit at least once. But she didn't.

As for the girls at the convent school, they didn't seem to like me. They thought I was strange. First of all they were all very polite, well bred, uncommunicative; they lived by rules. I was totally impulsive, romantic, undisciplined. My knowledge of languages, history, and literature was much greater than theirs, but my ignorance in grammar, spelling, geography, and arithmetic was overwhelming. The girls knew I had foreign parents; they knew I was Jewish although Catholic, they knew I had traveled in several countries, they knew I had read books they were not allowed to read, that I spoke Polish, that my father was a sculptor and my mother a writer.

They were nice to me, but from a distance, viewing me like some strange object from another planet. As for me, I couldn't even distinguish them one from another. They were a bunch of giggly girls, some fat, some skinny, some blond, some dark—a mass of active and healthy-looking girls, all dressed alike, all talking in polite accents, all whispering behind the nuns' backs, all taking prayers and chapel visits very lightly as rather a boring thing, all very French, very organized, very adult in their ways of talking. And in that mass I was trying to locate another Sonia.

I was also being prepared for my solemn communion, and at least I had one advantage now—I could be dressed like a bride and walk through the streets of Paris in broad daylight.

The religious ceremony was in the ancient church of St.-Etienne-du-Mont, just behind the Panthéon, in the Latin Quarter.

And that day I took part, with dozens of girls and dozens of boys, carrying tall lighted candles, in the outdoor procession all around the Panthéon. The girls were all in long white dresses, gloves, and muslin veils which the wind blew and tangled, had white rosaries hanging from their wrists and held white prayer books. The boys were freshly combed and cologned and wore, for the most part, their first long trousers. They had dark blue suits and white ties and, on their forearms, white sashes with fringe. My father said the ceremony was an echo of the Bar Mitzvah and the sash on the boys' forearms was like the Jewish *tallis*.

My father would always point out to my mother and to me all the resemblances between the Jewish and Catholic religions and he would quote the Pope who had said, "Spiritually we are all Semites." He would show me in the prayers of the mass all the passages from the Bible and from Jewish prayer books. "Holy, holy, holy"—"*Kadosh, kadosh, kadosh,*" he would say.

"The Catholic religion has its roots in Judaism," he often told me. But he felt that the Catholic religion had gone further than Judaism, that it had taken the best in Judaism, had explored it and made it richer and more human too. He believed that by being a Catholic he was a more complete Jew.

One day the Great Rabbi of Paris had come to call on my father and they had closed the door to my father's studio and talked for hours.

When the Great Rabbi left, he had shaken hands with my father and seemed very friendly. Later my father told us that they had discussed religions, the Messiah, Judaism, Hasidism and prophecies, and that the discussion had been pleasant and interesting.

I think that this rabbi had liked my father and had not felt so far from him. He looked that way when he left.

And many years later I was speaking with another rabbi—from America—who had met my father in the last years of my father's life. The American rabbi said to me, "It is now years since I talked with your father in Paris, but I will never forget him. He was a most extraordinary man, and I must tell you, Tereska, we talked about his conversion and about Judaism and Catholicism. Your father was the best Jew I have ever met."

❦ That summer we went back to Lectoure and then to Héas.

Lectoure—if I had a home town it would be Lectoure. Paris is too big, too splendid, to be a home town. But Lectoure, the small Roman city nestled inside her high walls in the shadow of her fortress-cathedral, that could be my home town.

That summer in Lectoure, my father was painting most of the time: peaceful landscapes of narrow alleys joined at the rooftops by stone archways and luscious still lifes of Mya's kitchen table, spread with her morning marketing—onions, a few pears, a bottle of wine. My mother was still rewriting and correcting her novel. I read and watched the gypsies.

For choice of reading I had a vast library. Next door to Mya lived a middle-aged bachelor, the town's banker. He had never married and had only one passion: books. These books, thousands of them, were first editions, bound in expensive leather. He had all the French classics and many translations of foreign classics. M. Lagarde never lent a book of his to anyone. They were much too precious to him. But for some reason he trusted me. Maybe he felt I loved books as much as he did. He was a very shy man who never talked much and, walking in Lectoure's streets, never looked at anyone to avoid having to stop and make conversation. He was slightly overweight and baby-faced and wore, in Lectoure's heat, an uncomfortable dark suit, stiff shirt, collar, and a vest.

M. Lagarde let me come to his library whenever I wanted and choose any book I wanted. He never asked me which book I took. I didn't talk much to him. I would enter, smile, choose a book, shake hands politely, and depart. Then I sat all day next door in a wicker chair built like a small alcove or a big egg. I loved that chair. I felt protected on all sides in it; it was like a womb or a sarcophagus. I would put on my white cotton gloves (part of the convent school uniform for going to chapel) so as not to dirty the precious pages of M. Lagarde's precious volumes in any way.

When M. Lagarde passed by on his way to the bank or his way back home, he would shyly glance at me, and seeing me holding one of his books, my hands covered in white cotton gloves, would throw me a quick smile.

In the books I tried to bury the pain. Now I couldn't write long letters to Sonia about what I was reading, telling the story, discussing the characters, comparing it with other stories. Never again would I be D'Artagnan or La Esmeralda or Fabiola. I had lost Sonia. I had lost all the fascinating lives I could take on. But I still had books.

Whenever I got tired of reading, I went to see the gypsies. Lectoure had many gypsy caravans which camped under the walls of the *Bastion*—a public garden planted with tall trees. Lectoure was kind to gypsies. Some towns chased them, didn't allow them in, but Lectoure let them stop and build fires, wash their clothes and hang them on lines between trees. Nobody cared, or bothered them, or paid any attention to them—except, maybe, for me.

Long hours I would sit on the *Bastion* wall watching the gypsies. I would imagine their journeys across Europe. I would marvel at their dark faces, at their colorful clothes, at their dirty, ragged children so full of bounce and life. I would dream. I too was a gypsy. I lived in a caravan with one of the clans. I camped at the Saintes-Maries in Camargue for the annual pilgrimage I had heard of. I was the mistress of one of the tall, handsome, wild-looking men. I liked the idea of being someone's mistress because of reading Alexandre Dumas. A mistress was exotic and romantic.

In August, Mya, Romeck, and my parents decided that this time they would all rent the smuggler's house in Héas for a month. Mya and my mother packed a crate of food, all the things we would need and wouldn't be able to find in Héas, where there was not one single store: cans of sardines, sugar, salt, coffee, cans of meats, matches.

Héas could provide us with fresh milk, some tomatoes, eggs, and cheese. We could gather the wild spinach that grew there in abundance, and fish the best trout in the Gave. And at the entrance to Héas, where the large rocks had fallen during the avalanche, grew enormous, sweet, perfumed raspberries. The place was called *Le Chaos,* and we went there often with Mya and Romeck to gather our dessert.

Once a week people from Gèdres, the town two to three hours' walk below Héas, came up bringing mules loaded with mail and large round loaves of homemade bread which would last us for a week without getting stale. If we had needed something very urgently, we would have had to walk down to Gèdres. But it never happened. There was nothing we ever needed that was not in Héas.

My mother didn't like climbing mountains. She had always had very fragile ankles which twisted easily. So my father stayed with her at the house in Héas. They would read, sit near the Gave, or walk to the chapel, while Mya, Romeck, and I resumed our routine: up every morning around four o'clock, hot coffee drunk quickly, and out into the most beautiful nights, with flashlights to guide our way, with sometimes a moon or bright stars and sometimes only a deep, silent fog.

Only Héas could replace Sonia.

My grandparents from Lodz were selling their fur store and their apartment, their furniture and books and carpets, and were emigrating to Paris. They were to arrive in the fall.

My father had rented an apartment for them in a Jewish district near the Grands Boulevards, on a street where mostly furriers from Poland lived. He felt that it would make things easier for the émigrés.

It was a very small place compared to the vast apartment in Lodz, but my grandfather Ludovic would be retired now—more or less—and couldn't afford a big rent.

He did bring with him some furs from Poland. He said he would sell them directly to dealers, buy more and sell again—just to keep busy.

My grandmother had brought her most precious possessions from Lodz and soon the small apartment took on a strange air of Lodz.

In the dining–living room and the bedroom hung hand-made lace drapes, the floors were covered with expensive fur rugs, the furniture was *acajou*. There were silver candelabra and yellow and red cut-glass vases from Czechoslovakia, many family photos and all the portraits my father had done of my grandparents, my mother, and of me over the years, and had given my grandparents. To those he added a portrait he had done of me that past summer in Héas. I was reading, head bent, a book on my lap, wearing a blue dress and a small white canvas hat. I liked that portrait particularly, because it had been done in Héas. It was like having Héas in Paris with me.

The Germans must have liked it too. They took it, with all the rest of my grandparents' precious last possessions, when they occupied Paris. Nobody knows what happened to any of it.

While my grandmother brought to Paris her silver and her piles of sheets and blankets and knicknacks, my grandfather brought what was most precious to him. My grandfather only sold furs for a living—his real interest was stamps. Now, in Paris, working less, he had more time for his stamp collection, and he devoted himself to it.

I remember Sundays, which we always passed with my grandparents. My grandmother was a great cook, and on Sundays she would make each one of us his favorite dish: gefilte fish for my mother, liver pâté for my father, and steak tartare for me. My grandfather, his white mustache tinted with brownish spots around his mouth from his cigars, sat at the dining-room table smoking one after another, while my grandmother prepared the meal in the kitchen. He would lift a stamp delicately with tweezers and examine it under the porcelain chandelier he had brought from Poland. His right hand always had a slight tremor in it, so it was hard for him to pick up the stamps, but he managed. He kept the nails on his small fingers very long and used them to handle the stamps. I would sit next to him for hours looking at his collection and learning about stamps.

Every Sunday afternoon he went to the stamp market in the gardens of the Champs Elysées. Soon he started taking me with him. We walked along the Grands Boulevards to the Opéra where we caught a bus to the stamp market.

The Grands Boulevards were like one big whore—selling themselves all over in cinemas and stores—glittering and fake and cheap. They were long, vulgar displays of clothes, jewels, bags, theaters. I was fascinated. There was nothing like it on the Left Bank. I insisted each time that we walk all the way from the Rex Cinéma, near where my grandparents lived, to the Opéra. It was quite a walk but my grandfather didn't mind. Very tall, with an imposing white beard, he walked slowly in his well-cut Lodz coat with a fur collar, a homburg on his head, carrying a cane studded with thousands of tiny nails he had hammered into it as a hobby.

I looked at every store window and at every display of pictures in front of the cinemas. I was still not allowed to go to movies more than two or three times a year, so they were most exciting. But on the Grands Boulevards at that time most theaters were showing what must have been the equivalent of the Forty-second Street films in New York. I was very puzzled by the poster photos. There were lots of half-naked girls in beds and men with whips and nudist films. Although I knew how babies were born, it wasn't connected for me in any way with nakedness, sensuality, or violence. I had no idea what these strange scenes meant.

One day when we took the bus at the Opéra, I stood on the outside platform as usual, looking at the passing streets, and my grandfather went inside to sit.

The platform was crowded and someone was leaning at my back and pushing. At first I didn't pay any attention. Then I distinctly felt a hand on my back, sliding downward. I moved—but the hand found my loins again. I moved again, getting scared, and threw a glance backward. A man was standing behind me and his hand kept returning however I tried to avoid it.

I was terribly scared. I didn't know why, but I was terrified. Fortunately, just then the bus arrived at our stop, my grandfather came out on the platform, and I squeezed my way through the crowd out of the bus.

I went back to the convent school. I had had only one term there before summer, but somehow when I came back in October I already felt like a *ancienne,* an old pupil. Each year school started with three days of retreat. There were no classes, but twice a day there was a lecture in the chapel by a Jesuit father and in between these lectures we walked around the garden in silence, meditating, reading religious books, writing our thoughts in small diaries or praying. Whatever we did was done in silence.

I liked the retreat. It was fall and the leaves were slowly turning red and gold on the trees. The chrysanthemums were opening all over the garden in a burst of yellow, copper, and mauve. The sister-nuns were raking the alleys and burning leaves.

During retreat all was very quiet in the garden and in the

house. I liked that dreamlike stillness. The only sound one heard was the chapel bell, or a bell which rang at the inside entrance to the school whenever a nun was called to the parlor. Each nun had a specific number of rings and knew in this way when she was wanted. We would listen to that iron bell clanking and count: two, Mother Superior; three, *Mère* Marthe; four, *Mère* Anne-Marie. . . .

There was a girl I noticed during the retreat. She had been in a lower class the previous term, but had been switched to my class because she was said to be very bright. She too was about eleven years old. She wore her short hair cut just like Sonia's, straight, with a bang across her forehead, but her hair was very blond and her small face was always set in a mischievous smile. There was something about her which made me notice her among the other girls.

She had a tomboyish air. Her socks were always falling down her legs and a nun always gestured for her to pull them up.

Once, during retreat, she forgot about the rule of silence and exclaimed loudly: "Gosh! I lost my prayer book. Who stole it? I bet someone stole it!" with a very slight foreign accent I couldn't place. Half the girls started giggling, while the other half went "*Chut, chut,*" with their index fingers across their lips.

A few days after the retreat we were standing in the garden at the ten o'clock recess. The girl, whose name I now knew was Lucilla, was eating a piece of bread spread with jam. She turned to me and asked some question, then said, "I like you; let's be friends." Impulsively I jumped at her, putting my arms around her shoulders. It shook the bread from her hand and it fell to the ground on the jam side. I thought, Oh my God, here goes my first friend in this school, but Lucilla bent down, looked at her spoiled snack and only shrugged and said, "It's all right, never mind."

We spent the rest of the time talking. Her name was Lucilla de Castro, and she had two sisters in the same school, Mariana and Isabelle. She also had two brothers, but they were in some school in Switzerland. The three sisters were boarding at the school and Lucilla said she would take me upstairs to show me the dormitories and her cubicle.

Lucilla said she was Peruvian. She spoke Spanish, "But," she said, solemnly, "I am not Spanish. I hate all Spaniards. They invaded Peru. I'll tell you all about it."

Her mother lived in Paris and her father lived in Lima. Lucie, as she was called, didn't say more about it on that occasion.

Before class there was a short prayer and I noticed that Lucie opened her desk and, hiding behind the lid, was learning her geography lesson while we recited an Ave Maria.

When it was her turn to answer geography questions, she knew all the answers perfectly.

During the after-lunch recess I came back to school early to spend the recess in the garden with Lucilla. I asked her about that geography lesson and she smiled her tomboy smile. "I never learn my lessons, they are boring. I just glance at them during prayers and as I listen to the nun when she explains the lessons, I remember it enough for the next time." She had a fantastic memory and was the best pupil in the class.

Soon we were great friends. With her I didn't feel the emotional exclusiveness I had felt toward Sonia. It was more of an open, pleasant friendship which became very strong but was more normal for two girls of eleven. We didn't dream and act out fantasies, but we talked a lot and very intimately about our lives, our problems.

Lucilla was impressed by my artist parents and my Jewish origins. I was impressed by her stories of Peru, of her brothers and her mother.

Her older sister had very white skin, very dark hair and eyes, and was a pet pupil of the nuns. She never answered back, she was quiet and polite, she embroidered beautifully, she sang well, and she never broke the rule of silence in the corridors. Because of that, I didn't like her. The youngest sister was cute and gay and spoiled.

Lucilla was a very good student but extremely undisciplined. She enjoyed disobeying orders and was the first rebel I had met. The idea of not obeying the nuns or teasing them had not entered my head. Now I could see there was a point in sneaking out of the study hall to meet in the lavatories to talk, or drawing pictures behind my raised book while *Mère* Helen was teaching us English. The point was that it was fun.

Mère Helen was Irish. Her English lessons were very boring, especially when she insisted that we read Shakespeare when we couldn't even ask in English for a pound of green beans. Lucilla taught me a trick. Whenever I didn't want to sit through an English lesson, she said: "Just tell Mother Helen that you don't believe in hell; that will do it, you'll see."

I tried it. *Mère* Helen had just started asking us about English grammar, when I raised my hand and said, "*Ma Mère,* I have a problem. I am sorry to interrupt but it bothers me a lot."

Mère Helen was not so young. She wore metal-rimmed, round eyeglasses, which she now pushed down her nose, and said in French, with her Irish accent, "What is it, Thérèse? I am listening."

I said: "*Ma Mère,* I really try but I just can't believe in hell. How can God allow it?" *Mère* Helen's face got very red and she said, "All right, let me explain it again."

She explained it again ten times a year. There was always a girl who "couldn't believe in hell" and then we had no English lesson but a lesson about hell, which was much more fun. Lucilla also taught me to slide on my stomach down the bannister leading to the basement where our dining room was. She taught me to sneak to the kitchen and beg the sister-cook for a piece of chocolate or a cookie. The sister-cook could never resist her. Lucilla had ways. She looked so starved at those moments and would put on such smiles. Then, when the sister finally gave in, Lucilla would jump up and kiss her on both cheeks and the sister would beam all over.

Another girl in my class was called Annie. She was very tall and at twelve she already looked fifteen or sixteen. She had very straight hair, cut just below her ears, and a big nose and lips like the Bourbon kings, the lower lip slightly pendulous. I know now who Annie looked like—and Annie's mother, too—: General de Gaulle. They had the same height, the same big noses, the same Bourbon lips, the same shape of head. In school Annie was inattentive. She tried to imitate Lucilla's wild ways, except that while Lucilla was rarely caught, being too nimble for the nuns, Annie's loud voice and laughter got her caught and punished each time. "Annie, you'll stay in class during recess," said *Mère* Anne-Marie sternly. "Annie, you'll copy your Latin theme three times."

At her home I discovered another Annie, a lady, a perfect housekeeper, gentle, smiling, serving me tea, polite, reasonable, knitting herself a sweater, discussing her future. She wanted to marry a colonial officer and live in Algeria. She wanted six children. She knew their names already. She was against birth control, flirting, two-piece bathing suits.

Her father was a lawyer and she lived near the Luxembourg Gardens. At night we always left school together and she walked me to the corner of my street. We talked there for a while under a street light before she went on and I turned toward my house. We called that corner *La cour des adieux* after the place where Napoléon had said his last good-byes to his troops before he left for exile.

How often we sat at *La cour des adieux* on a bench under the chestnut trees. One day we devoured there a whole kilo of *pain fantaisie*, the long French bread, and drank together from the bottle a gallon of milk. We were thirteen and very hungry . . .

Because of my friendship with Annie and Lucilla I was now rushing home for lunch, swallowing my food in a hurry, and running back to school to be on time for the one hour, after-lunch recess. I became very good at dodge-ball, which we called *la balle au prisonnier*. We also jumped rope. Two girls would hold a long rope and turn it while the others lined up to get under it and jump until they missed a step. Or we would play hide-and-seek in the large garden.

The older girls played tennis and ignored us little girls. They wore their hair long in the back, held with a ribbon or a barrette. They whispered among themselves and all had a crush on one mother-nun they liked particularly. If that mother-nun was the one who supervised recess that day, they would surround her and talk animatedly with her for the whole recess. They talked about books or plays they had seen, or travels, or even politics. I heard them mention Mussolini a few times, but I wasn't interested in the older girls.

Because I had been accepted by Lucilla, I soon became accepted by all the other girls. Perhaps it was also because I myself was changing. The school had transformed me into a real French girl. Before I came, I had been the high-strung, too-sensitive child of foreigners living in France. I was a mixture of cultures, the only child of an artist. But now I had become another French girl—French and Catholic—wearing the schoolgirl uniform: two braids, the ends clasped by a barrette, the navy blue dress with a round white collar, the light-gray stockings and black patent-leather shoes. Curtsying when shaking hands with any grownups, studying Latin, singing in the school choir (although I couldn't carry a tune). Playing jokes on the nuns, learning "good manners" at the special classes we had just for that, learning to knit, to embroider, to sew. I hated Latin and learning to sew. I giggled with the others at the *leçons de bonne tenue* when an old nun taught us how to undress "modestly." I had *fous-rires*—uncontrollable giggles with Lucilla, until our cheeks ached.

My parents didn't recognize me. Where was their dreamy, sensitive, lonesome child? I was turning into a regular tomboy, like Lucilla. I had no time anymore for posing for my father or for sitting around when his friends came. I had lessons to learn, homework to do. I had to rush to school to play ball. At nine o'clock I was exhausted and fell asleep without even reading in bed.

Lucilla always had wild ideas. Her latest had been for three of us to arrive in class one morning with my face white with talcum powder, Annie's covered with yellow powder, and Monique's eyes enlarged and outlined with a black crayon. It was for *Mère* Helen's English class that we got ourselves up that way. We waited for her reaction, but nothing happened. Maybe she was wiser than we thought. She looked at us as if there were nothing special on our faces and never made any comment. So all we could do was go and wash.

One day one of my mother's friends had a premature baby and we went to the clinic to visit her. In school the next day I told the class about the tiny baby, born in the seventh month of his mother's pregnancy, lying in a glass incubator. A nun heard me and the next day my mother was called to the school parlor.

"Madame," the Mother Superior said, "do you know that Thérèse is very well informed about the facts of life?"

My mother said of course she knew, that she and my father had told me all about these things a long time ago.

"I am glad that at least she had been informed by you and not by some other child," said the Mother Superior. "But, madame, she absolutely mustn't tell other girls in this school about what she knows. Most of the girls are very ignorant on this subject; their parents wish it so and our own belief is that it is much too soon for them to know about such things. Why, your daughter is only twelve years old! Girls don't really have to have such knowledge until they are fourteen or fifteen, or even just before they marry. I know that things are changing, we have to adapt ourselves to a modern world, alas, and I don't want to sound old-fashioned—we really want to go forward with the times— but surely twelve years old is much too young. I know that Thérèse has been brought up very differently from our other girls, but you must tell her very sternly never to speak to her companions about the birth of babies, not in such a way—you understand!"

The Mother Superior was quite pale and my mother said that I would be told this. She spoke to me and I swore I wouldn't discuss any of these matters in school. But Lucilla had taught me not to take what the nuns said so seriously and we often hid in the lavatories, the best place to talk in peace, and had long talks about the way babies were born. Lucilla had some ideas on this subject, but her information was confused and I straightened her out on most of it—on whatever I myself knew.

I didn't know as much as the Mother Superior thought, anyway. There was one thing that had bothered me for quite a while and I couldn't ask anyone about it or figure out by myself what it was.

Every time I went to confession, while waiting my turn with the other girls, I read the list of venial sins and the list of mortal sins. Each time I stopped at the sin listed as "Sin against purity." What exactly did that mean, and had it anything to do with this thing that was bothering me? This thing that was bothering me, how could I tell it to the chaplain? I was certain that I had invented it. I was sure no one in the world had thought of doing anything like that with himself. It had started when I was still reading the genteel books by the Countess de Ségur. A scene in one book had provoked it. Since then I had done it again, from time to time, but how could I know if it was a sin or a personal invention of mine that no one had ever heard of?

What consoled me was the thought that if one didn't know, then it couldn't be a sin. A sin had to be voluntary—and I certainly didn't want to sin.

I still thought of Sonia very often and prayed for her every day. How could the Holy Virgin accede to my wish that Sonia become a Catholic like me, if I couldn't speak to her about religion and encourage her in her aspirations? I told Lucie all about Sonia and her divorced parents and what had happened. Then Lucie told me about her parents. It was one day when we were hidden in the lavatories. There were three or four toilets next to each other. Lucie and I sneaked into one and there, seated on the floor, we could enjoy about twenty minutes of undisturbed conversation.

Lucie explained to me how she had come to live in Paris away from her father. Her father had threatened to kill her mother. He always slept with a revolver under his pillow, Lucilla said. Mme de Castro got more scared every day. She had five children by this man and she didn't love him. He was cruel, made scenes, and always said he would kill her one day. Finally she decided to leave him, to run away. She had an uncle and aunt living in Paris. So when M. de Castro was away on business, Mme de Castro gathered her children, packed some suitcases, took her Inca maid with her, and embarked on a boat. She had written to her uncle in Paris who was awaiting her. The De Castro family had now been living in Paris for several years, in an apartment they had rented on a small street in the elegant Sixteenth Arrondissement, rue du Colonel Renard. I had reason to remember the name of that street, later.

Lucie was quite matter-of-fact about this story. She didn't moan about it, she didn't indulge in self-pity. That was how things were—that was all. She also told me about her grandfather in Peru who was a captain in the fire brigade, and all she could remember of her life in South America. She made me swear that I wouldn't repeat this to anyone.

As we were coming out of the toilet, we were suddenly faced by the Mother Superior. She looked at us severely and told me to follow her. There was a bench covered in red velvet outside the chapel. Mother Superior sat me there, next to her, and asked me in a very pinched voice what we had been doing together in the toilet. I said we had been talking. What about, she asked. I said I couldn't tell her. That got her very interested. I didn't know what to do. I realized that she thought we had been having some very sinful conversation, but I couldn't tell her about Lucilla's father and mother. I had sworn I wouldn't.

What seemed to me a very long time passed. Mother Superior was pressing me to tell her and hinting darkly that I could be expelled if I didn't speak up. Finally I remembered something Lucilla had told me which I felt she wouldn't mind if I revealed. I said, trying to make sure I wasn't betraying Lucie's confidence, "She was telling me about her family, *Ma Mère,* she was explaining about. . . ." I stopped, and Mother Superior said sharply, "Go on!" "She told me—she said—that her . . ." I stopped. Would it be all right? Wouldn't Lucie mind?

"Yes," said Mother Superior, bracing herself for the worst.

"She said, *Ma Mère,* that her grandfather was . . . a captain in the fire brigade in Peru."

Mother Superior looked at me. I was pale and looked very upset by what I had said. "Is that all you were talking about in there?" she asked in a gentler voice.

I nodded, close to tears. Then I looked up at her. She was smiling. She patted my hand and she said: "It's ridiculous to lock yourself in such a place. Nice girls choose different places to have conversations. Don't let me ever again catch you going to the bathroom with another girl. Now, back to the study hall: Go!"

I curtsied and left in a hurry.

🌷 The convent school had three faces—the faces of the seasons we spent there.

In the fall, everything was romantic-looking, the air smelled of fallen leaves, the sky had a certain light grayness, it was cold in the classrooms because the heat had not yet been turned on, and we wore cardigans over our light blue smocks.

In winter, the school was very warm and, under the electric lights, turned on early in the afternoon, the classrooms, the corridors, and the hallways had a special glow. It was quiet inside, as if all noises were stopping at the doors and windows. Night fell while we ate our *goûter* at four o'clock. I always stayed in school after the three-thirty bell. If you wanted you could stay until six and do your homework in the study hall. Those who stayed ate the *goûter* together—bowls of hot coffee with milk and chicory in which you dipped your bread and butter. Generally *Mère* Marthe sat at the table and talked with us while we ate. Lucilla and I sat together and always had lots of things to tell each other. After the *goûter* there was a half-hour recess. In winter it was spent inside, in a playroom. We always played the same game: holding hands, making a circle, and singing old French songs:

A la claire fontaine
M'en allant promener. . . .

or:

Meunier, tu dors,
Ton moulin, ton moulin
Va trop vite, ton moulin, ton moulin
Va trop fort. . . .

or:

Ma mère m'a donné un mari
Mon Dieu quel homme, quel petit homme,
Ma mère m'a donné un mari
Mon Dieu quel homme, qu'il est petit!

There were hundreds of songs—beautiful songs, full of irony, poesy, and wisdom.

In December we had a *papier mâché* grotto, imitating Lourdes, erected in our study hall. A "good girl" would be the Holy Virgin standing in the grotto in a white dress and veil, hands joined. Sometimes it was Mariana, Lucie's so-well-behaved sister, or another girl, a blond, silent student who never said a word that wasn't perfectly polite. She had a pretty round face, a camellia complexion, Dresden blue eyes, and a sweet smile. She was so sweet always that we wondered if she were real.

In each class there were little altars with candles burning. We walked by them in procession singing hymns, dressed in our navy blue uniforms with round white collars, long white tulle veils, patent-leather shoes, and good-behavior ribbons across our chests. Those ribbons—how we all strived to get them. There were three: a yellow, a red, and a blue. You got one or another according to how good you had been all week. Since becoming Lucilla's friend I hardly ever got ribbons.

Then spring came and our school put on its third face.

All the windows were opened, a light breeze came in and moved the white lace drapes softly.

The sister-nuns were spring-cleaning, everything smelled

fresh. In the garden green tongues pierced the black earth and the trees were covered all over with delicate little buds.

On holiday I would go and visit Lucilla in her family's furnished apartment on rue du Colonel Renard. Lucilla loved to read as much as I did and her family's foreign background and bohemian habits fitted me well. I met her mother, who looked like a tropical bird—small, delicate, very feminine. She wore lots of rings on her very narrow hands, and many ruffles and furs. She spoke with a singing voice in a mixture of French and Spanish.

I met her brothers, who were always changing schools, in Switzerland, in England, in Germany—good-looking boys, very well mannered and elusive. The mother was always traveling or being sick, but not in a serious way, and the house was run by the Inca maid, who looked like a real Indian and had raised Lucie's mother, and who had a total, primitive devotion to the family.

At Lucie's home I ate marvelous, different food. I ate small pink bananas, and avocados and sweet potatoes and guava jelly —things people ate in Peru, Mme de Castro said, and I tasted everything and loved it because it was new and different.

After some time they all moved to another very large furnished apartment on one of the avenues starting at the Place de l'Etoile. They seemed to have a lot of money, were always extremely well dressed in expensive clothes and went to Biarritz in the summer. I never understood what they lived on. Lucie said that her uncle supported them.

During the winter my father had a group of people gather one evening a week in his studio to study the Bible. My father felt that Catholics didn't know the Old Testament enough and, as he knew it so well, having been brought up until the age of sixteen with much biblical study, he asked a few friends if they would like to gather at his house to read a passage

together and to study it, comparing various commentaries.
Most people who came were French Catholics. Jacques had
entered a Trappist monastery near Lyon, so he wasn't there, and
Olivier was in India. Among those who did come was a young
priest who brought several friends of his. I didn't go often
to these meetings, as I was doing homework and going to
sleep at a regular hour, but I attended a few. My father was very
much the center of the discussions. He explained the meaning of
certain words in Hebrew, and how the Jewish commentators
had seen a passage, and what it meant in the history of the time.

The family priest had friends who owned a château near Lyon,
next to a large farm which they ran. They had heard of my parents and wanted very much to meet them. They had enough
room and, as we didn't have enough money to go to a hotel, they
invited us to come and spend the summer on their farm. My parents were glad because we couldn't go back to Poland. They
would be able to visit Jacques in his Trappist monastery not far
away, and I would have two months in the country.

So we went.

The word "château" had cast a spell over me during the five
or six hours' train trip from Paris. I was going to spend the
summer in a château, very much like those heroines of my
childhood with Sonia: Camille and Madeleine de Fleurville, the
crinolined sisters with their pony-drawn carriages, nurses, and
governesses. "Château" in later years had also meant Alexandre
Dumas and passionate love affairs, silk rope ladders thrown
out of windows, masked balls, musketeers.

This château had the added romance of having belonged to
a famous poet, Lamartine. Verses I had learned by heart at
school the year before could have been inspired here, written
here. On the train I tried to remember even one, but I couldn't.
Actually I hated Lamartine's consumptive poetry. Still, to live
in the same house where he had lived would be wonderful.

At the station our host was waiting for us. He was very suntanned—not the elegant tan people acquire on vacations, his tan
was deep and dark and inflicted on his skin by a merciless sun
rather than cultivated conscientiously by an eager city man. The
sun had carved tortuous lines all over his face as my father would
over a sculpture with a burin. These lines didn't prevent his
looking young and handsome. He had broad shoulders and dark
curly hair, some always dangling in his eyes. He was very strong-
looking, with peasant hands and intellectual eyes. He didn't
talk much, but when he did, his voice was firm, self-assured,
pleasant. This was Georges.

His wife Maggie was ebullient, and talked and talked as
she greeted us effusively. She seemed to have unending energy.
At the same time, all her flow of words gave me the feeling that
she might be shy and trying very hard to conceal it. She, unlike
her husband, was not at all good-looking. She was tanned in the
same merciless way, wore glasses, and had a nose that was too
long and a mouth too thin. Yet she was youthful, full of charm,
tall and well built. I examined her on our way to the château.

"Excuse me," said Maggie, "you must excuse me. I hope you
are not too tired—such a long train journey, I am so sorry. But
you see there is this milk I have to deliver to the hospital, it will
take only a few minutes. Generally I take it in early in the morning, but today as you were coming around eleven, I thought it
would save me two trips. Oh, look! Right there you can see
those very old wooden houses, fourteenth-century. Aren't they
beautiful? We have twenty cows. We keep some milk for ourselves and sell the rest. Georges bakes our own bread, we are
three kilometers from the town, quite isolated from anyone. I
hope you won't find it lonesome. I can take you to town every
morning when I go down, but I am afraid it is so early. . . ."
She talked and talked, very quickly as if afraid she'd never have
time for all she had to say. Georges didn't speak, his strong

fingers held the wheel tightly. From time to time we were jostled all over the seat, which felt as if it were stuffed exclusively with stones. The car was a sight anyway. I had no idea what make it was, as I couldn't tell one car from another, but I could tell that it was very old and had not been washed since it had been bought. It looked as though it were used not only to deliver milk but also to plow fields, to take the twenty cows to the market, to transport years of harvests. . . .

Georges stopped in front of what must have been the hospital, a red brick building with a large garden in front. Maggie jumped out with great agility and started pulling big, clanking cans of milk out of the back of the car. Her hands were like men's hands—not men's hands, peasant's hands. The fingers were like vine branches, brown and twisted and knotted. But the most extraordinary thing about Maggie was the way she was dressed. She wore an elaborate silk dress with a crumpled *jabot,* thick beige cotton stockings, and very muddy high-heeled shoes. It was a strange mixture, her attempt at elegance and obviously a farm wife's life. Now the car was approaching the property and Maggie said excitedly, "*Là là!* You can see our house now, on the hill, the pink house. . . ." There was no other house wherever one looked. It could then only be that small, elegant pink eighteenth-century château, blushing between tall cypress trees. One second we saw it and the next second it was hidden by a small wood, by a hill, by the curve of the road.

❦ Georges slowed down in front of two stone pillars. He turned off the road and the car entered a narrow lane bordered by thick, tall walnut trees. On both sides there were fields, and cows in the fields. It was warm, the air smelled of bees, of hay, of blackberries. After a few minutes, we saw a large imposing ironwork gate, half open. Disorderly wisteria was climbing all over it and Maggie said: "The children must have been playing here and pushed the gate. Let me out, Georges, I'll open it more or you won't be able to pass." She had her hand on the doorknob and she opened the door of the car, her long legs clad in the beige cotton stocking and run-over, high-heeled shoes already halfway out. As she pushed the gate back, we heard calls of "*Maman, maman, papa, papa,*" and a little blond boy three or four years old appeared, hair falling over his face and down his neck. He was wearing a torn shirt and too-tight, faded shorts. His face was beautiful, sensitive. Behind him was a little girl, two or three years old, with dark black eyes and a very round face, dressed in a tattered dress too long for her. Half falling from her little arms, she carried a blond baby, a smiling, red-cheeked angel, with diapers so full they hung from him under the weight of their contents.

"Jeannot," said Maggie as we got out, "and this is Josée and the baby is Christian." She frowned at her daughter. "Josée, why do you carry him? He is too heavy for you." "*Maman,* he was crying," explained the serious, round-faced baby girl.

"Come and help me, Jeannot," said Maggie. "I have vegetables in the car. Take them out to the kitchen. Josée, put down Christian and help your brother." Josée put down the baby in the middle of the alley, the baby started crawling around, he picked up a stone and sucked on it, laughing. The contents of the diaper overflowed all over his pink, fat little legs. Shyly I asked, "Madame, would you let me play with the children? Could I help you feed them?" Maggie smiled. "Feed them? You can have them all day, you can wash them and take care of them, if you like. I don't have the time. They are all yours . . . besides, you can call me Maggie."

I looked at the château. It was a three-story pink building, with very clear and simple lines, almost perfect in its austere simplicity. There were long French windows, a curved *perron* descending from both sides of the main door, and at the top of the house a porthole in the roof in which sat a stone bust of a lady, looking serenely at the landscape. Maggie said, in her rapid, excited way, "You must come in and wash up. I'll make lunch very soon. I only need some wood to light the stove. Excuse me a minute."

"Jeannot," she called to her little son, "leave these baskets for the time being and run with Josée to pick up some wood for the stove. I am all out of it."

As Georges helped my father carry our two suitcases he pointed to the entrance of the house. "The legend says there is a treasure buried here. It was buried during the Revolution. When we bought the house it was written in the contract that if we find the treasure it is ours."

I knew at once that I was going to like it there. I loved those three beautiful dirty, barefooted babies and I couldn't wait to take care of them. There was a sense of freedom and of isolation in Chanteloup. In the strange château I came upon broken-down furniture and cold stone floors. Then suddenly I would see a beautiful old oak table, a marvelous ancient buffet with a bunch of wild flowers stuck in a wine bottle on the top, and two half-burned candles on either side of a primitive wooden Madonna. The wallpaper was peeling but a painting which hung in the dining room looked like an old master. For a brief second I caught a glimpse of the view through an open door of the master bedroom. The room was empty of furniture except for a very large, unmade brass bed. And on the floor all over, piles and piles of clothes, shoes, books, garden tools, thrown all over the place as though after a hurricane. The little children came in, their arms full of faggots, smiling but serious. Maggie said, "All right, put them in the kitchen. Josée, run out and bring Christian." I had never, never seen anywhere such little children being kept so busy and being so obedient. Whatever their mother said, those tots did at once and never seemed to mind.

We had our first lunch around a table that could easily have seated twenty people. Georges presided. He said the *Bénédicité* before the meal, then took in his arms a loaf of bread the size of a sea turtle in the tropics. He pressed it against him with one arm while at the same time cutting a slice from outside toward himself with one strong stroke of his knife. He explained to my astounded mother how, twice a month, he baked those loaves. He would get up that day while it was still dark and mix the dough in a special ancient wooden hutch which he showed us standing along a wall. The flour came from his own rye fields, and he baked the bread in a stone oven over a fire. He told my mother she could come and watch him next time. The oven was outside, near the farm.

What a bread! I have never tasted any so good, not even the shepherds' bread in Héas. It was as dark as theirs but fresher, lighter in texture. The lunch was not very tasty as Maggie had no more idea about cooking than my mother, but Maggie didn't let her total ignorance stand in her way. After all, without know-how she cooked for an average of twelve people at each meal, and on a wood stove, too.

Around the table sat Jeannot and Josée eating with great appetite and very silently. Georges believed that at meals children should listen but not talk unless talked to. The baby sat in a high chair next to his father, who from time to time picked up some potatoes or meat or cheese from his own plate and fed the baby little morsels, cooing at him at the same time.

I only then noticed that Maggie must be pregnant again. She was so slim that her small round belly looked incongruous. How old was she? No more than thirty, maybe less. We found out all about our hosts at that lunch. Neither had ever lived this kind of life before. Georges was raised in Ethiopia, the son of a French salt-mine engineer, and as a child had played with the Negus's children. His mother had died when he was very young.

Maggie was the only daughter of a wealthy, middle-class druggist from Lyon. She never cooked so much as an egg until her marriage. They were very devout Catholics, and wanted a large family. They wanted to live like peasants; this was their dream life: a patriarchal life close to nature. With them lived a maiden aunt and a few students sent by an agricultural school for their practical training. There were also always many friends who had come from Paris or Lyon.

Georges and Maggie, I soon found out, were totally unconcerned with the niceties of bourgeois life. Maggie was unbelievably messy, yet her children were totally healthy despite her complete disregard for hygiene. Flies came and went freely in the kitchen, food was left around carelessly, cats jumped up and licked the children's cereal before they did. Chickens wandered in, a dog rushed to steal a piece of meat, but the children, in their torn clothes, their overgrown hair, their running noses and overflowing diapers, had rosy complexions, fat little arms and legs. They looked perfectly happy and free and were friendly to everyone.

After lunch Jeannot grabbed one of my hands and Josée the other. They took me around to show me the farm.

In Héas, in Lectoure, in Poland, too, my summers had been organized somewhat around myself. With Romeck and Mya, my aunts, cousins, grandparents, things were always done to entertain me, make life pleasant, amusing, interesting. I was at the center of the adults' lives, a little girl people listened to, smiled at, gave presents to. But here in Chanteloup I blended into the hard peasant life lived by the La Fays. They had no time for me at all. Maggie had no time for her own children. When I spent my entire days with the three tots, it was not playing, as at first I thought it would be. It was my real life, my total responsibility. Maggie was up at five o'clock at the latest every morning. She prepared breakfast for the men going out to the fields. At six she fed the chickens and dogs and drove to town with the milk. She had no help at all, no maid would accept work in a twenty-room house with no heating, no gas, no hot water, no refrigeration, no washing machine, three babies and another one on the way. When I came down around eight o'clock, I fed the children, washed and dressed them, then took them out for long walks all over the countryside. The children were so unspoiled, so warm and gay. I never heard them cry or complain. Anything one did for them they appreciated enthusiastically. They were very bright. At mealtimes the conversations around the large oak table were always interesting. Silent and big-eyed, Jeannot and Josée listened attentively to their parents and friends discussing literature, art, politics, religion. Maggie had so little time for her children, but she managed to be loving and secure with them. She didn't have time to wash their faces much, but she had time to answer their questions, to educate them at every opportunity.

Very soon I discovered Maggie's and Georges's educational beliefs, and I saw how those children, seemingly so free and unwatched, were at the same time carefully guided by very concerned parents. Once, while helping Maggie shuck peas in her large kitchen, I asked her, "Tell me, Maggie, when do you actually start your children's education?" Maggie said: "As soon as they are born. In the cradle a baby starts being educated. That is where he begins to learn about the world." When I pressed her for more information, she said: "When Christian cries, Tereska, and I don't pick him up because I know that he is not hungry or in need—at that moment he learns that one doesn't get things in life by having tantrums. Already then, as a tiny baby, he learns to wait his turn. He learns to control his desires." Jeannot and Josée, I could see, at the age of three and four understood responsibility. They were capable of self-control and it didn't make them unhappy or withdrawn. On the

contrary, I had never seen such affectionate and friendly children, so full of life, so eager to enjoy it. With the baby Maggie
was particularly tender. She had so little time for him all day, but
while she breast-fed him, sitting at the table among all her
crowd, she held him against her with a love so apparent I could
feel it as if I were cradled in her tender arms. Maggie was full
of warmth and generosity and gave of herself with a total disregard for her own comforts.

In Chanteloup my father transformed an abandoned barn
into a studio. Georges brought him a few acacia tree trunks and
my father started sculpting happily. My mother wrote another
book in her room. Her first novel had been accepted by a French
publisher. She also helped Maggie and Georges by watching
the cows. She loved being a shepherdess and sat for hours under
a tree with a book to make sure that the cows didn't break out
of the pasture. A dog was there to help too. Everyone worked at
Chanteloup, but on Sundays, and some evenings, we all gathered
around Georges, talking and having fun, too.

From our several summers there, I remember some nights of
revels. There were six children around then and later five more
were to come. Certain weeks there must have been a dozen
guests staying at the château. Later Maggie acquired a gas stove,
a great improvement in her material life, and a big refrigerator.
She felt that her life was practically luxurious with these two
modern inventions. Georges's brother, who was a priest, often
came from Lyon, and he and all the guests would decide to have
a costume ball some nights.

In the vast attic, where the stone lady looked out of her porthole, Maggie found trunks full of ancient evening gowns, embroidered vests, silk shirts, straw hats, ostrich plumes, beaded
purses, and velvet coats. Generations of past ladies must never
have thrown anything away, just as Maggie herself never threw
out the most torn piece of clothing. "It can always be useful,"

she would say, adding it to the piles on her bedroom floor.

It would be a warm August night and Chanteloup's windows would be all ablaze. A sort of "Court of Miracles" was in progress, with strange counts and duchesses in very crumpled and tattered ancient costumes, going in and out, singing, joking, calling to each other. One guest had disguised himself as a baby, with an Irish-lace bonnet on his head and a pacifier in his mouth; he was wheeled in a broken pram by Georges, who was dressed as a nurse in long skirts, a false bosom, and pince-nez.

My father was dancing, as he often did. He was a marvelous dancer. Once, he told me, he had been asked by Diaghilev to join his ballet, but he had refused because he couldn't dance and sculpt as well. Now at these parties he improvised dances in the style of modern ballet, surrounded by all the admiring guests. Jeannot, Josée, Christian, Luc, Noëlle, and the last baby stood around all night in their pajamas adorned with touches of their own: some had flowers, feathers, jewels; some old hats and lace collars; their eyes wide open fighting against their need to sleep, their mouths full of laughter, admiring and enjoying. We had fireworks and a candlelight dinner on the grass. We had music from a piano someone played inside the house, the sounds of Chopin coming through the open windows. We danced and ran in *farandoles*. We sang old French songs— *"Auprès de ma blonde"* and *"Trois jeunes tambours"* and *"A la claire fontaine,"* and many others. The wine we drank was from Georges's vineyards.

Maggie was carrying her seventh or eighth child, who most likely was going to be born, like all the others, in the bed where he had been conceived. And Georges would most likely deliver it himself, as he had done before when the midwife arrived too late. During the night I picked up one little child after another, asleep in the grass or on a step of the *perron* or the living room floor, and carried him to his bed.

I learned how to milk cows that first summer and I became quite good at it. I also helped with the *vendange* in September when the grapes were ripe. I gathered eggs hidden all over the various barns by the chickens; I helped feed the pigs and plucked a chicken on a feast day. I acquired all kinds of knowledge, not only about child-rearing, but about planting seasons and farm animals.

It is curious that I remember so well to this day the taste of the food prepared by Maggie, while I have totally forgotten the best meals I've eaten in some very expensive restaurants in Paris, in London, in New York, in Moscow, in Hong Kong, and other places. I have not the slightest remembrance of food at the Tour d'Argent, or its equivalents. But right now, so many years later, I can feel on my tongue, on my palate, Maggie's soup, Maggie's dish of very salty cod, Maggie's hard-as-cement plum tart, Maggie's very stringy beef specialty. Maybe it is because she had only one soup, one way of preparing cod (the only fish she ever bought), one tart, one sort of meat cooked one way. To this day I can taste that soup. Every day of his life Georges ate it. It was made of any vegetables Maggie had that day, all boiled together, not much spiced, and to this she added the stale bread left over in her kitchen. We were all hungry and that bland soup tasted wonderful.

Because Maggie and Georges were always broke, because it never rained when it should have and always when it shouldn't; because they had eleven children and many friends and the most generous dispositions, Maggie would buy only the cheapest meat in the market, the cheapest fish. Because she also never had the time to sit and relax and learn the culinary art, her tarts were like rocks, her meat like rubber. But she had time to read to me from Paul Claudel, her one arm cradling a baby, stirring the bread soup on the stove with a wooden spoon with her other hand. Somehow she was also holding a book. How? With what? I don't remember. I sat in the kitchen peeling potatoes or feeding another baby while Maggie introduced me to her beloved author, who became my beloved author, opening up to me the worlds of Violaine, Prouèze: Claudel's heroic women, Maggie's spiritual sisters.

We also went to visit Jacques at the nearby Trappist monastery. My father, being a man, was allowed inside, but my mother and I had to wait for Jacques to come outside to see us.

He came, a strange-looking Jacques in a long white wool robe with a hood, looking very calm and happy. He still had red-rimmed eyes and his round head seemed even rounder now with the hair so closely cropped. He told us that Minie had decided to become a nun and had applied to the "Sisters of the Poor." He was allowed to write to her from time to time.

When we went back to Paris, life was much more regular. Those years before 1939 were a long stretch of growing up, going to convent school, spending summers in Chanteloup or in Lectoure and Héas. But the world outside began to enter my life: there was a war in Ethiopia, a cruel war, and I hated Mussolini. Then I started hearing the name "Hitler." At first it was hard to understand. Why did that man in Germany hate the Jews so much? I was hearing of boycotts, of Jews being beaten up in the streets, of their stores being looted. Over the years the news got worse. There were many articles in the papers about Jews losing their civil rights, being expelled and tortured. I remember reading these articles and crying. My parents were very upset. They discussed Hitler and Germany, wondering what was going on and where it was leading.

In France there was Léon Blum and a near revolution, with cars burned in the streets and Frenchmen fighting Frenchmen. Then there was a war in Spain and that summer of 1937 in

Héas when I saw streams of refugees from Spain crossing over and coming down the mountains. Mya spoke Spanish fluently and she organized relief for them in Lectoure.

❦ In school there was one nun called *Mère* Marthe and I fell in love with her. To me she was like a real mother, wise, energetic, secure. Mother Marthe must have been in her early forties. She had a narrow face, small dark eyes, and a ruddy complexion. She was understanding and comforting. She knew about any problem that could face a girl of fourteen or fifteen, and she knew how to give a girl confidence in herself.

She encouraged me to write, she said she liked what I wrote, and showed that she liked me.

My best friends in school were Lucilla, the tall Annie, and a girl called Monique who was flitty and immature but who loved poetry and whose father had written a book about Erasmus. We four were always together. Lucilla invented forbidden things to do, like smoking cigarettes on the roof of the school. Annie was very proper and unimaginative, but very stable, good-hearted, and full of admiration for Lucilla's and my wild ideas, and Monique amused us with her adoration of Katharine Hepburn and Camembert cheese.

I lived in a French world, but at home we had several friends who were converted Jews and foreigners. Some of them were Polish, some were Egyptian, some Russian, some English or American. There was a Father Cohen, a Dominican monk, and a Father de Menasce from Egypt who had written a book called *When Israel Loves God,* and an *Abbé* Glasberg from Poland who later was involved with the illegal boat *Exodus,* and many more.

Mère Marthe was modernizing things in school. She subscribed to a movie magazine so she could talk about films with us and know what we were talking about. She had the school buy dance records and let the boarders dance with each other some evenings. She discussed politics and the latest novels of François Mauriac. All the girls thought she was extraordinary.

Often during study hall I would climb the stairs to her small study to talk to her. She always made me feel proud to be Jewish. She spoke to me as if I had the great honor of belonging to the physical family of Jesus, something special that no other girl in our school had, and a privilege. I never felt anti-Semitism in all the years I studied there, not from the nuns and not from the children.

Except once—there was a girl whose family was something aristocratic in Rumania. Her mother had been a lady-in-waiting to the Queen, or maybe it had been her grandmother—I don't remember. Her mother had gone to school in France, as befitted a girl from Rumanian high society, and had been a classmate of our Mother Superior. That was why Claude was now sent to our school.

Claude was small, fat, dark, and had an oily skin, but very attractive dark eyes. She was in my class, and, as she was a new girl, she didn't have time, I guess, to find out that I was Jewish. The fact had been accepted as normal for years now and I don't think anyone discussed it particularly.

One evening I was sitting next to Claude in study hall, helping her—or she was helping me—with a lesson. Under the guise of asking each other questions about that lesson we talked about all kinds of things, getting acquainted. Apropos something or other, Claude began making nasty remarks about Jews.

It was the first time in my life that anyone had spoken that way in front of me. I listened to her for a minute and then said, "Don't talk this way to me, Claude, I am Jewish!" She blushed and stammered and said she hadn't known, and apologized. She never made another remark of that kind; anyway, not in front of me.

I was Jewish. This was something I knew very deeply. I could be as French and Catholic as any other girl in my school, but it didn't change the fact that I was also Jewish. I was aware of it in the same way that I was aware of the color of my eyes, of the shape of my hands, of the temperament which was mine and not Annie's or Lucilla's. I would discuss with my friends my parents' Polishness and Jewishness the same way Lucilla discussed her Peruvianism or Monique her parents' having come from a provincial French town. Monique's grandmother was from Toulouse in the south, mine was from a town called Kalisz in Poland. Except for that Rumanian girl who hadn't known it, everyone else in school accepted as totally normal— accepted as totally as I did—that I was a Catholic Jew, that my parents were Polish.

Some girls liked me and some didn't. It would never have occurred to me, if someone were mean, the way children some-times are—if someone pulled my braids or made an unpleasant remark—that it was because I was Jewish or my parents for-eigners. If a girl didn't like me I felt that it was *me* she didn't like, my own personality, and I accepted it. I didn't like all the other girls. Some I found stupid, some silly, some old-maidish, or I didn't like some habits they had.

Several times, especially in the earlier grades, girls had asked me with awe in their voices if, being Jewish, my family had had any connections with Jesus's family. Nobody ever, even before the Good Friday services had been revised to discard any anti-Jewish lines, pointed to me as being Jewish and said I had killed Christ. Maybe the French are just too logical to think in those terms.

I have often heard since that the French are anti-Semitic. If they are, I was totally unaware of it during years of convent school. I did sometimes hear children say "money-loving as a Jew" but the same children said as often, "stingy as a Scotsman" or "drunk as a Russian." I knew these were only sayings. My own grandparents had the same way of talking about the "goys": "drunk as a goy," "stupid as a goy." I didn't feel that I had to take it literally or personally. What I felt was pride in being Jewish in the same way I was proud that my father was an artist. The other girls' history started on the first page of the *Histoire de France* with the Gauls and Vercingetorix, but by that time my history had already existed for centuries. We had had kings and prophets and the Bible was being enacted, told. It was wonderful to be French because France had such a great civilization, but it was even more wonderful to be French and Jewish and Catholic and Polish, because it was like having many treasures instead of only one.

Since Minie's departure we had had several other young women, mostly from Switzerland, staying with us for a year at a time, studying French and helping with the housework.

One of them was Vally. She was in her early twenties and was pretty in a sort of mawkish way. She slept in my room and often at night we would talk together. Vally had left a fiancé in Switzerland and always talked to me about him and their dates, and what went on during those dates. One thing in particular which bothered me was Vally's description of her fiancé's kisses. She said he used his tongue.

His tongue? What did she mean? The fiancé apparently was trying very hard to put his hand in various places and Vally was trying as hard not to let him. Their behavior was very puzzling.

As always I went to my father for explanations.

He said, yes, some people did kiss with their tongues, and, as for the rest, he thought Vally was a silly girl. At the same time he answered some more questions of mine about how children were made and what exactly the father had to do. But I still couldn't visualize it. It was all very technical for me. I must have been about fourteen years old at that time and such questions were on my mind.

I was going to see more films now, sometimes with Vally, sometimes with Annie or Monique. I remember only a few movies from that period—some Greta Garbo films, *Mutiny on the Bounty, The Charge of the Light Brigade,* some René Clair movies, Charlie Chaplin in *City Lights, Mayerling,* Katharine Hepburn in *Little Women.* With my parents I went to the Odéon to see classical plays—Corneille, Racine, Molière, Alfred de Musset—but mostly we went to art shows, and always to the Louvre.

Sometimes there were gatherings of artists to which my parents took me. Some were at the painter Desvallières's large and incredibly disorderly studio. But it was a disorder which made me think of Boileau's verse:

Un beau désordre est un effet de l'art.

In the vast room, under the glass roof which filtered a strange, translucent light, Desvallières, who was an old, distinguished-looking man, and took himself very seriously, had gathered a small flea market of extraordinary objects. There were African masks and ancient fans and old clocks. There were wigs and ribbons and medals, complicated tools and glass balls and marionettes and wax dolls. In this décor his friends sat, drank coffee, discussed art, and read poetry.

There was a good-looking poetess who spoke continuously about her poetry. There was another poetess who had a mad look. She seemed to hate every woman present and to think of herself as a vamp. Of course the poetesses couldn't stand each other. Desvallières had a gift for attracting strange people: little, baby-voiced actresses who simpered around older men, disheveled violinists, esoteric writers, pushy, ambitious young men who came and looked around to see if there was anyone present who could be useful to them, and left very soon if there was no one.

There were also people of real talent and personality and, however weird the atmosphere was, those evenings were always fascinating for me.

🌷 I had seen Sonia again.

When I was almost fourteen, she appeared suddenly, accompanied by an aging governess. I was sitting in the garden of our house reading when I heard my name called. I looked up and there was Sonia, my Sonia—but no longer my Sonia. She was so different I couldn't believe it. She threw herself into my arms with a somehow theatrical joy. She wore lipstick and powder, although she was barely fifteen, and her clothes were in the latest style, with that adult touch she always liked, but even more so. I looked like a baby next to her, in my anklets and convent uniform. the two braids on my shoulders. Sonia said that her father had hired that governess, who was English, to take care of her and she had persuaded her to come to see me. It was funny that now, at fifteen, she should have a governess tagging behind, while at eight she had roamed the streets by herself. But later Sonia said something about going out with boys and her father being angry, so I thought that maybe this governess was there to guard Sonia from becoming too free.

We talked for about an hour, but it was not the way it had been before. In my mind, I kept comparing Sonia to Lucilla, to Annie, to Monique, and I couldn't adjust to her. We were miles apart—she with her fashionable clothes and lipstick and her slightly affected way of talking, and I in my new life at convent school, my regular hours, homework, navy blue uniform, and childish friends.

While Sonia was going out with boys and flirting and learning the Lambeth Walk, I was learning Latin, playing *La balle au prisonnier* and giggling with Lucilla or teasing *Mère* Helen about hell. Suddenly Sonia and I had nothing to say to each other. I was looking at her hair, which had been so straight, so smooth, like a helmet around her head, and which was now done in curls, and I had to fight back the tears which were ready to burst from my eyes.

When she left I ran to my room, closed the door, and cried.

When I was almost sixteen, I decided I would become a nun.

I was sometimes moody for reasons I didn't quite understand. Even being with my father didn't help. I felt the world was a frightening place. It was no longer the secure dream world of my childhood, the peaceful world of Héas. I heard about revolutions and wars, about people being massacred and hated, about hunger and disease. I heard of a man in Germany inciting people to kill and burn other people because they were Jews, and of a man in Spain driving Spaniards to kill other Spaniards. In the streets I saw bums sleeping on the sidewalks in winter or lining up at convent doors to receive a crust of bread.

Levin came again to see us in Paris and he told us about a terrible depression in the United States. Many people had lost all they had and had committed suicide . . . He was back from Palestine, where the Arabs were fighting the Zionist settlers. The world seemed a scary place and I—how could I face that world? My own family had pushed me away cruelly because I believed differently from what they believed. My own grandparents had never written to me again, nor had my uncles, aunts, and cousins.

My parents hadn't done anything mean or bad. They had only acted on their personal beliefs, and for that my mother's parents had to flee Poland like criminals, and my father's parents had acted as if we were dead. I knew how much my parents had suffered because of that intolerance. Why couldn't people live in love and peace in one united world? When would they learn? It all seemed futile—to love, to marry, to have children if it was to expose them to more hatred and wars.

Maybe it was better to become a nun like *Mère* Marthe. When I had loved Sonia, I had loved her passionately, and when I loved *Mère* Marthe I also loved her passionately. So if *Mère* Martha was a nun I thought that I should be one, too.

We had long talks and I knew that she had a special affection for me, that she felt I could "give the best of myself," as she would say. I often had the impression that she was sad and lonely and that she really had only me to talk to. Most of the girls at the school took the nuns for granted. The nuns were there to take care of them and if they had devoted their lives to teaching the girls, then it was their duty to do it. They didn't feel any particular gratitude to the nuns as I did toward *Mère* Marthe. They didn't go after school to talk about everything that was on their minds.

Mère Marthe knew all my thoughts. When she felt I was depressed, she would send me little notes in class:

> *When will my Tereska learn to govern her soul? And not to allow "depressing" thoughts to "depress" her? But as I know it is hard to do, don't hesitate to come and talk to me. Don't you know yet that it is with the heart of a mother and of a best friend that I follow the ascending march of the soul of my Tereska.*

*So should I tell her to come this evening at 5:30 (if I am not
in the parlor), otherwise at 6:00. So come, or take your pen....*

I had dozens of these little notes written by *Mère* Marthe,
and so many letters. I kept only a few.

*So, my Tereska, should I, after the dear little note of tonight,
make my own apology and another comment? Although I am
very "sarcastic," to use Shakespeare's language, I would never,
be sure of that, never make fun of anything you tell me, should
it come from your head or your heart. So please cross that
mean word from your vocabulary and put it away from your
mind. You know that you are my Tereska.*

She always called me Tereska, my Polish name, instead of
Thérèse, the way everyone did. And because she did, I started
liking Tereska better than Thérèse.

In the spring and fall we often walked along the garden
paths and I told her all my fears, all my hopes. Once she said:
"You are going up the hill, Tereska, and I am coming down.
I will pass you the torch." Perhaps nobody would talk this
way today, perhaps today it would sound mawkish—but what
is it to be mawkish? She meant what she said. She said it with
all her heart.

But when I told her that I was thinking of becoming a nun,
to be like her, she had the honesty to discourage me at first. She
said I was an only child and that my parents would need me
one day. She said I was too young to think of it. She said I had
to wait and pray and see.

The idea of becoming a nun didn't please me at all. It was a
very painful idea. I wanted to do it, but I hated to do it. I
couldn't stand the thought of losing my father, of losing my
freedom. Although I had moments of depression and fear about
the world, I still loved life and I loved the world. I loved plants,

animals, the sun, sandy beaches, mountains. I loved to read and to watch films and to go places.

I loved having friends, writing letters, talking, walking along the streets of Paris. But if I became a nun I would lose all that and more. I would dedicate my life to one thing only, and I knew that when you dedicate your life so totally to one thing, you put yourself in prison.

I didn't tell my parents my intentions. I was afraid of hurting them. I knew they would not dissuade me, but I knew that I was their only child and, in our situation, cut off as my parents were from the greater part of their families, this would be a blow.

My father never complained about anything. He was even-tempered; he seemed contented. He sculpted all day in his studio, which no one ever entered when he was working. Even my mother, who could never make the smallest decision without my father, would never disturb him then. But sometimes, if my father asked me to come in to pose for him, I would sit quietly in the way he wanted and look at his face as he worked. His face was all concentration then. He didn't look gentle any more but somehow fierce. He would blink his eyes and bite his lips. His hands with their very long, strong fingers modeled the clay or held a burin tightly. His hands were covered with cuts and bumps because he was absent-minded and would hit his fingers with the hammer or scratch the skin with the gouge. He had the hands of a workman, not those of a delicate poet. But he had never been a delicate poet. He was like his hands, strong and beautiful and marked by cuts and hurts.

And if I became a nun I would add to his cuts and hurts, and he wouldn't complain.

My friend Annie wanted to get married as soon as possible and to have many children. She was the most "square"—to use a modern term—of all my friends, but I liked her good sense, her logic, her healthy laughter. She could cook, sew, knit. She was organized and dependable. It was at her house that I went for the first time to a party for boys and girls.

I had never met any boys at all. I had no brothers; I went to a girls' school; Lucie's brothers were in a boarding school, Annie didn't have any, Monique's brother was younger so he didn't count. My cousins were in Poland and kept away from me by their parents. When I was in Chanteloup, the boys there were either four or five, or much too old for me; in Héas there was no one my age.

My parents never gave any thought to my situation. They felt I was too young for such things, anyway. But Annie's mother was preparing for the future and she had organized a *matinée dansante*. The boys invited were all sons of friends. I don't think Annie had anything to say about their choice. The catered event took place one afternoon, and all the mothers sat in an adjoining small living room.

The girls had to wear long dresses and I didn't have such a thing, so my mother borrowed one for me. It belonged to the daughter of a writer friend. It was a thin blue wool dress, very simple, long, tied at the waist with a large dark blue velvet ribbon. I was the only girl in a woolen dress and so simple, but I didn't mind. I knew my dress was very elegant. I didn't like the pink or white taffetas and velvet dresses of all the other girls.

Annie lived in a large, old-fashioned apartment on the rue Gay-Lussac, which was to be the scene of the student revolution in Paris in May 1968. All the paintings on the walls were from no later than the eighteenth century, all the furniture was Louis XV or Louis XVI. There were two living rooms, a library, an enormous kitchen, and a vast dining room.

There were about two dozen young people there—from fifteen years old to about eighteen. All the girls were very self-conscious about their long dresses and their hair fresh from the hairdresser. But I didn't care about what impression I would make on the boys, as I was going to be a nun, so I had a great time. My head wasn't stiff with curls. I had just pinned my braids around my head and as I soon realized that the boys couldn't dance any better than I could, I relaxed completely and enjoyed the fancy small sandwiches and various lemonades.

The boys were at the pimply age, but nice. They tried to seem very worldly and to act polite, as their fathers did. I decided to make them relax, too, and told them stories about the convent school to make them laugh while we were trying to dance. I didn't miss a dance, or a little sandwich either.

The next day Annie said, with a somewhat prim expression, "I didn't know you were going to be so successful with boys."

I hadn't known, either.

When I went to Chanteloup for Easter I met another young man.

I drove to Chanteloup that spring with some friends of my parents who were going and had offered to take me along in their car. There were five or six of us in the car. We stopped one night along the way in the lodge of a Benedictine monastery where the next day, at three or four o'clock in the morning, we went to the Gothic chapel to hear the monks sing Gregorian chants at matins.

The next day we got to Chanteloup. There were five children and Maggie was pregnant again. The fields were full of buttercups and daisies, the woods were full of violets and lilies of the valley, the barns were full of baby calves and little pigs. Jeannot, Josée, Christian, Jacqueline, and Luc looked the same: overgrown blond hair falling in their eyes as they climbed my knees and clamored for stories.

We all went together, holding hands, to the hay barns to

look for the eggs which the chickens always hid there, and for long walks of discovery.

In the car, on the way, there had been a young man of about twenty or twenty-one sitting next to me. I hadn't paid any attention to him. Once we got to Chanteloup he asked if I would like to learn to drive. He said he could take me in the car and teach me. I said yes enthusiastically, and he gave me one lesson, but we didn't continue, because after one lesson I got bored with all the gears and pedals. It was too complicated. Besides, I didn't want to waste time. I wanted to spend every minute with the children. I loved them so much and we had such fun together.

Emile came and sat near us sometimes on the grass in front of the *perron* and listened when I told stories to the children. Or he would come when I fed them their dinner or gave them their baths. He didn't bother me, as he was a quiet, nice-looking young man, and I didn't mind having him around. I just didn't really see him.

About two weeks after we returned to Paris, Emile's mother asked my parents if she could come to see them. She had, she wrote, something very important to discuss. We were intrigued. My parents didn't know her well and wondered what it could be about.

When she came I was upstairs in my room with Annie, doing homework. I heard the lady come in, and out of curiosity I opened my door. I heard my name mentioned a few times, so I made a sign to Annie to keep quiet and came down a few steps to listen. Nobody could see me there.

To my amazement I heard that Emile had fallen in love with me and that he wanted to marry me!

I thought this was hilarious. And he didn't even have the courage to tell me himself.

My parents called me, told me what had happened, and asked what I wanted to do about it.

By then my mood had changed. I didn't think that it was hilarious any more. I began to take it seriously. Of course, I had no intention of marrying Emile, but I could visualize a beautiful romantic scene between us with me telling him my secret: that I wanted to be a nun.

But as my parents didn't know about it, I had to speak to Emile privately. I told my parents that I would give Emile my answer myself, and that he should come to see me.

He came. I remember the dress I was wearing. It's funny what one remembers, because I don't remember his face. He climbed the stairs to my bedroom, smiling, and as soon as I saw his smiling face I had a feeling that things might not be as easy as I had thought. I had prepared such a beautiful speech, all about my vocation and a life dedicated to God, but Emile sat next to me on a chair and seized my hand. He said: "I am so glad to be here. I have waited for this moment. You can't imagine, Tereska, my feelings since I met you." He went on and on. I opened my mouth a few times, but Emile wouldn't let me say a word. He smiled all the time and said: "You are so young—no, don't interrupt me, please. Let me explain first. I have to make clear to you. . . ." All this time he was squeezing my hand and I found it most unpleasant. I tried to pull my hand away, but Emile held tight. I tried to look out my window into the garden and to think of something else and just ignore him until he stopped talking. Why on earth had I had the idiotic idea of telling him to come and speak to me? Why couldn't I have told my parents that I was not interested in Emile and had them convey it to him? I was furious at myself.

Suddenly there was a lull. Emile was catching his breath. I might have a chance. I really didn't want to hurt his feelings. I said: "Listen, Emile, I am sorry, you didn't let me say a word. I must explain why I asked you to come here." Now I could make it all simple and clear without offending him. A religious young man such as he should be pleased to know a future nun, after all. So I said: "My parents don't know it yet, that's why I couldn't speak in front of them, but, Emile, I have made up my mind to enter a convent as soon as I am twenty-one years old. So you understand that I can't think of marriage."

He looked at me as if I were out of my mind, but then something quite unexpected happened. Emile sank to his knees in front of me, buried his head in my lap, and started sobbing.

It was horrible, horrible. He still held my hand and my hand was under his face getting all wet with his tears. I was afraid I was going to be sick. I was sure of it. I knew I would be vomiting from disgust in a minute. I tried to say something but I couldn't say a word. I didn't know what to do. I couldn't get up—he had his head on my knees, he held my hand.

Is this love then? It can't be. Love is pure, ethereal. But this young man had an odor coming from all those tears and the smell made me feel even sicker. I couldn't stand to look at his hair, at the nape of his neck. I thought that I hated him. Was I heartless? Here a young man was crying for love of me and all I could think was that he smelled; that I hated him. If only I knew what to do. How does one end such a situation? If only I were worldly and wise. If only *he* were worldly and wise, as I had imagined he would be, saying perhaps, "It is beautiful, Tereska, and I admire your decision. It breaks my heart but I can't take you away from God." Instead . . . this . . .

Finally he looked up at me, his nose all red, and said, "You'll change your mind, I am sure. I'll wait for you. You are too young to know what you really want." By now I was determined to enter a convent, any convent, if for no other reason than to escape Emile forever.

At last he stopped crying. I don't remember how, but finally he had to blow his nose and to do that he had to let go of my hand. He repeated several times that he'd wait as long as necessary and that I was too young to make such an important decision as a religious vocation. I didn't answer, so he must have become a little bored, too, because he said good-bye and left. Then I stood in the middle of my bedroom and started trembling. I stood there and shook all over. My parents came to my room and saw me in that state. My mother undressed me and put me to bed and my father sat on my bed and put his comforting hand on my head. But it didn't help.

For hours I lay in bed in a cold sweat, shaking all over as if I had malaria.

For months after that when I was walking in the streets, if I saw a man who looked like Emile, I would be so afraid it might be he that I would start trembling again and would cross the street, my knees ready to give way under me. It took me long years to get over it.

My father received a letter from his father.

It was a great day for us. A door was opening, a hand was stretched out toward us. My grandfather Isucher in Zgierz couldn't bury his son alive any longer and wrote asking my father to explain why he had done such a terrible thing. My father answered with a long letter in Yiddish.

Then my uncle Samuel wrote, and my uncle Alexandre. The family was slowly coming back.

My father wrote to everyone, but my grandmother Salomé never wrote. I knew that my father wanted so much to hear from her.

All year letters went between Paris, Zgierz, and Lisbon, and my father said that maybe, who knows, we might still go back to Poland one day. In one of his letters, my grandfather repeated the story of the rabbi who years before had predicted that one of his sons would be a Christian. But the letters weren't accusing or insulting any longer; they were trying to establish a bridge of understanding. My uncle Samuel sent us photos of his daughter, a beautiful girl called Clara—my cousin Clara.

Levin returned to Paris, but this time with his wife. That was when I found out that his first name wasn't Levin, as I had always thought, but Meyer. He had gotten married in Chicago and his wife was pregnant. They were on their way to Spain, to the war. Levin was going as a war correspondent and his wife was going to work in a Republican hospital laboratory. She was a chemist and the first woman of her kind I had ever seen, a modern woman in the American sense—totally independent, hard-drinking, chain-smoking, tough. I thought she was very good-looking. She was tall and had very clear features, everything sharply outlined: the nose, the cheekbones, the jaw. She didn't act as though she were married and pregnant.

She was nice to me and spoke to me as if I were on her level, a woman like her and not a schoolgirl. I found it fascinating to be talked to that way. All the adults I knew always spoke to me as if I were still a child. It was not in the tone of their voices, they didn't baby talk in that nasal, ridiculous voice some people use with children; but they talked from a certain height of adulthood, as if they were bending down toward my adolescence and ignorance and vulnerability. I knew that none of them would hurt me because I was younger and smaller than they were.

With Levin's wife, it was something else. To her I was just another female and the difference in our ages didn't matter.

As soon as she got to Madrid she wrote asking me to send her Gauloises cigarettes from Paris. She couldn't find them in Spain and couldn't function without her favorite brand. She wrote to me about the war, too—about the bombardments and the spirit of the people fighting the fascist troops. I kept her letters and was proud that she trusted me and asked me to do something for her—I was grateful to be able to do something for her while she was working for a great cause.

🌷In the summer my parents and Monique's rented a villa together in Normandy on the Trouville beach. My parents had become friendly with Monique's parents, especially with her father, who was a very cultured man, a writer and a humanist. The villa was quite large. Monique and I shared a room at the top of the house. It was like having a sister, getting up together, washing our hair together, sunbathing, swimming, reading, talking late at night.

It was a very pleasant summer, and I started writing a novel there. Every day at four o'clock I left everyone at the beach and came home, my brown skin still hot from the sun and covered with sand and salt. The house was quiet and dark. All the shutters were closed against the heat. I sat in front of the table in our room, still in my bathing suit, my braids hanging down my back. During the whole summer I wrote regularly every day until the two families came back from the beach and Monique would erupt into our room with her hands full of shells, dripping puddles on the floor, laughing, talking about the last Katharine Hepburn movie. It was still her passion.

All was well. Monique's brother was fifteen and led his own life. Monique's father discussed philosophy with my parents. Her mother was a great cook and we ate mussels that we picked up on the rocks at low tide and small, silvery eels which burrowed in the sand at the edge of the retreating waters and which we caught with our hands.

Then the newspapers began printing large headlines—large, black, frightening headlines. In another world there were men called Hitler, Chamberlain, Daladier. Countries were mobilizing troops. Monique's father predicted war and all its horrible consequences. I couldn't believe it. I didn't want to believe it.

Trouville was beautiful. Many people had left and it was a very warm summer, with grandiose sunsets. The beach became almost deserted, and Chamberlain, with Daladier, went to Munich. Then all was well again. There was not going to be a war—that was all I could remember. There was not going to be a war. I didn't know why Monique's father was so gloomy. I was happy. There was not going to be a war.

The Great Powers would find a way now to stop Hitler, some way other than war.

We came back to Paris.

I had to work hard that winter because in June I would take the *Baccalauréat,* and it was a hard exam. Lucilla was in Paris too. She went to another school, but we saw each other often. She was the same but had grown into quite an attractive girl— seventeen, very blond, with a small face, dark eyes, a smiling mouth, an upturned nose, and a lovely, graceful body. She was as full of life and gaiety and mischief as before. She still had her pretty Spanish accent and her mother still looked like an expensive bird and they still lived in the same richly furnished apartment near the Etoile.

During the winter my grandmother Salomé died in Zgierz. She died without having written to my father since the time she heard of his conversion, without having ever seen him again. We didn't know how lucky she was to have died then, in her own house, surrounded by many of her children, with her husband at her side.

It was during that winter that we heard and read of the "night of the broken glass" in Germany, when the Nazis burned Jewish houses and synagogues to the ground, arrested thousands of Jews, and expelled all Jewish children from the schools. I was wild with anger. I wanted to murder Hitler the way a young man had assassinated a Nazi in Switzerland. But the "night of the broken glass" had been the Germans' direct answer to an attempt by a Jew to fight back. A boy my age had shot a Councillor at the German Embassy in Paris.

My father was saying that Jews must have their own country; that was the only way out; it was logical, and there was no other solution. Somewhere at that time I read a sentence from Dostoievsky which impressed me very much, only where Dostoievsky had written "Russian" I thought: "Jew." And wondered. It was:

> Beyond all doubt the destiny of a Russian is Pan-European and universal. To become a true Russian, to become a Russian fully, means only to become a universal man . . . our destiny is universality.

Was not this the highest plateau of mankind?

There was something deeply poignant about the wanderings of the Jews, their universality. This had a significance of its own, like a symbol of a higher calling, higher than patriotism or loyalty to an individual country. Was this possibly the Jews' mission, which they would lose if they had a country like everyone else?

My grandparents who lived in Paris were very busy making preparations. They too felt that time had passed, that people were forgetting, and that they now could go back to Poland, at least for the summer. That summer of 1939 they would go for a visit to spend time in Lodz again.

In June I took my *Baccalauréat* examination. Soon after, my grandparents left for Poland and Monique's parents rented a villa with us—this time in Brittany.

So by July we were happily settled in Dinard, expecting a long, lovely summer.

Hitler invaded Poland on September first.

On September third, war was declared by France and by England. It was on my birthday. I wrote in my diary, in the dramatic style I used then:

Sept. 3, 1939—The War
This horrible word, which until now was for us a page in a history book, a movie, a tale for an adult, this word has become a reality for us, the generation that novelists have called "The Children of Peace."

While Polish towns are burning, France and England are going to defend Liberty. Our fathers, our brothers, will fight. The whole world is becoming chaos . . . the war. . . .

Since eleven o'clock this morning, "German" means "enemy." The gas mask will be our 1940 fashion. How long will it last? Will we awake from this nightmare, old people? Will we be separated for years from those we love? Hope has run away, shielding her face. Happiness has disappeared with this last summer, because a man was insane and this insane man is leading Germany.

My father was still a Polish citizen. He had never asked for French nationality although he had lived in France since he was sixteen years old. Now he was forty-seven. He had never served in any army but he said that his duty as a Jew was to fight Hitler, so he volunteered for the Polish army formed in France, and was accepted.

We came back to Paris. Everyone lived in fear of imminent bombardments, and those who could left. My father asked my mother and me to go and stay with Mya in Lectoure while he was in the army.

I was heartbroken. I didn't want to go away. I wanted to stay and continue my studies. I had to enter the "philosophy year" to pass the second part of the *Baccalauréat* the next June, the equivalent, I think, of the second year in an American university.

I didn't want to leave *Mère* Marthe or Lucilla and Annie and Monique, my whole world, Paris, my books, my room. It was one thing to go to Lectoure for a few weeks' holiday and another to settle there for the war's duration.

And we had no news from anyone in Poland. My grandparents who had gone back there—where were they now? Were they alive? And my grandfather in Zgierz and all my uncles, aunts, and cousins? Poland was in flames—that was all we knew.

But my father was so insistent that finally we packed to go. My father, in his ill-fitting sky-blue uniform, came from Rennes, where he was stationed, to see us. He looked like those old photos of soldiers in the 1914 war. He was forty-seven years old and all the other soldiers were twenty, twenty-five, thirty at the most. I wanted to cry when I saw him, he looked so sad. He didn't look like a soldier. The military was not his calling. He looked like an artist disguised in an army uniform.

I went to see *Mère* Marthe to say good-bye to her. The convent school had also moved. They were now in a château near Paris, lent to the nuns by some friend. All the boarders and all the nuns lived together on a large estate. We walked around the grounds in a drizzling rain. *Mère* Marthe held my hand and said I shouldn't even think of a convent now that my father was away. My place was with my mother.

Lucilla had left for Biarritz with her family. Annie was with her grandmother, who had a large house where I had often gone for holidays in a village two hours from Paris, and Monique was staying in Paris, because her father taught at a lycée. We left for Lectoure.

That time I hated Lectoure. I hated its narrow streets and suffocating air. It was so quiet, so provincial. You couldn't walk in the only main street without wearing gloves. When you passed along the ancient houses bordering the sidewalks, curtains would be slightly pulled aside by invisible hands.

Mme Dalie had died recently. In her nineties, she had still gone every day to the *enclos* to weed the patches, to pick fresh lettuce, and to gather strawberries. One day as she was going down the steep stairs leading to the *enclos* she fell and rolled down to the landing. When Mya and a maid arrived and picked her up, her head was bleeding on her white hair. Mme Dalie opened her incredibly blue eyes, pointed at the shaking maid and said to her daughter in a clear voice: "*Mya, donne-lui un petit verre d'Armagnac, elle en a besoin.*" Then she died.

The Spanish refugees were still in Lectoure and Mya was still taking care of them. Romeck had decided to separate completely from his wife and enter a monastery. He couldn't marry Mya because he couldn't get a Catholic divorce. He told me that he felt he was now an older man and could devote his life to studies and meditation. That kind of life attracted him. His wife was willing to separate and he would provide for her from his pension as an ex-professor.

Mya spent her days with the refugees and I went to the local lycée. I hated that lycée too. I wanted desperately to go back to Paris. I was miserable at the idea of spending my life in this sleeping town. How could we know when the war might end? It might even take the whole year, or two years. I couldn't possibly live for two years in such dullness. And no one was bombing Paris. Life was safe in Paris. I wanted to go back.

What saved me was that my grandparents suddenly came back—back from Poland in the midst of the war!

In November or December we got a telegram from Paris. They were already home in their apartment near the Rex Cinéma. We packed and left at once.

My grandparents were like people who have come back after an earthquake. We couldn't believe it. They couldn't believe it.

My father got a special leave and everyone we knew in Paris gathered at my grandparents' apartment to hear what they had to say. The Germans had let them out. My grandfather had gone to the *Kommandant* after Poland had been occupied. While Jews were being beaten in the streets and shot without warning my grandfather spoke to a German officer and showed him his French residence card, explaining that he and my grandmother didn't belong there, it was a mistake. They lived in Paris. Could they go home? He didn't offer any bribe, he didn't moan or threaten, he just stated an administrative error.

Something must have gone on in that German's brain: here things were not in order. The order was that people living in Poland and those living in Lodz should be under German control—but as yet not people in Paris—or maybe he was a decent person and saw a "correct" way to save two Jews. He allowed them to leave for Austria and Italy, and from there they took the train back to Paris. So here they were, intact.

But everyone else in Lodz—that was something else. The things my grandparents told us didn't let me sleep at night—and these reports would seem like a paradise compared to what was to come.

About the rest of our family my grandparents couldn't tell us much. Everyone lived in terror. My uncle Alexandre had been an officer in the Polish army and they had heard that he hadn't come back after Poland fell. My aunt, Sonia, his wife, was alone with two small children, probably half-starving like everyone else. My Lodz grandparents didn't know my father's family well so they had little news—only hearsay. About Zgierz they didn't know anything. Communications were cut. People hardly left their houses, they told us, and if you went out in the streets you might never come back. It was a miracle they had escaped.

Then, a month later, my uncle Alexandre arrived in Paris. He had been taken prisoner by the Germans, had escaped, had somehow gotten to Sweden, and since then he had tried every means to bribe someone in Poland to get his wife and children out. He had some money in a French bank and rented an apartment in Paris. Then he started going around like a madman following every lead for a way to help them escape.

In January, I think, my aunt Sonia and her two children did get out of Poland, too, and came to Italy, where my uncle met them. Then we found out how my grandfather Isucher had died. My aunt knew. My grandfather was alone in his big house in Zgierz with only one of his daughters when the German had come. An officer said that he knew my grandfather had a very valuable library, a collection of rare books, and that he had come to take them away.

My grandfather stood there in front of the German and said, "As long as I am alive not one of these books will leave this house." As he said it, he had a heart attack and fell dead. The Germans took the books away.

Some of us, at least, were together. All the others in Poland—who knew what had happened to them, or what would happen? Would they be alive when it was all over? Life in Paris was more or less normal. It was the period later called *la drôle de guerre,* the phony war. We had blackouts, we had rationing, but not a shot was fired. Paris wasn't bombed. The soldiers were sitting behind the Maginot Line, waiting.

I went to the Lycée Henri IV, transformed temporarily into a girls' lycée, and studied for my philosophy year. We were given gas masks, which were very convenient for transporting our yarn to the lycée; we knitted under our desks. The wool came out very neatly from the gas mask holder. Of course we left the mask itself at home. I didn't study much that year—my mind was elsewhere. I was restless. Classes at the lycée were large and impersonal. I felt anonymous. I had been accustomed, for years, to the small—seven or eight girls—classes at the convent, where the nuns knew each one of us well and the atmosphere was much more like a large family than a school. I sat and didn't listen, and dreamed. I often skipped classes and instead went to a movie on Boulevard St.-Michel. The lycée was in the Latin Quarter, next to the St. Etienne du Mont Church where I had had my *communion solennelle*.

On weekends I saw my grandparents, my uncle and aunt, and my little cousins. They talked of Poland and of the tragedy there. Once in a while my father came home on leave. Once in a while I went to see *Mère* Marthe in the country. I felt useless, unattached. How long could it last, this drifting, drifting of our lives, drifting of the war? What were we accomplishing while people were being tortured in Poland?

Then it was May, and Hitler struck again. He invaded Belgium and advanced on France. Refugees from Belgium, and all the north, poured into Paris. At the Gare St. Lazare a center was opened for them. Finally one day I left school and went to the Gare St. Lazare. I found a nurse, who seemed to be in charge, and said, "Can you use me? I am free and I am willing to do anything." She gave me a baby's bottle filled with milk, showed me a baby crying, sitting on a blanket, and said, "Take that baby and feed him."

I was hired. No one asked me any questions, not even my name. They didn't have time. Refugees were arriving on every train; others came to the Gare St. Lazare by car, and some on foot. They were dirty and hungry. Some were sick.

Each night I came home exhausted but happy. At least I was not feeling so useless any more. I told my mother that I had quit school and she didn't ask me to go back. She understood.

My mother worried all the time about my father. Where was he, was he all right? We had no news of him. The armies were fighting, the Germans came nearer to Paris every day, but the newspapers wrote not to worry, that the armies were executing strategic retreats.

From strategic retreat to strategic retreat they were getting so near Paris that my mother, my uncle, my aunt, and grandparents all decided to leave, to go south like everyone else. It would only be for a few days, then we would come back. It was almost summer anyway, so why not go south to a nice resort and spend the summer there—and my father could join us as soon as it was over.

A cousin of my mother's, Norek, had also come to Paris. He and his wife and child had left Warsaw in the summer of 1939 to visit Belgium, then the war had started and they had stayed there. Now they had arrived in Paris with other Belgian refugees and, as Norek was quite close to my mother, he took over the decisions for the family. It was he who decided that we should all go to St.-Jean-de-Luz, near the Spanish border, and rent a place there for a few weeks. We packed, but not much, as we were only leaving for the summer.

We arrived in St.-Jean-de-Luz—my mother, my grandmother and grandfather, my cousin Norek and his wife, and their ten-year-old girl, Ryśia. My uncle Alexandre and his wife and children went to Biarritz. St.-Jean-de-Luz was already beginning to get crowded. It was early in June and many people from Paris had come down. The hotels, which would have remained closed for another three weeks, started opening, as well as the restaurants, the bars, and the shops. It was a strange atmosphere—part festival, part panic. The newspapers announced that all the students there from Paris who were going to take their exams for the *Baccalauréat* could take them, on June eighteenth, in Bayonne, a nearby town. So I began to study again and registered in Bayonne for the exams.

By chance we found a small house and all of us crowded into it.

My mother had written to my father's army address that we were going to St.-Jean-de-Luz and had told him to write us in care of a Parisian friend who had a summer home there. We were very happy when we finally heard from him. It was only a postcard saying that he was with his regiment somewhere near La Rochelle. At least he was in the south, too, and we hoped that he would join us.

Magnolia trees were in bloom everywhere. The region was beautiful, the weather was perfect, but all we heard about was more strategic retreats. No one believed yet that France could lose the war.

I went to Biarritz and saw Lucilla. Her life hadn't changed so much. Her family had always gone to Biarritz every summer.

Back in St.-Jean-de-Luz I studied, read the papers, and listened to the news on the radio, all the time worrying about my father. More and more refugees were arriving from all over France. The highway leading into St.-Jean-de-Luz was crowded with cars piled with mattresses and luggage. People came on bicycles, on foot, in horse-drawn wagons. They slept in the streets, in the parks, on benches, on the beach.

My cousin Norek was the first to get scared. He went to Bayonne, to the Portuguese Consulate, and got us all Portuguese visas. I didn't understand why. Why would we need them? We wouldn't leave France.

On June eighteenth I took the exams. On June nineteenth I was walking in a street in St.-Jean-de-Luz when a friend from Paris saw me and stopped me.

"Did you hear General de Gaulle on the radio yesterday?" she asked.

I hadn't heard. I didn't know what she was talking about. She said, "He called to all French people to join him. He said that France had lost a battle but that France had not lost the war. He is forming an army in England."

I looked at her. Was it really the end then? And who was General de Gaulle?

She continued, very seriously, "Tereska, you are Jewish. Take your mother and your grandparents, and leave. The Germans will be here soon. They'll be all over France. It will be terrible for all of us, but it will be worse for you. Hurry and leave."

Regiment after regiment started arriving. Many were Polish troops. They looked exhausted. The soldiers dropped wherever they stopped. My mother and I walked from Polish soldier to Polish soldier, asking each one if he knew my father. Just before the Germans came my mother and I were walking and we saw four young Polish soldiers sitting on the sidewalk looking puzzled and tired. My mother asked them if they knew that the Germans were coming in a few hours. They didn't know. They didn't understand French and had no idea. They had lost their unit. If the Germans catch us, they'll shoot us, they said.

So we went with them from door to door, asking people to give them civilian clothes. We outfitted the four of them completely and they threw their army uniforms into the sea. Then my mother found them a guide and gave him some money to take them across the border into Spain. They left, and to this day I hope that they got out safely.

Later two British warships appeared and it was said that they would take anyone aboard who wanted to leave. The troops, and some civilians with them, started boarding.

I went home and told my mother that I was leaving. I was going to join the army General de Gaulle was forming. My mother began to cry, then my grandparents. My cousin Norek said I was crazy, that I was a child, that they didn't take children in armies, that I couldn't be so heartless as to abandon my mother at such a time, that no one even knew if my father were still alive. Everyone talked and cried and argued all night.

In the morning the warships were gone and small white posters appeared all over the town. Groups of people congregated in front of them. Reading them, some cried silently, some became red and angry. The posters said that the Germans were going to enter the town in a few hours and that the mayor asked the population to be dignified and calm.

My cousin Norek took his wife and child and left for Spain and, after that, Lisbon. But my mother, my grandparents, and I stayed. We couldn't leave. We wanted to stay and wait for my father. He knew we were in St.-Jean-de-Luz and might come.

A delegation headed by the mayor carried tricolor flags and flowers to the monument for the 1914 war dead. A hush fell over the town.

🌺 The first Germans I saw looked unreal—like actors on a stage. I was standing in front of our house when all at once two motorcycles zoomed by. The men wore helmets—the kind I had seen in photos and newsreels—and greenish-colored uniforms and black boots. More motorcycles passed with a deafening noise; rows and rows of roaring motorcycles with those men wearing those helmets and boots.

The Germans were occupying St.-Jean-de-Luz.

Years later I saw a Cocteau movie, *Testament d'Orphée*. In it were some men on motorcycles who reminded me of those Germans.

My grandparents were hysterical. They had escaped the Germans a few months before and now the Germans had caught up with them again. But we still had had no word from my father.

I cried at night. Where was he? Was he alive? I didn't want my mother to know that I cried. I never cried around her, even as a child. It didn't help me and it didn't help her. When I was upset I had my father to go to; I had *Mère* Marthe.

My uncle Alexandre had already left, saving his wife and his children once more by going to join his brother Samuel in Lisbon. Finally my grandparents persuaded my mother to leave too. We had Portuguese visas, but how long would they be valid? If we were out of France, we could help my father join us. By staying we could only become prisoners together. We needed Spanish transit visas, which could still be had only at Hendaye. There were no more cars or buses, or any kind of transportation, so mother and I walked and hitchhiked on horse-drawn wagons until Hendaye.

We got the visas—the last ones, I think—and returned to St.-Jean-de-Luz the same way we had come. Then we packed and somehow got to the Spanish border—how, I don't remember. We had only our suitcases. My grandparents were stiff with fear, my mother so pale. At the border my mother was holding her passport when I noticed that her right hand was trembling violently. I thought it was from fear, but fear had caused more than a passing trembling. At that moment my mother's old disease, the *encéphalite léthargique* which she had caught on the train from Poland to Paris when I was four and which had been dormant in her all those years, raised its head again. That trembling never stopped. It increased over the years and spread to her whole right side. She now had Parkinson's disease.

At the border the French flag was seen no more. The French customs official stamped our passports. A few Germans were standing there, laughing among themselves. The French customs man whispered to us: "*Les salauds, ils ne resteront pas longtemps!*"

We crossed to the other side—to Spain.

There were taxis there and we got into one. As we were driving through the town of Irún on our way to the train station, a unit of German soldiers in uniform marched by. Our Spanish driver stopped the taxi, got out, and saluted with his arm raised. That was Franco's Spain. My grandparents almost fainted in the taxi; they thought the driver was going to hand them over to the Germans. But he got in again and drove us to the station.

Before our train left we had an hour or so to wait. My grandparents stayed in our compartment and I went into the town with my mother to buy some food, as we didn't know what we would find to eat on the train. Irún was still partly in ruins after the Civil War. Everywhere we saw houses that had been bombed and burned. People looked very poor. As we were buying our bread and fruit in a grocery, a man, hearing us talking in French, approached and said, "You are refugees from France? Please let me pay for this food. I was in France during our war and people were good to me; let me at least do this now."

He wouldn't hear of our paying for the food, and he added more fruit and cheese and sausages to our purchases.

That is how I realized I had become a refugee.

Part IV 🌷 Exile

We were sure that we were going straight to Lisbon to my uncle Samuel. We had no money and no idea of what else we could do. But at the border the first thing we were told by the Portuguese officials was that none of the refugees, and there were quite a few on the train, could go to Lisbon. The train was going to stop in a place called Figueira da Foz and we were to stay there and not set foot outside until we had visas for another country and were going to leave Portugal.

It was a terrible shock. Where was Figueira da Foz; how would we manage there without money? My mother and grandmother started crying and I went out into the corridor to hide my tears. We felt trapped and lost.

It was night when we got to a town where the train stopped and we heard voices calling out "Figueira da Foz, Figueira."

Everyone on the train seemed to be getting off here. People were calling to each other in French, English, Polish, Czech, German. They were pulling down from the racks expensive suitcases, even tennis rackets, cameras, and hat boxes. Most of these refugees were rich. This was not a group of haggard refugees such as the ones I had seen on the roads arriving at St.-Jean-de-Luz.

Some famous actors and writers were supposed to be on that train. It had been whispered while we were crossing Spain that Danielle Darrieux and Maurice Chevalier were there, hiding behind dark glasses. If they were, I didn't see them—but I did recognize a French actor I had seen in several movies, including Jean Renoir's *La Grande Illusion*. His name was Dalio, and he was traveling with a pretty young woman who looked like a starlet.

Everyone seemed to be dressed for Portugal already. Men were wearing light suits and women had straw hats ready, and sun glasses and cotton dresses. It was amazing. But the most amazed were the group of young Portuguese men waiting at the station to help us.

They had heard that a train of refugees was arriving. For days they had seen newsreels of the fall of France, of the bombed-out, starving people, unwashed and in torn clothes, stumbling along the roads dragging their crying children and their broken suitcases. So young men from the best families in Figueira da Foz volunteered to come to the station to meet us when the train arrived in the middle of the night. They came, eager and quite pleased with themselves, in their white tropical suits, ready to carry our bundles.

But who came out of that train? Actors, bankers, businessmen with their elegant wives, some famous faces, people carrying pig-skin luggage, women with crocodile bags and Scottish blankets. It was an embarrassing moment. Then the elite of Figueira composed itself and ran toward our luggage, determined to help anyway. When a young man who looked ten times richer than my grandmother had ever been got hold of her suitcase, my grandmother refused to hand it over to him and cried to my mother in Polish, "Guina, he is taking away our things. He'll steal them; don't let him take anything." We had a hard time persuading my grandmother that it was all right, that the young man was a volunteer and wouldn't steal her worn-out old suit-case.

We followed our helpers to the Casino where a large room had been set up with tables covered with food. It was touching how the Portuguese had tried to make our arrival pleasant. A few people who had come on an earlier train were sitting there and were apparently waiting for us too. Among them we suddenly saw our cousin Norek, his wife Lucia, and his daughter Ryśia.

Norek was like a son to my grandparents and they were overjoyed. He was a jolly-looking man—that is the only way one can describe him adequately. Since the war he had lost his apartment in Warsaw, his job, and all his money, and had now been in exile for a year. He still looked jolly. He had a round, friendly face and was always laughing and telling jokes—never the same ones. He was bespectacled, rather on the well-padded side but strong-looking, in his early forties. His wife was a kind, very well dressed and well groomed woman. Ryśia was spoiled, as many little Polish Jewish children of wealthy families were. But she was very intelligent and affectionate. I liked her very much.

Norek and his family had left a few days before we had, but he had stayed longer at the border, longer in Spain, and had finally arrived only a few hours before us. Now that we were all in Figueira and had had coffee and cakes and fruit, more tables were set up and official-looking Portuguese had us come up to the tables, family by family, to fill out questionnaires and be given addresses of hotels and pensions where we could stay. At one table sat a Polish official who might have been from "The Joint" or some other American Jewish charitable organization and who asked us if we had any money. Those who didn't, he said, would be helped. A fund was available and a certain amount of money could be given to each person each month.

We couldn't believe it.

Norek, who was a lawyer and the only practical person in our group, suggested that we, all seven of us, stay together and pool the money we would get. This way we would have a reasonable sum to live on. Of course we all agreed. It was wonderful to be together.

That night we stayed at a small *pension,* but Norek said that
the next day we would have to start looking for a cheap place
to rent, furnished, where we could cook our own meals.

Figueira was a seaside resort on the Atlantic Ocean where we
would have the most beautiful beach to use. And we had worried
about being shut up in a concentration camp. The next day we
walked around and admired the town—not without heavy
hearts still. Even though Figueira was beautiful, full of palm
trees and hibiscus and mimosa and masses of purple bougain-
villaea, we didn't know where my father was and were sick with
worry about him. We had lost everything, our past, our house,
our friends, France. It was like being terribly unhappy in the
midst of a carnival.

We had to be very careful with money so as to be able to
stretch our allowances to last us all month. Norek found us a
cheap apartment with a room for my grandparents, one for
my mother and me, a small one for Norek and Lucia, and a dark,
windowless sort of cubicle where poor Ryśia was to sleep. That it
was windowless didn't really make such a difference because
we had no view anyway. The apartment was under the roof
and had no windows, only some skylight openings in the ceilings. The room I occupied with my mother would double as our
living room and my grandparents' room would be our dining
room. We moved our things in, then wrote to Lisbon to uncle
Samuel telling him of our flight from France, our trip and our
arrival, and waited for his reply—for him to come to Figueira.

I started to learn Portuguese at once. It was a little like Latin
and my years of Latin helped me. Our landlord had a daughter
named Maria de Lourdes who was my age. We had arrived in
July. It was very hot and each day I went to the beach
with Ryśia. We talked together and swam together. She was
a little like one of the Chanteloup children to me and I liked
playing mother to her. She helped me, too. It was comforting

to see her nice round face during our walks, nice to answer
her questions. It helped me not to think all the time about
my father.

Once I bought a French newspaper, a few days old, and there
were printed lists of students who had passed the *Baccalauréat*
in Bayonne in June. My name was among them.

We waited and waited for my uncle, but he only wrote us
a letter. He never came to Figueira. I think that, even then,
it was because of my parents' conversion. Lisbon was not so far
from Figueira and he knew how much we wanted to see him.

The night of the Fourteenth of July, Bastille Day, we went to
a ball at the Casino—a ball organized especially for the French
refugees, but all the Poles and Belgians and Dutch and Czechs
were there too. It was the first ball I had ever attended, and the
saddest. I kept thinking of Paris, Paris occupied by the Germans,
where all celebrations for the Fourteenth of July had been forbidden by Hitler. Nobody wore evening clothes to this ball and
everyone looked preoccupied. Soon the refugees tired of dancing
and sat around talking about the only things on their minds—
visas, consulates, the Clipper, whether the doors of Brazil were
wider open than the doors of Chile. What about going to Canada? or Argentina? Someone had heard that for a thousand dol-
lars you could get visas for such and such a country. How long
before Hitler would take over Portugal?

We left at two o'clock in the morning—Norek trying as usual
to cheer us up with his innumerable jokes, Lucia patient and
kind and as always impeccably dressed, never looking tired or
hot or depressed, and my mother always worrying, worrying,
repeating, "Where is Marek? Where can he be? When will we
hear from him?"

We heard that same night. My father was with the Polish army
in Scotland. He had left France from La Rochelle with his regiment, on a boat going to England. The boat had been repeatedly

bombed and nearly sunk. My father had written Uncle Samuel begging him to help my mother and me escape from France, to send us visas. The last he knew was that we had been in St.-Jean-de-Luz.

We cried that night. I even cried in front of my mother. We read and reread my father's letter to my uncle and wrote at once to Scotland. Now, I told my mother, I absolutely had to join General de Gaulle's army in England. We didn't have to stay in Portugal any longer. We could join my father.

In the meantime my mother had written to her friend Jacques Maritain, who was in the United States with his wife, and he arranged to have us sent four visas to enter the U. S. A. People in Figueira da Foz at that time were paying fortunes to get American visas. No one knew when Hitler's armies would cross Spain and invade Portugal too. This was the last place refugees could stay. Beyond there was only the ocean.

But I stood firm on that point. I was not going anywhere but to England and to the Free French Forces. My mother wanted to be near my father, too. There was only the question of my grandparents. London was being bombed day and night; this was the time of the Battle of Britain. The Portuguese were sure that England would fall at any moment, it was only a question of time, and many Portuguese were pleased at the idea of Germany's victory. We couldn't possibly drag my grandparents to England. Finally it was decided that they would leave for Canada with my uncle Alexandre and his family, who were all in Lisbon, while Norek, Lucia, Ryśia, my mother and I would take the first opportunity to go to England.

It wasn't so simple to "go to England" at that time. Portugal was officially neutral, but unofficially its heart was with Mussolini and Hitler and Franco. There were spies everywhere in Lisbon—spies for every country, every dictator, and for the English and Free French too. We had to apply to the British Consulate and wait and see.

France was now ruled by the Vichy Government, which had the blessing of the United States. They didn't like General de Gaulle, who was considered too independent, not docile enough. The Vichy Government, I learned from the papers, had taken away my French citizenship because I had left France, so now I wasn't even French. But I knew that if I wasn't Vichy French, I was Free French, and anyone who joined the Free French lost his nationality anyway.

In Figueira da Foz the refugees went to the bullfights and to the Casino and to the movies. We swam and sun-bathed. It was an easy life. Only at night were we reminded of the war, when everyone sat glued to the radio listening to the B.B.C.

On the beaches of Portugal in 1940 one couldn't wear just any kind of bathing suit. It was all regulated: men had to wear full one-piece suits, no trunks were allowed. The exposure of their bare chests was considered indecent. Women, of course, had to be modestly covered, but even that was not sufficient. They were also not allowed to wear their terry cloth robes half open over their bathing suits. A robe had to be closed or it had to be off. To wear it half open was considered provocative. The Portuguese all obeyed the rules, but the refugees gave a lot of trouble to the "morals police" patrolling the beaches.

Finally the town of Figueira had a brilliant idea.

One morning we arrived at the beach and noticed two new wooden posts stuck into the sand about half a mile apart. On each post there was a sign *"Bagno de Sol."* The refugees were told that between those two posts they could keep their robes half open and men could wear trunks. I was even allowed a two-piece bathing suit—but only between those two posts. In this way the morals of the rest of the beach's visitors were safeguarded and we were permitted our own disgusting practices.

But the next time my mother went to confession in Figueira's church, the priest told her that he had heard (from the local morals police?) that her daughter was wearing a very indecent two-piece bathing suit. My poor mother had many faults, but she was not particularly prudish. She laughed and said that my bathing suit looked very decent to her. That was the end of that. The priest shrugged and didn't talk any more about my bathing suit.

On the beach young men often came to our *Bagno de Sol* to flirt and talk to the refugee girls. It became "the" place to be seen. Often now a young man called Carlos came to talk to me. He was always asking me to go driving with him in his sports car, but, remembering Emile, I was scared stiff and told Ryśia always to hang around, never to leave me alone with Carlos.

On the one hand I liked Carlos; he spoke good French and was terribly handsome. It would have been nice to drive in his car, to go and have ice cream with him. On the other hand, I still wanted to be a nun and I was afraid any dating might again end in a painful scene.

I have snapshots of Carlos on the beach with me, and Ryśia "hanging around"—he was a magnificent-looking specimen of manhood and I looked very small and slim next to all that chest and muscle. Portuguese girls my age were already developed like mature women, but apparently Carlos liked my type better.

It was a long, hot summer. Under our roof in the rented apartment it was stifling. We were seven people living in three rooms and more and more we got on one another's nerves. Once Ryśia got into an argument with my grandfather. I don't remember what about, nothing important certainly. Ryśia was a spoiled little girl. It was hard for her to have lived this refugee life for a whole year, first in Belgium, then in France, and then here. She didn't go to school. She was cranky; she hated her dark cubicle of a room; she had no friends her own age. In Poland she had been a rich little princess, with too many toys and every wish immediately granted. Everyone had listened with admiration to her every word. Suddenly she seemed to be in everyone's way. All her belongings were packed into one suit-case. People around her talked only of war and persecutions and visas and voyages. My grandmother had never been an easy per-son to live with, and now in those three rooms she was worse—complaining, bickering, nagging. My mother cried all the time and acted as if everyone should think only of her problems.

I can't remember what happened that day except that sud-denly a violent fight started. Ryśia must have been impolite to my grandfather or to my impossible grandmother. Maybe Norek would have liked to be as rude himself and the idea frightened him into threatening to hit Ryśia. He, who had never touched his adored and spoiled little brat, now pulled his belt out of his trousers. . . .

I heard the belt hissing and heard Ryśia howling and my mother crying. Lucia screamed, "Norek, are you crazy?" and ran to protect her daughter. My grandmother repeated in Polish, "Oh! To have lived to see such a day! Oh! My God protect us! The child shouldn't talk this way to an old man! What are we doing here? We should leave. We are a burden to all of you! We should have remained in Poland! Better for the Germans to murder us!" . . .

I was frozen in my corner of the room, unable to cope with the situation. My grandfather had some sort of an attack. I had never seen him in such a state. He was always such a dignified, calm man. His face got beet red and he roared at the top of his voice, pounding on the table. Then he clutched his long white beard and I saw with horror that he had pulled out whole tufts of his hair. The tufts were stuck to his fingers.

I couldn't stand it. I never could stand scenes and screams. I had not been used to it. They always affect me very much—they frighten me. I have never understood how anyone can completely lose control of himself. Sometimes in Lectoure Romeck had had rages, but it was nothing compared to what seized my grandfather that day.

After that I was very depressed. I wanted to get away, to leave, to stop wasting time in that golden cage while the terrible war was going on. I felt that I was young and healthy and that I should be doing something worthwhile, not swimming in the Atlantic and listening to Portuguese *saudades*. Beautiful Portugal was totally unreal.

There were cafés in Figueira where the refugees gathered. They called the street where all the cafés were the "Champs-Elysées" and people sat there and gossiped all day about each other: who was having an affair with whom, and that sort of thing.

The Polish Consulate was set up in a library on that street. All the news and messages were tacked onto a board in the library window. Every afternoon crowds stood in front of that library commenting on the announcements in five or six languages. Toward the end of August there was an announcement on the board that a boat would be leaving Lisbon sometime in September taking people to England. My mother was delegated by the family to get permits for Lisbon, then to go to the British Consulate for English visas. I stayed in Figueira, hoping she would manage. Norek felt that my mother, having a husband in the army in England, would be the most likely to convince the British to admit her and her daughter, and her cousins, too. Every afternoon when I came back from the beach I sat with Norek, Lucia, and my grandparents in one of the cafés on the "Champs-Elysées," eating sunflower seeds, which were very cheap, and listening to the refugees talk.

Most of the people around me were totally different from anyone I had known up to then—different from all my parents' friends in Paris, from Mya and Romeck, from the people in Chanteloup. I was astonished to find them so critical of each other. I felt that many were selfish, interested only in saving their own skins. They didn't seem to have any ideals, any faith except in success and money. Maybe if I had known them better I would have penetrated this front and found fine hidden qualities. But I didn't know them. I only heard their jokes, their remarks. I thought they were cynical and I felt strange among them, listening to their tales of great prewar parties and complicated intrigues. Until then I had belonged to my world—Jewish, Polish, Catholic, French world. Somehow each one had fallen into place in my child's life in such a way that I knew who I was even if what I was may have seemed complicated to others. Even after the scandal, when my parents' conversion was discovered, I still knew who I was, I fitted where I was. In Figueira da Foz for the first time I started not belonging.

Officially no longer French, I was adopted by the Poles. I wasn't rejected any longer by the Jews as the refugees in Figueira didn't care about my mother or my religion. But on the other hand I couldn't fit myself into the old-fashioned, reactionary Catholic Portuguese society either. I realized that until then I had been many things and suddenly, I was nothing.

My mother had no such problem because she had lived in her youth among people of very much the same type as those surrounding her: wealthy assimilated Jewish families. Also, she was very attached to her cousin Norek. In a way she was back in her world, a world that accepted her conversion with total indifference, which made life easy for her. But I felt that the people around me didn't know where to put me. I wasn't really French, I wasn't really Polish, I wasn't really Jewish, I wasn't really Catholic. I didn't flirt like other girls my age; I sat on the beach with my little cousin and built sand castles with her. I looked fifteen years old at the most, and I spoke of going to England and joining the Free French Forces. They thought I was insane not to go to the United States, when we had the incredible luck of having received our visas—and for free. They kept telling me that England wouldn't last until Christmas, that London was in ruins; but I was going to London. Everything I was saying or doing or not saying, was considered strange in the world of Figueira.

My mother came back proudly with our English visas and at the end of September I met Carlos in the street one day and told him we were leaving the next day for Lisbon, and then for London. I can still see him standing there, very pale, not saying anything and looking sad.

We arrived in Lisbon. My uncle Alexandre was there, and I saw my uncle Samuel for the first time since I was ten years old. We had to stay in Lisbon a few days until our boat was ready to leave. During those days my uncle Samuel said he would show me the city. It was a beautiful city. During each tour my uncle took me to the place where the Inquisition had been and told me, over and over again, how the Church had forced the Jews to convert and how those who didn't agree to convert were tortured and chased out of Portugal. All during those tours he would only talk about the Inquisition, looking at me with accusing eyes.

I listened, but I didn't say much. I didn't want to get into any arguments with him. I felt very bad about the Inquisition but there was little I could do about it. I wanted to see Lisbon, to see the Castelo and the very old quarter of the Alfama, to see the hills, the churches, the museums. It was so wonderful to be in a new city, in a new country. I was curious about a thousand things and soon I would be in the army, being blitzed, doing all I could do against Hitler. I was tired of hearing about the Inquisition.

But I guess my uncle had to get it all off his chest, and I was the next best person after my father.

In October we left Portugal, headed for Gibraltar. Norek, Lucia, and Ryśia were coming too. My grandparents stayed in Lisbon with my uncle Alexandre, who was taking them to Canada.

The name of the boat was the *Neuralia*. It was the first time in my life that I had been on a boat. This was a rather small one, but it had all the graces of the nineteenth century—rococo decor, red carpets, carved columns, Hindu stewards in turbans. The baths were elaborate affairs filled with sea water. The lounges reminded me of Jules Verne's books. One expected to see appear some tall colonial Englishman in very narrow trousers, neatly capped, holding a pipe, or some frivolous countess wearing a pouf and twirling a lorgnette on a gold chain.

We were in first class, in a lovely all-white cabin, served and blanketed on deck, all without any money at all. That was one of the mysteries and ironies of wartime which I had only started learning. "We have lost everything," as my mother repeated all the time, with deep sighs, and maybe because of that fact, anonymous powers suddenly started taking care of us. We had lived on a luxurious beach for three months and, because we were refugees, the casino and the movie houses in Figueira were free for us. Without any money of our own we had survived for three months, rented an apartment, bought food at the open-air market. Now we were traveling first class on an English pleasure boat used for elegant passengers going to India.

Sea gulls shrieked, flying in a long, tenacious trail behind the *Neuralia*. On deck I made a friend. She was fifteen and had lived in Warsaw at the beginning of the war, she told me. She also told me atrocity stories of the first months of the German occupation. For hours Iza and I stood on deck talking. She had very blue eyes which sometimes turned green, sometimes gray. She was about my size but sturdily built, with long, opulent black hair and beautiful white teeth. She was full of life, full of energy. She seemed always ready to bite into things, as if life were a big red apple. We got along at once and perfectly. It didn't bother us that I was a little older. I could talk to Iza about anything and everything. Although she was Polish, she spoke French well. She had also learned some Italian in Italy and some Portuguese in Lisbon. Around us, as in Figueira, it was a Tower of Babel— people calling to each other in every language under the inscrutable eyes of our turbaned stewards. I was perfectly happy on that boat and happy that we had left behind the false peace of Portugal, that we were on our way to England.

As we approached Gibraltar we saw dolphins jumping in and out of the waves, and then we saw the Rock. The air smelled different, sounds came to us with a different intensity. Here there was already something of Africa.

A British officer came to the lounge and told us that everyone had to stay for a week in hotels in Gibraltar until our second boat arrived to pick us up. My mother started crying. "What will we do in such a place, and without money? How terrible, how awful," she wailed. But Ryśia, Iza, and I were delighted. It was such an adventure to be able to live at the foot of that immense Rock.

We disembarked and were taken into the town.

Lots of people crowded the streets but there was something strange about the crowd. I looked all around and realized that there was not a single woman, or even a girl, in the streets— only men, mostly in British uniforms. Gibraltar's women had all been evacuated. The town was an enormous barracks and the few civilian men were hotelkeepers, shopkeepers, workers from Spain who crossed every day at Algeciras, Hindu merchants, providers of fun and purchases for the soldiers. Later we did notice a few women but they never seemed to leave the two or three cafés where they sang or danced or sat with the soldiers.

We were assigned a room in a very poor hotel where my mother was scared to go out to the bathroom on the landing or down the stairs.

Iza was with her parents in another hotel. We managed to meet and walk around, holding hands, not very certain of our safety among so many men—and they really were like wolves. When we passed all heads turned. They whistled, they yelled, they smiled, they called out, they made obscene gestures. It was frightening. We probably had nothing to fear—they were just lonely and at war, and would not have hurt us in any way. Yet the experience was very unpleasant.

We walked to a higher level on the Rock where there was a park planted with flowers and trees I had never seen before and from which the view seemed unlimited. From one side of the Rock we could see Spain clearly, from the other side, Africa.

Finally our boat arrived—the *Reina del Pacífico*. She was a gray battleship filled with Polish army units. There were five or six families waiting to embark on her for the trip to England, which we were told would take two or three weeks in a convoy, trying to escape mines and bombs.

So once more we were on board ship, mostly among Polish soldiers. There were also a few young Frenchmen who had escaped from France to join General de Gaulle and I told them proudly that I was going to join the French army too.

After dinner we often sat on the top deck with those Frenchmen. I'll never forget those men. It was dark around us. The sea was stormy. One of them was twenty-five years old. His wife was twenty-three. He had left her and their four children in France. He didn't even have a photograph of his children. Another one had a brother who was a prisoner in Germany. His old parents were all alone. The third Frenchman was seventeen years old. He had run away to Gibraltar to join the army.

The men told us these things simply, without fancy sentences. Sometimes they sang. They whistled. I looked at the sea. Dear God, I thought, I ask only one thing of you. Let me get to England and join De Gaulle's army.

The trip took three weeks, what with safety drills and alerts. When the ship entered British waters at Liverpool, she slowly advanced between rows of sunken boats. Everything looked as gray as the color of our ship. The sky was gray, the town in front of us was gray.

When night fell we heard sirens and the roar of planes overhead, and bombs bursting all around us. It was our baptism. From the start I was never scared of bombs. I felt very sure that I wouldn't be killed by a bomb. I think that was the reason I never feared the blitz, the V-1's and V-2's, and why, in another war, years later in Israel, alerts during those Six Days left me so indifferent. It wasn't courage; it was a certitude that my death when it came would come another way.

In the morning we got off the boat in Liverpool. Until then we hadn't even known the name of the town facing us. But in the morning they told us where we were and we were transferred directly from the pier to a bus waiting for us. Once more we didn't know where the bus was going. Things were done secretly, probably because of the war.

We drove all day. We passed nameless towns. All signs with names had been removed in case of a German landing. In the streets the women I pointed out to Iza wore slacks. I had never seen women wearing slacks, except white flannel ones on beaches, or jodhpurs for riding; slacks for everyday wear were something new.

Everyone seemed determined and grim and from time to time we saw bombed-out houses, burned houses. But it was only as we approached the outskirts of London that we saw masses of ruins everywhere. It was getting dark and soon we couldn't see anything. The streets were totally dark, not one light could be seen behind the blacked-out windows. Our bus lights were dimmed and the bus drove on very slowly. Then there were the sirens again, rising to a sort of tragic howl.

The bus stopped and we were told to get out. We were led down some steps to a shelter. We froze all night in that shelter, without any heat; nor had we had any food since morning. Around four o'clock Iza and I organized a few people to join hands and dance in a circle, singing, to warm ourselves a little.

That was my first night in London.

Part V ❀ London

In the morning we got into the bus again and off we went to what we discovered with surprise was a screening camp. The British called it "Patriotic School." Patriotic School was a sort of compound where the women and children slept in certain dormitories, thirty or forty together, and the men in others. During the day we were checked and interrogated and re-checked and processed to make sure we were not spies.

The grounds were large. We were not allowed to write to anyone in England or to communicate with anyone outside the camp, but we could walk around inside the fence. Iza and I walked together whenever we could along the frozen paths. We continued our discussions about the world and the way it should be organized in the future. It was really very simple and we had it all under neat control. If governments only had enough good sense to listen to our plans, there would never be wars again, never hunger, never injustices. Men would love men—everyone would be everyone's brother.

Once the British were satisfied that we were genuine refugees, they let us out and we were directed to a hotel in London where room and board were provided by the Polish Refugee Committee.

The first thing I did was to rush to Free French headquarters and register for the Women's Army which was just being formed. My mother wrote to my father in Scotland and we hoped he would get leave and come and see us.

Now there was a wait of a few days until I was called for the army medical examination and I amused myself by counting all the beds I had slept in since the war started. This one was the twentieth. We lived in the hotel to which we had been assigned. It had once been fashionable, in a fashionable neighborhood— but once was long ago. The hotel's former grandeur hung in dusty, discolored green velvet drapes. The carpets looked as if they had leprosy, and mice ran joyfully at night in our room. Most of the guests were Polish refugees like us. In the hotel I was considered Polish, as the Poles had generously adopted me, putting me on their lists. With us were a few older single men: a doctor, an ex-lawyer, a few ex-businessmen, two or three couples with small children, and a few young women who had been on the boat with us. There were also a few English spinsters and ex-army officers.

Iza and her parents, as well as Norek and his family, had left for Scotland. No one who didn't have to stayed in London.

The air raids started so punctually every evening that you could have regulated your watch by them. It was always at dinner time and I never saw anyone interrupt whatever they were doing because of the sirens. I think that the English staying at the hotel must have set the tone. The first time we ate there the siren started howling and I looked around. I saw an English guest raise a hand to pick up the salt shaker, another wiped his mouth with his napkin, a lady said to her neighbor: "My goodness, six o'clock already." They went on eating, with their solemn, stiff manners. The Poles looked at one another and immediately gave a perfect imitation of British *sang-froid*. The sirens kept screaming, then stopped, and we heard the drone of planes overhead and here and there an explosion.

We ate and talked, shook salt on our boiled cabbage and potatoes, wiped our mouths, and checked our watches.

After dinner you could go back to your room or sit in one of the ancient decayed drawing rooms, under dusty chandeliers, on squeaky, threadbare couches. Someone tried to play the out-of-tune piano, some played cards, some read *The Times*. If anyone was determined to go to a shelter, there was always the underground station five minutes away.

At first my mother was very frightened and wanted to go to the shelter in the underground, but I told her that I wouldn't go, so she gave up the idea and stayed at the hotel. She would rather stay with me than be alone in the crowded, dirty subway station. Later on she got used to the air raids as everyone else did.

But she was very upset that I was going to leave her and go into the army. My father was away, I would be away, and she had never before been all alone in a foreign city, under bombardment, without money and not knowing the language. Her Parkinson's disease was getting worse. Her hand shook badly, then slowly the shaking started spreading all over her right side.

We had no money at all. When we wanted to take a bus or go to a movie, we used part of the money we had had when we arrived. It wouldn't last us long, even at a few pence each time. But once I got into the army I would have my pay and could give my mother part of it. Part of my father's pay was also going to be transferred to my mother. But my father was a private first class, as I would be, so our combined pay would not amount to much.

On November sixth I read that Roosevelt had been re-elected in the United States. We were overjoyed. Everyone hoped that Roosevelt would be able, finally, to bring America into the war to help us. The night before we had had the longest air raid yet. It lasted fourteen uninterrupted hours. I wrote in my diary:

It is the most disagreeable feeling one can imagine, listening to the night planes droning above one's bed, while cannons and bombs compete for noise or, rather, uproar. One day the war will be only a memory, but I'll always remember those night air raids in London and the waiting while the plane comes nearer. We think . . . will the bombs fall on our house? The droning draws nearer still. It passes above our heads, it goes away, it diminishes. We breathe with relief until the next time . . . and this keeps on—ten, twenty times a night. Thousands of people sleep in the underground. They are afraid to stay at home or even to go to a regular shelter. Every night they bring their mattresses and blankets. They sleep on the dirty ground, in the stuffy air, among the drafts of the station, in the smoke. When I take the subway as early as three or four o'clock in the afternoon, I see these people already settling in on the stairs, in the corridors, on the platforms—children, women, old people. All the poorest mob of London goes down into the subways to sleep every night.

When the raid is particularly bad, as it was yesterday and tonight, I dream of the peace in Héas. I remember the picnics with Mya and Romeck. I see the Cirque de Troumouze and the eternal snows. Ah, if only the war could end, end quickly!

We awaited my father's arrival, but he didn't come. On November twentieth I was called for the medical examination which was my first taste of army life.

In a large room an army nurse was processing two dozen naked women and girls. In convent school nobody ever undressed in front of another person. The boarders slept in cubicles separated from one another by white curtains hanging from the ceiling to the floor on all four sides of each bed, leaving room for only the bed, a chair, and a dresser. Each girl undressed inside her cubicle. I had slept at school on a few occasions and had never seen so much as the naked shoulder of another girl.

The one and only naked girl I had seen had been fairly recently. In St.-Jean-de-Luz, in the last days when the refugees were pouring in, the daughter of a cousin of my mother's arrived. She was about twenty years old, married, and had been living in Belgium. Her husband was in the army. She stayed with us for two or three days. One afternoon it was very hot and she went to my room to sleep. When I knocked to come in, she opened the door for me stark naked. I looked at her and it struck me for the first time how beautiful a girl's body can be. It had never occurred to me before. A beautiful body up to then had been an Ingres or a Renoir nude—paintings—nothing made out of flesh. At that moment in St.-Jean-de-Luz I had thought, with wonder, how perfect, how lovely! Now in the army center I was in a room with two dozen women, some pretty, some ugly, feeling quite embarrassed about having to undress with everyone.

Nobody knew anyone else. The women spoke with different French accents, some from the south, some from Brittany, some from Paris. Many seemed quite vulgar. I couldn't decide who they were or from where they had come, or how. The nurse hurried us. We had to pass tests, answer a lot of questions, fill out forms, see the doctor, get shots. We didn't talk much. I was so worried that I might not be accepted that I couldn't think of anything else.

I noticed only one girl. She was tall, muscular, and slim, and spoke French with a foreign accent. I knew, because when the doctor told her to go to the bathroom and bring him a sample of her urine, she said that she couldn't do it. She went into the bathroom a few times and each time came out with an empty jar. Everyone in line laughed, even the doctor, but she didn't seem embarrassed. She shook her short dark hair and opened her very green eyes wide, repeating, "I am sorry, I can't. Nothing comes out." I heard that her name was Micheline. She was about my age; I liked her. I remember smiling at her, that day, and her smiling back.

A few days later I got my papers. I had been accepted and was to report to Waterloo railroad station at eight o'clock in the morning. My mother was in tears. She had hoped that at least I would be stationed in London, but now it looked as though we were going away—and I didn't even know where, or for how long, and I hadn't seen my father.

The night before I was to leave, we decided to be extravagant and go to a movie together, even to buy two buns to eat before the movie. We chose at random a film playing in the neighborhood. It was a war story about a father whose three sons go to war, one after the other, and the three of them die, one after the other.

We walked out of this movie in a very black mood. All night I cried silently in my bed. After all, I had never left my parents. All I knew of life was the convent school. I couldn't even say good-bye to my father and I worried about leaving my childish mother alone in London, with the air raids.

The English barracks weren't so bad. I liked getting up early, getting dressed in my uniform, polishing my buttons, going out to drill and marching for hours in the English countryside. My understanding of English was not too good, as *Mère* Helen had taught us to understand only Shakespeare; any other style was unfamiliar, but after a few days I was able to understand the commands.

We had British uniforms and lived in a huge hotel, the Savoy, in Bournemouth, a seaside resort. The place was full of A.T.S., and for a month or so we were learning their way of life, their way of marching, saluting, and all regulations. Then, when we knew it all perfectly, our captain said, "We'll go back to London now, girls, where our barracks will be awaiting us, and French officers will come to teach you all the drills and commands and regulations the French way." Our captain was once a famous tennis champion. That must have been why she had been made an officer at once. She was in her late thirties, I think, and always walked slightly bent to one side, as if she were still dragging her racket in one hand and was exhausted after a match.

The first days I had trouble remembering to call our corporal, our sergeant and our captain by their grades. Each time I talked to them I would say, "*Oui, ma mère,*" instead of "Yes, captain," any figure of authority being so firmly implanted in my mind as a nun.

In the dormitory I was with Odile, Micheline, Sophie and a dozen English girls. We got along well together. We ranged in age from seventeen to twenty, although Sophie had cheated about her age to be accepted and had told the army she was almost eighteen. Sophie was a small, shy, and very quiet girl. She was of Russian origin—her grandfather had been a famous Prince Kropotkin. She had been born and raised in France, and was at school in England, by chance, when the war broke out.

Micheline, who spoke French with a Norwegian accent, was the athletic girl I had noticed at the medical examination. She had a Norwegian father and a French mother. They had lived in Norway before the war but Micheline was born in France, so she could choose her nationality, and she had decided to join the Free French Forces. She would say, "*J'adore la France,*" in her funny accent, and open her green eyes wide. It was a trick she had—to open her eyes like that. They appeared to be overflowing with laughter. Micheline was very gay and always made us all laugh.

Then there was Odile. She was incredibly pretty—small, delicate, with brown eyes and light brown hair, a mouth like a ripe fruit, a perfect skin, perfect teeth. Odile had a long, aristocratic family name, excellent manners, and a protective attitude toward all of us, as though she were visiting us from her château and found we needed her help. But it was not done in a snobbish way—she was very friendly and sincere. Odile told us that she had been in England since 1939, boarding with an English family to learn the language. When France fell she decided not to go back but to stay and join General de Gaulle.

🌷 We had been together one week and everything was still new. We had observed each other, chosen our friends, and were learning how to get along. One day I remember most vividly. I was lying on my bed in the dormitory, reading *Gone with the Wind*. It was afternoon and we had been up since six o'clock and had gone through several drills, then lunch; now we had an hour to rest. I was wearing my khaki skirt and shirt, but my tie and jacket were hanging on a chair next to my bed. Micheline was polishing her jacket buttons and singing "Clementine." Odile was writing a letter. Sophie was dreaming with her eyes open, stretched out on her bed. This picture is very clear in my mind.

To whom was Odile writing that day? It couldn't have been to anyone in France, because we couldn't write to any country occupied by Germany—only send messages through the Red Cross. I had arranged with my cousin Clara to send my letters to her in Portugal and she would mail them to France from there. Before leaving Portugal I had written to *Mère* Marthe, to Annie and Monique, telling them in guarded words that I was joining General de Gaulle's army in England. We had even established a simple code, so that now I could tell them a few things in that code. General de Gaulle we called "the doctor," Pétain was "the grandfather," England was "Alice," and so on. I could write to *Mère* Marthe via Lisbon that "I am at Alice's working for the doctor and hoping that her grandfather is not going to make any more mistakes." Maybe Odile had such a system, too, and was writing in her code on that day.

I remember so well: Micheline was singing "Oh, my darling, Oh, my darling, Oh, my darling Clementine," and Sophie had just asked me, "How is that book? Do you like it? Can I read it after you?" when the door of the dormitory opened and an A.T.S. called out: "Is Tereska there?"

When I answered she said, "Someone to see you downstairs," and was gone.

I jumped up, put on my jacket, knotted my tie. Who could it be? Maybe the captain or the sergeant wanted to see me. I ran down the stairs quickly and there in the hall stood a Polish soldier. It was my father. We hadn't seen each other for long months, almost a year, and I couldn't believe it was true. He also wore a British uniform, with the Polish eagle on his cap, and on his shoulder was sewn a small red badge with "Poland" written on it.

I hugged him and he hugged me and I cried against his shoulder, not caring whether anyone saw me. Only then, hidden in his arms, hearing his voice again, did I realize how terrified I had been all those weeks we thought he might be dead. Only then did I know how much I had missed him and how lonely it had been there in the huge, anonymous barracks, how scared I really was of the captain and of the military discipline. While I sobbed, my head on his shoulder, I thought, at the same time, "Stop, you idiot, you are going to worry him. He'll think you are unhappy and he mustn't be alarmed because of you."

He said, "Darling, you can ask to be allowed out and we'll go to the town and sit somewhere and talk. They'll let you go if you explain that you haven't seen me for so long."

He knew all about the army and they did let me go out.

I held his arm tightly as we walked along. He looked so young that no one gave us a second look. He could have been any soldier walking with a girl in a uniform. We found a tea-room and he ordered tea and muffins. I sat and looked at him, still unable to believe that he was there near me. He told me how his unit had already been on a boat at La Rochelle last June and how in the middle of the night they had been awakened and transferred without any apparent reason to another boat. The men all grumbled and cursed the army for never giving them any rest. But once they were on the other boat there was an alert, and the first boat was blown to pieces in front of their eyes.

He told me of a long march from Brittany to La Rochelle, of German planes machine-gunning them, of hunger, wounded soldiers, and defeat. I imagined him walking and walking, so tired, so lonesome—my poor, courageous father who wanted to fight Hitler.

He told me how he had worried about us, how he had thought that we had remained in France while he was safe in England. And I told him all about Portugal and Uncle Samuel and the Inquisition and Gibraltar and my friend Iza—but I didn't say much about the army. What was there to say? There were drills, there were marches. Some girls were nice, some were strange.

My father told me he had been to London and had seen my mother and her trembling hand. He looked so sad, so upset by her sickness. He had this last day and then he had to go back to St. Andrews in Scotland. He told me about St. Andrews —how the Polish soldiers awoke one dawn and found themselves lying up to their necks in water. It had rained so hard during the night that their tents were flooded. My father drove a truck and was the oldest of all the soldiers. The others were all young Polish peasants and workmen. All they talked about was women and drinking. "I have done some drawing," he said, "in my free time. I go out into the countryside and draw trees—beautiful Scottish trees; each one is different."

He sounded so sad and I knew how he felt among the soldiers

and how much more at home he felt among just trees. Then the time came when he had to go and he took me back to the Savoy. We didn't talk on the way back, we were both too sad. I held his hand and thought that I might never see him again. He could be killed in an air raid in Scotland or he could be sent to Africa and we would be separated again for years. We didn't belong to ourselves anymore, we belonged to armies.

After dinner, back in the barracks, my father gone, I sat with Sophie. I felt at ease with her because she was even more out of place there than I was. At least I pretended to have a good time and sometimes, such as when we marched six abreast, in step— one two, one two, at some early hour, along a cliff high above the sea—I did have a good time. But Sophie, I am sure, was lost, always lost, her face wore such a sad, puzzled expression all the time. It only lit up when she looked at Véra.

I hadn't actually spoken to Véra, but I had noticed her many times. The first time was in Waterloo Station as we gathered on the platform, a small group of women with tricolored ribbons attached to the buttonholes of their coats. Véra had arrived dressed in the latest Paris style, high-heeled shoes, blond perox-ided hair down to her shoulders, a face like an actress. She was accompanied by an effeminate-looking young man with dark eyes and very long eyelashes who was carrying a copy of *Vogue*. He gave her the magazine, saying, "Véra, for the last time, be frivolous."

I noticed Véra again when we were given our uniforms. None of them fitted. Odile's was too long, mine was too large, Sophie's jacket sleeves hung below her knees, Micheline's was too tight. But Véra appeared in a uniform that fitted her perfectly; only her hair was too long, the sergeant said. She had to cut it shorter so that it would not touch her collar.

Many of us had our hair cut shorter that week, including me. I came out with a very modern style, just below the ears. Odile refused to cut hers, so she gathered it in a small bun and pinned it. But even with shorter hair, Véra looked as glamorous as before. She had a very unusual way of walking, very erect, with her head and shoulders thrown back and her chest projecting aggressively. She was older than most of our little group. She had been married twice, she told Sophie. She must have been thirty-two or thirty-three years old but she seemed older to me —anyone over twenty-three seemed to me quite ancient.

Véra had a very distinctive voice—one could hear it clearly from afar—and she wasn't impressed by either the corporal or the captain. During drills, during meals, I had noticed her, heard her. When Véra came into the room where we were sitting, Sophie whispered, "Isn't she beautiful?" I agreed. She looked like Marlene Dietrich.

Odile said: "Don't get involved with her, Sophie, she's not your type. She'll only get you into trouble." But Odile always gave advice that no one listened to.

Two women joined us in Bournemouth and we were told that the older one would be our warrant officer. Her name was something Beaulieu. I never heard her first name and it didn't matter as everyone immediately called her only Beaulieu. She was short and stocky, and with her mannish haircut, her uniform, her tie, her flat shoes and, especially, her low, harsh voice, she seemed more like a man disguised as an older woman than a woman. She had once had blond hair, but it had turned peppery, now, and her eyes were gray, with a funny expression in them—as if she were on the lookout for something.

The other girl must have been in her late twenties. She, too, was stocky, heavily built, with large shoulders and strong legs and hands. Her name was Chartier—that is, her family name. We forgot her first name at once too and called her Chartier. Her voice was also low, like a man's, but she had large, beautiful blue eyes with a sad expression in them. In spite of the expression she was not sad, but friendly in the manner of an older brother who was there to protect us young girls.

After two weeks I more or less knew each of the two dozen women who made up the first group of the "Corps Féminin." The captain planned to insist that headquarters change that name to something less likely to provoke jokes.

General de Gaulle had enough against us as it was. He never wanted a feminine corps in his army. He considered that a woman had no place in an army. But there were all those Frenchwomen in England and they wanted to join him, so something had to be done to organize them. It was Warrant Officer Beaulieu who explained this to us one evening.

Beaulieu was on the best terms with our captain and she obviously liked Chartier very much too. They were always together and there were hints that Chartier would become a corporal as soon as we got back to London and our own barracks.

Three days before our English training was over Beaulieu chose a few girls to go ahead with her to London to clean and prepare the barracks for all the others. I was among them. So were Odile and Micheline. We packed our belongings in khaki duffel bags and put them on the truck which would take us to London. All traveling would be in army trucks. I was glad that we were going back to London. I would see my mother and I was very anxious to show myself to her in my uniform. The truck took us to the fashionable West End and stopped in a narrow elegant street—Hill Street—behind the Dorchester Hotel. We jumped out and pulled down our bags. We were in front of a large townhouse. Beaulieu told us that it belonged to the Rothschild family. They couldn't use it during the war and had offered it to us.

Inside it was completely empty. There was a large hallway with a grand staircase going up to the other floors. There were vast rooms, a library without any books on the shelves, and in the basement a large kitchen and pantries. Upstairs were more empty rooms and bathrooms.

We looked around. Our voices reverberated in all the emptiness. The house had not been used since the start of the war and was very dirty.

"Roll up your sleeves, girls," yelled Beaulieu in her harsh voice. "Come on, get to work, *'et qu'ça saute!'* " That was her favorite expression—*"Et qu'ça saute,"* we soon learned, and also *"Ah! ça n'arrangera pas les bidons, ma pauvre fille, ça n'arrangera pas les bidons!"* This was her own particular slang for use when someone had made a mistake.

Beaulieu set us to scrubbing the hallway, the stairs, the kitchen, the bathrooms. I had never scrubbed anything before and I hated kneeling on the cold floor wringing out a dirty rag over a pail of murky water. But I saw aristocratic Odile working like mad without complaining, and Micheline cleaning the oven while singing *"Mon légionnaire."* Even Véra had joined us.

Véra was married to an Englishman, an RAF pilot, and she had joined him in England. Before the war she had been a journalist living in Paris. She stuffed large bags with straw for our mattresses until we got something better to sleep on. Once again I realized the physical courage of Frenchwomen—the courage I had seen in Chanteloup where Maggie always worked so hard. From upper-class Odile to the little peasant girls from Brittany, they all knew how to work. They could clean a house, they could sew and cook and never complain that it was too hard for them.

At night I was exhausted—but Odile hardly looked ruffled. She smiled, her gorgeous lips parting over those regular, white, pearly teeth, and only said: *"Ouf!* Enough for today," then gracefully bent to one side and fainted away.

Chartier was right there, holding Odile's head in her lap, calling for water, and looking disapproving. "*Ah, ces gosses de riches,*" she said—these spoiled rich kids, they are no good.

But Odile came to as quickly as she had fainted. Her peachy complexion hadn't even changed color very much and Micheline whispered to me, "Do you think she really fainted? I think she faked it." "Oh, Micheline," I said, shocked, "how can you suggest such a thing? Of course she fainted, poor girl."

Beaulieu arrived and bent over Odile. "What's the matter with you?" she asked. "Couldn't you have told me if you didn't feel well? '*La prudence est mère de la porcelaine*' "—another of her funny expressions.

Odile sat up and said, "I am sorry, it was nothing, I am sure. I just have some trouble with my back, that's all. I can walk now, it's passed. Please, everyone, don't stand here around me."

That night in the barracks room where we slept on the straw mattresses spread all over the floor, Odile, lying under a gray army blanket next to me, said, "I can tell you, you won't repeat it. I trust you and you'll understand. A few months ago I had to jump from the roof of the house where I lived with that English couple. I must have broken something. I lay all night on the ground. I couldn't move. Now I have these pains which come back once in a while."

I said, "My goodness, but that's terrible. Didn't you go to a doctor? And why did you have to jump from the roof? Why didn't anybody come to your rescue?"

Odile said, "It was that horrible couple. They were after me. Let's not talk about it."

I didn't understand what she meant.

In the morning, before we began our cleaning again, we had our first drill in French with Beaulieu. She took us outside in the street and taught us the French steps and commands and way of saluting. It was all different from the English way and she told us to forget everything they had taught us at Bournemouth.

"The drill, my children," she yelled at us, "must be perfect —'*Ça doit être au bouton.*' One of these days the Queen is going to inspect us, so we must be prepared. It will have to be '*au bouton.*'"

Beaulieu beamed with pride, her cap sitting jauntily on her head. "You are the first unit of the women's corps," she said, "so you'd better be good. All the new ones who come in from now on will look up to you as their models."

Odile stood very erect, her eyes shining. I knew how she felt, and how Micheline and Véra felt. We all felt very patriotic. We didn't mind the drizzle or the cold barracks, the straw mattresses on the floor, the hard work. We could hardly believe our luck being in General de Gaulle's army. We had not seen him yet but we knew he was in London with us, that he had saved France's honor, that only because of him France was not really a defeated puppet of Germany in Pétain's hands.

In a few days the barracks took shape. We got iron beds, sheets, towels, tables, and benches. More girls arrived and soon we were almost a hundred women.

One night Beaulieu, one hand in her skirt pocket, bought drinks at our bar in the lounge for her favorites. In the evening we had a record player going, and a few French records. The one played most was called "Violetta." Chartier joked with Beaulieu; a few girls sat in armchairs and read old issues of *L'Illustration* and *L'Intransigeant*. Odile sewed on a dress to wear on her leave.

I lent my copy of *Gone with the Wind* to Sophie and she read it, frowning when she came to English words she didn't understand. Véra sat on the arm of Sophie's chair and put a protective hand on Sophie's head. She smiled. "How are you, my kitten?" she said. Sophie lifted adoring eyes toward her.

It was noisy at night and the lounge was thick with smoke. The music blared, girls were screaming, singing, smoking, dancing. Beaulieu's voice could be heard outside in the streets, I am sure. There was lots of drinking going on at the bar. All the windows were painted dark blue, crisscrossed with sticky ribbons of tape, and we planned soon to put up black drapes as a further blackout precaution. Every night the sirens sounded but we only went down to the shelter if the women wardens on the roof told us that the bombs were falling in our neighborhood. If it was in the middle of the night we got up, put our mattresses over our heads and went, in our pajamas, down to the basement until morning.

Fortunately I was chosen to work as a switchboard operator. I worked one day out of two and during my twenty-four hours in the switchboard room meals were brought to me. I couldn't leave even during the raids, so I didn't have to go down to the shelter. Véra and Sophie took the switchboard the alternate twenty-four hours. The girl who worked with me was nicknamed *Poisson Rouge* by Véra, maybe because she had as much brains as a goldfish.

Véra always nicknamed people. One girl she called *Poupée* because she looked like a doll. Across the street from our barracks there was a modern apartment building. At the front door stood a very faggy-looking doorman, and Véra called him "The Peruvian Ambassador." Véra attracted around her a whole little court of admiring girls. She read their fortunes in the palms of their hands, she analyzed their handwriting, she told them about prewar life in Paris, she taught them dance steps. But her most adoring admirer was certainly Sophie.

Beaulieu and Chartier were on the fringe of the admiring

crowd, attracted, like everyone else, by Véra's sparkles. But at the same time I felt a certain unexplained hostility in them toward her.

By January 1941 we all had jobs. Odile was secretary to an officer, a Lieutenant Delorme with whom she seemed very impressed; Micheline worked in the decoding section of the "Committee of the Interior"; Sophie was on guard duty; Chartier was now a driver and, as predicted, a corporal.

We all hoped that next spring the Allies would open the second front—that the war would soon be over.

❧In the meantime the war was on, very much so. At the end of December 1940 I wrote in my diary:

December 1940—Written at night after an alert

The anti-aircraft guns are thundering above our barracks. Suddenly a sharp whistle. It feels as if all the air around us was displaced. The house shakes, a deafening blow explodes. We look up . . . a second whistle . . . a second blow. We stand up . . . a third and stronger whistle throws us to the floor. The bomb comes down, down, and lands. All the glass windows shatter with silver-toned ringing. The shutters bang against the windows. An enormous din fills the street, then silence. The lamp on the ceiling goes out, comes on again, swings madly.

"I am scared," whispers Sophie. People are running in the street. Beaulieu rings the bell. There are knocks on our door. I run and open it. Two firemen rush toward our telephone. "Allô—Allô! The house at No. 6 is burning." Beaulieu sends everyone to the shelter. I am on guard at the switchboard with *Poisson Rouge*. Again there are knocks. I open the door. More firemen ask for coffee. With Odile and Chantal I go out carrying a pail full of hot coffee.

We are wearing our helmets and walking on a carpet of broken glass that crunches under our shoes. It is midnight but the street is as light as at noon. The whole sky is burning. It is a sea of fire. The sky is an orange-colored lake, the sky is red, the sky is blazing. The cannon thunders, a rain of shrapnel falls all over the street. The house that was hit is around the corner. There were seven people under it. Two have already been pulled out—dead. A horrible smell . . . the gas pipes have burst. We walk back to the barracks, stumbling over paving stones, rocks, wood, glass, iron.

Above us the sky gets redder all the time. We climb to the barracks roof. I think of Nero watching Rome burning. An extravagant brazier in front of our eyes. Toward London's docks, thick black smoke. Fleet Street is in flames.

Hours later: Again we go out with coffee. It is as strange as a dream, a nightmare, but we feel proud to be here, to be in the streets of heroic London. This is why we joined the army.

It was early in January 1941 that I met Janek. My father sent him to see us from Scotland. I don't remember when he first came; maybe he saw only my mother then, or maybe she called me at the barracks to tell me that a Polish soldier had come to London on leave with a message from my father. The message said that Janek was a friend of Jean de Menasce, a Dominican monk we knew, a writer, who was in Switzerland. He was one of the several converted Jews we had known before the war and who were in orders.

When I saw Janek in London the first time, I was, above all, disappointed. He was small, barely taller than I, and quite plump. In his heavy uniform, he looked smaller and plumper. There was something pathetic about him—a sadness, a vulnerability. He spoke very softly and smiled with a solemn child's smile. My father's message or letter, or my mother's phone call, had prepared me, in my imagination, to meet a tall handsome man, because my father had said that this friend of his was a poet. But the little fat boy with sad eyes didn't look like a poet. It took some time before I found out more about Janek and learned the strange way he had taken to come to England.

This strange way was once again connected with a Catholic Jew—with Father de Menasce. Wherever we were, in whatever time—peace or war—the threads running through our lives were always attached, in one way or another, to Catholic Jews.

Janek was studying in Switzerland at the start of the war. After the fall of Poland he became very depressed. It wasn't worry for his family, because his family had left Poland just before the war and was safe in South Africa. Janek's depression came from a sense of the absurdity and cruelty of the world. Man was just no good and nothing would change him. After thousands of years man had not learned a thing. Men still lived in little boxes, separate from other men, suspicious and hateful, each one building a wall around himself, uniting only to fight and kill each other in more and more cruel wars.

Such a long time and man had not even achieved a world government, one country, one God for all. Instead of giving up insane nationalism, there was more and more of it. Janek's depression became acute and he decided he didn't want to live any longer in such an awful world—like the young Frenchman quoted by André Gide in his diary: "I can't play in a world where everyone cheats," and then killed himself; so Janek, too, was going to kill himself. But before doing so he, for some reason, talked to Jean de Menasce in Fribourg, and the monk told the very depressed young man: "All right, Janek. I understand how you feel and why you want to die, but there is a war going on and the outcome of this war will have tremendous consequences for humanity. You are Jewish. If you want to die, at least die fighting against Hitler. Go to England, join the Free Polish army. Don't waste your death!"

This appealed to Janek, and he escaped from Switzerland into the unoccupied zone of France, where he got in touch with an underground organization which could guide him to England. Many young men were taking these roads out of the countries under Hitler's rule. Many died and many were taken prisoner. Janek, who wanted to die, had no trouble whatever. He found a guide at once. The price was reasonable, the guide was trustworthy, and he got Janek into Spain. Then in Spain Janek once more had all the luck. He crossed Spain without any incident. He wasn't caught and sent to Franco's jails. He arrived in Lisbon promptly and there got a boat, as we had, to Gibraltar. He joined the army in Scotland. He met my father, who told him to go and see us when he got to London. Soon after, Janek was transferred to a job at Polish headquarters in London, so we saw him often. I liked him because he was so gentle and sensitive, and wrote beautiful poetry—but I found him, with his small plump body, totally unattractive as a man.

I have often heard people say that women are attracted to ugly men. Maybe this is true only of older women. Young girls, on the contrary, can dismiss a genius if he is small, or fat, or unsightly in any way. They can be friends with such a man but can rarely fall in love with him, or be attracted to him physically. Perhaps it is an instinct in young girls which makes physical perfection so important that sex is easier for them to visualize.

My life was completely involved with the army. It had cast a sort of spell over me. I had gone straight from a convent school existence to its glittery, noisy, sexy, nervous atmosphere, and very soon I couldn't live without it. It was a kind of intoxication. However disturbing it was, it also had a reality to it that convent school or the gatherings at my parents', discussing God and St. Thomas Aquinas, or poets' readings at Desvallières's studio had never had. One was a part of an ethereal, idealized world, where art, mysticism, religion, and goodness were everything; the other life was a tough, vulgar, sweaty world of crude words, soldiers' dance halls, bombs, and drinking. I found I was becoming fascinated because, as rough as it was, it was real, it was life, and I had an overwhelming curiosity about that life.

All the younger girls had been assigned one dorm together: the bookless library. At that time about a dozen of us between eighteen and twenty years old lived there. Our dorm was soon nicknamed by Véra the "Virgins' Dorm," and everyone called it that, even after there were very few virgins left.

Sophie, silent Sophie, was there, smiling shyly and mostly listening to the others. Odile would give us all advice in her aristocratic voice; Micheline was telling jokes she had heard from her boss, a big, heavy, flat-footed naval officer who had taken the pseudonym of Kieff because, he said, he had been an opium smoker—or was it hashish?—in Indo-China.

Another girl was Chantal de Villeret. She was eighteen and had long, white-blond hair which she too rolled into a bun rather than cut. She had very delicate skin which got all red, pink, or blue, or covered with a rash, at the slightest emotion. Chantal was the only girl in our dorm who never undressed in front of the others. She never even so much as took off her khaki skirt if there was anyone around. She got under her blankets to dress and undress and kept that extreme modesty all through the war.

Then there was another girl who was about twenty, but certainly was not a virgin. She was divorced and a Parisian. She told very spicy stories and although she was not good-looking in the ordinary sense, she had what is called *du chien,* a sort of raw sexiness. She had a lover even before we were really settled in the dorm, and soon it was not one lover but two, three, and four lovers, who generally didn't know about each other.

If Odile gave us maternal advice, Denise had advice of a different kind—about contraceptives, ways to handle men, how to be tough. Sophie would listen to her in wonder and shake her head in disbelief. Chantal would blush deeply and she would hide under her blankets. Micheline laughed but took Denise's advice very seriously. Odile bent her lovely head toward me, saying, "Poor Denise, she is so vulgar!"

We had fun in that dorm. In the evenings before lights-out, we sat on our beds or walked around naked—except for Chantal —shining our uniform buttons or our shoes, or sewing, or reading, but mostly gossiping and laughing.

One night an army chaplain assigned to our barracks wandered into our dorm by accident, looking for the girl in charge of the chapel. He blushed and gasped and ran out, and all of us sat on the floor or on our beds, naked and convulsed with laughter. We were still young enough, innocent enough, childish enough, to find it hilarious to have been discovered naked by a blushing young priest. At times we were like boarding-school girls, a life still so near to us; at other times, more and more, we were women soldiers.

We had a chapel on the first floor of the barracks and the girl in charge of changing the flowers and preparing everything for the mass on Sundays was a colorless, old-maidish woman of thirty-five or forty, who looked ageless, and wore the skirt of her uniform almost down to her ankles and her mousey hair in a tight little bun at the nape of her neck. How she had happened to join the army I never knew. She wasn't particularly religious either, but the captain had no idea what to do with her and taking one look had decided she would be the *sacristine*. I don't remember her name; but I do recall that she was always in a bad mood, muttering and grumbling.

The vast majority of girls in our barracks were Catholic, and most attended mass, if not every Sunday, at least on many Sundays. In the beginning I went every Sunday. In the army as in my French world before the war, nobody questioned my being both Jewish and Catholic—I had a Jewish family name, I went to mass—it was all my private affair. Religion was not discussed anyway. We were all French.

And I was beginning to have the classical religious doubts that most young people raised to be religious have at that age. I saw the chaplain a few times but I don't remember his helping me much. My father was rarely in London and when he came I didn't want to worry him. A few times I spoke to Maurice Schumann, who was, like my parents, a converted Jew, so I felt near to him. He was then the official radio spokesman for the Free French, but he had his own problems. Little by little I felt less need for formalized religion, for attending mass and for the sacraments, although at the same time I felt guilty when I did not go to church. Before the war everyone around me had been so religious: my parents, all their friends, the nuns. In the barracks religion was more of a residual habit than a deep faith.

What kept me going was very often the thought that my parents had given up so much for their religion, I couldn't fail them. I had to continue what they had started—it was important that Jews of Catholic religion exist among other Jews.

Many times I went to chapel more because of that principle than to satisfy a need in myself to affirm my own religion. Of my various identities at that time what seemed most firm was being French. It was still unthinkable for me not to be, at least, French.

Every night the alert sounded and we heard bombs exploding here and there. We didn't hear the explosions or the drone of the planes, they had become such familiar noises. Like the roar of the Gave in Héas, after a few days, I didn't hear

it anymore. Only if we heard shattered glass falling on the pavement, which meant houses quite near us were being hit, would
the door open and Chartier's or Beaulieu's head appear.

"Come on, everyone, take your mattresses and blankets. We
are going downstairs." If it was Beaulieu, she would add: "*et
qu'ça saute*," which might mean in English "get jumping."

It was right after the New Year—on January 4th—that Sophie
asked me if I would go out with her to have a cup of tea in a
nearby soldiers' canteen. She seemed very upset. I was not working that day so I said of course. The canteen was empty at that
hour. We sat down, and Sophie told me about Véra.

Véra had seduced her. I was astounded. I had no idea that
such things happened. Sophie didn't know much about it either,
but she told me more or less what had taken place on the previous night during the air raid as she and Véra slept in the
switchboard room. The electricity had gone out and Véra had
lit a hurricane lamp which she then covered with her blue silk
dressing gown. The lamp was standing on the floor and even
that small, unattractive room must have looked exotic in that
soft, diffused light. Sophie sat on her narrow camp bed and Véra
recited poetry to her. Véra knew many poems by heart. Her
favorites were Pierre Louÿs's "Songs of Bilitis." Many evenings
when Sophie and Véra had been on duty Véra had spent the
night reciting poems and telling stories about smoking opium
before the war, about some very strange parties she had gone to,
and about her lovers.

"You know," said Sophie, looking at me with her huge brown
eyes, "she always acted toward me as if she were a boy. I couldn't
understand it. It was as if she wanted to make love to me, to
seduce me. She always tells me how pretty I am, and such things,
and you know how nice she always is to me, how loving."

Sophie bent her head and a curtain of heavy, straight, brown
hair fell forward, hiding her pale little face. "I had to tell some-

one, Tereska," she said in a whisper. "I need a friend so badly.
I am so scared. I don't really know what happened, or what I
should do now."

After reciting poetry and talking for hours, smoking, drinking some beer, Véra sat down next to Sophie, put her arms
around Sophie's shoulder, and said, "You are a *belle de nuit*,
Sophie, do you know that? Some women are prettier in the
daytime, but you are a *belle de nuit*. You open at night, like
certain exotic flowers."

All that talk, all that poetry, the beer, the cigarettes, the
bombs, the blue light, the planes overhead, the occasional explosions, the loneliness, the love, and Véra's extreme elegance,
her sophistication, her blond hair, her soft hands, her soft mouth
—Sophie poured it all out to me. I could see it, feel it.

"She recited this poem by Pierre Louÿs," said Sophie, and
quoted:

> Elle entra, et passionément
> Les yeux fermés à demi, elle unit
> Ses lèvres aux miennes et nos langues
> Se connurent. . . .
> Jamais il n'y eut dans ma vie
> Un baiser comme celui-là

"In my life," Sophie continued, "there will never be anything
like this. I know it. It has hardly started but I already feel as if it
is finished and I mourn it." I still didn't quite understand. That
Pierre Louÿs poem, ". . . *et nos langues se connurent*," took me
back to my room at home, in Paris, to myself at fourteen, to
Vally, the Swiss girl, and her tales of her fiancé kissing her "with
his tongue." Then I had gone to my father for an explanation.
Who would explain things to me now? But Sophie described
it all, with many hesitations, skipping back and forth, shyly.

Véra had undressed her and caressed her as though she were a man and Sophie had experienced her first orgasm. She called it a "thrill." I don't think she knew the right word, and neither did I then.

But what was terrible was not what had happened the night before—Sophie would have been quite happy if that had been all. The terrible thing, which made Sophie bend her head and whisper and look so upset, was that the next morning Véra had been icy cold to her, had acted as if Sophie were her enemy, or worse, as if she weren't even there, ignoring her completely. That was why Sophie had wanted to talk to me, to ask me what to do. She was almost in tears. She was lost, bitterly hurt, and puzzled.

What had she done wrong?

And how could I explain it to her? I hadn't even known until that moment about lesbians. I had heard of *pédérastes* because once when I was in the Métro with my father before the war, we were walking along a corridor when I had noticed on a wall the inscription, in chalk: "*Jésuites pédérastes.*" I had asked my father what *pédéraste* meant and he told me it meant men who were sexually attracted to other men, and that some people couldn't understand a priest's chastity, didn't believe in it, and could explain it to themselves only as homosexuality. As I hadn't seen any inscription about lesbians, I knew nothing about that. I had no idea that there were women who were sexually attracted to other women. In spite of what I found out later to be a common belief, there was not the slightest atmosphere of lesbianism in the convent school—crushes sometimes on nuns, or between girls, maybe, but certainly they were exactly the same as the very platonic crushes that young girls have in schools all over the world and which are a normal part of their growing up.

But here, in our women's barracks, I discovered a very different face of love. Soon, after putting things together and listening carefully to Denise, I realized that Véra was not our only lesbian. Beaulieu was one, and there were others. I found out that there were as many categories of lesbians as of "regular" lovers. Véra certainly was entirely feminine in looks; she had been married twice, and had male lovers. Beaulieu and Chartier, on the other hand, were masculine-looking and -sounding, and never had anything to do with men.

There was an aura of secrecy around those lesbians. What they were was known and yet not known; it set them apart. "Normal" girls whispered about the lesbians. Nothing was really sure: was Sophie one or wasn't she? What about Beaulieu and Chartier? Did they do it together? What about that girl seen in a club with Beaulieu, at the bar? Was she Beaulieu's girl? What about Micheline, who was friendly with Véra too? What did it mean? No one knew more than gossip. Even when Véra talked it didn't mean much. She had a way of saying everything so that nothing was clear. Was she kidding? Was she being honest? Was she pulling your leg?

I was intrigued. I was very friendly with Chartier, with Sophie and with Véra, too. I told myself that as a future writer it was good for me to learn as much as possible about human nature. One day I would put it all in a book. But it wasn't as cold and calculated as that, of course. What drew me toward the "lesbian" group more than to the other groups was that perhaps I felt at home in an atmosphere of secrecy. I liked people who were "different," who were not one thing only. Véra's stories of her lesbian love affairs were much more intriguing, more exciting, more varied, than hearing about simple affairs between Chantal, Odile, or some other girl, and a man. An evening in a club with Beaulieu, Chartier, Micheline, and Véra had much more adventure in it than going out with Janek—as nice as he was—or some other French officer and his friends.

In my ignorance, the only advice I could give to Sophie was to try to stay away from Véra and to forget the whole thing. It was ridiculous advice, as Sophie was on day-and-night duty with Véra every twenty-four hours, and she couldn't forget what had happened even if she wanted to. I tried to help Sophie by introducing her to Janek, the little Polish soldier, but they didn't get along particularly well. Sophie was too shy for someone as shy as Janek. They didn't say a word to each other all evening. Besides, Janek in his own way was beginning to show that he liked me. I was quite at ease with him because I didn't feel anything toward him except a sisterly friendliness. I teased him and told him stories about our barracks.

Véra continued to be mean to Sophie. Sophie never knew in what mood she would find her. By now several girls had heard about the "affair," as Véra told things right and left. Discretion was not her forte. One day I was sitting in the lounge with Sophie and Chartier. Sophie looked very sad. She was such a little girl, all her feelings could be seen on her face. Véra sitting at the bar with Micheline. She had become very friendly with Micheline, who amused her with the put-on, innocent expression in her green eyes, her funny Norwegian accent, and the cupid design of her very red lips. Chartier put her large, strong hand on Sophie's knee and said, "Don't look so sad, my little lamb!"

Sophie blushed and said, "I am not sad."

"Oh, my kitten," said Chartier with her gruff, masculine voice, "it shows all over your face. No one is worth being so miserable about—no one!"

Sophie, still blushing, said, "But, Chartier, why is she so mean to me?"

"Because you are too serious about her, my kitten. Véra doesn't want to establish a relationship. She won't marry you. She just wants to have fun and thrills, and you want passion.

You picked the wrong person to be in love with. Look at Micheline—that's the girl for Véra."

And Chartier was right. A few days later the rumor all over the barracks was that Micheline was going to bed with Véra. They were seen together in the lounge, Véra's arm around Micheline's shoulders; dancing together cheek to cheek; laughing together and going out whenever they were free. Véra had a small apartment in town because she was married and her husband could join her there on his leaves. Micheline told me that Véra often took her there.

We had been in the barracks only four or five months but our lives had taken on patterns that were to last throughout the war and in some cases longer.

Odile was going out with her lieutenant, Roland Delorme. He was a naval officer, a man in his late thirties, married, with a family in France from whom he had no news.

Chantal de Villeret also had fallen in love with a married man almost twenty years older than she whose wife and children were in France.

I was going out with several officers but still had not fallen in love. In any case, they, too, were much older than I.

Micheline, when she was not out with Véra, went out with friends of Véra's, men in their thirties and early forties.

I think the independence of army life had matured us early, and when we went out we were interested in older men because they were more sophisticated, more amusing. They took us to elegant English restaurants, which refreshed us after the drabness of khaki life, and talked to us about their adventures and about Paris before the war. They educated us in many ways, and we knew it and wanted to be educated.

In our barracks only the little girls from Brittany, girls from fishermen's families, from the country, went out with young soldiers and sailors, and not even all of them did. On the whole, during their five years in London all the girls I knew were involved in one way or another with mature men, and their outlooks on life, art, sex, and politics changed because of it.

Micheline had become my best friend. We told each other everything. We ate lunch together. We went to work together. I knew that, like Sophie, Micheline had fallen in love with Véra. I was sorry for Sophie, who was very unhappy, but, as Chartier had said, I could see that Micheline was much better able to cope with a woman like Véra. Micheline was tough, but her toughness came from her lack of deep feelings. Nothing could hurt her for more than a few hours. Emotionally she was immune to real pain. Sometimes this angered me. How could she feel so little? How could she ask so little from people? How could she be so utterly happy with so little? At other times this very trait I disliked so much endeared her to me all the more. How wonderful it was: her lightness, her easy moods, her gaiety, her way of never making demands on people. Micheline was always ready, always willing; she never complained, and never felt sorry for herself, or if she did it was the way a little animal groans for a while in pain, and then licks its wounds and is back on its feet again. She was uncomplicated and wide-eyed about things. She would look at me and say very seriously, "Tereska, I have such a pretty body; everyone says so, men and women. So why shouldn't I use it?"

She would say just what the poet Ronsard had said but in her own words: "I am young now. I want to have a good time while I can. Why should I waste my youth? When I'm old it will be too late." And she would run excitedly to her next rendezvous.

. . .

I was learning to dance. Micheline was teaching me the steps in the barracks lounge. I had been transferred from the rather boring work at the switchboard to a job as a secretary for the Committee for Foreign Affairs at De Gaulle's headquarters, and it was much more interesting. I had been transferred because during an air raid I had been found by an inspecting officer washing my hair in the switchboard's bathroom. So every morning I took the truck to Carlton Gardens, laughing and singing with the other girls who worked there.

I didn't want to be a nun anymore; I was finally certain that it was not for me. But I didn't want to marry either. I felt that I was much too young to think about marriage. What I wanted was to learn about life. I still wanted to become a writer and had continued writing the same novel I had started in Trouville during the summer of 1939. I had taken the manuscript with me to St.-Jean-de-Luz, so I had it with me in London. It was autobiographical, and I had finished the first part. Now I was writing the second part, which took place during an unnamed war, in an unnamed women's army. I was also continuing my diary in a new notebook. I wrote portraits of Beaulieu, of Micheline, of Véra. Sometimes I was very unhappy and home-sick: I longed for *Mère* Marthe, for Lucilla and Annie and Monique; I longed for Paris and my former life. But then my mood would change and I would try to enjoy myself in the crazy noisy barracks. Janek was attracted by the girl I was then —full of strange stories and laughter. He asked me to lunch a few times at a little French restaurant in Soho and once brought me an English edition of the poems of Aragon, whom he knew I loved. A few times he read me some of his own poems. But I never gave him a thought when I wasn't with him.

I was very impressed by the lieutenant who was my boss at

the headquarters—not at all in love, just impressed. He was in the Free French Forces under a pseudonym, like many soldiers and officers who had left families in France and were afraid that there might be reprisals against them. But everyone knew Lieutenant d'Ollondes's real name—it was such a famous name, straight from French history, that I felt as if I were working for one of Alexandre Dumas's characters.

Lieutenant d'Ollondes was the kind of man who could never in any circumstances have been bribed. He was first at his desk every morning and last to leave, and, although he had lost his right leg, he continued doing sports, playing badminton, and taking long walks. At work he was meticulously fair to everyone, and that was lucky for me, because when I started working for him I was hopelessly bad, the worst secretary anyone could have. It was not only that I couldn't type, but also that I had no idea what a file or a card-index was. D'Ollondes was very patient, and took great pains to explain to me the work I had to do.

Army life very quickly became routine—drills every morning under Beaulieu or another officer, breakfast, bed-making according to regulations, then everyone off to her job—mostly in offices or as drivers, some as cooks, switchboard operators, guards, nurses. We worked hard every day until six or seven at night, with a short break for lunch. When we got back to the barracks we had dinner or went out to movies, nightclubs, or bars. During the first winter the alert sounded regularly, and many nights it was impossible to sleep, but the next morning we would be up and drilling in the park, whatever the weather. I remember being so weak sometimes from lack of sleep that year of the blitz that during the day I would fall into a sort of faint at my desk: my eyes would close and my head fall on my chest, then I would start awake again and stay awake for half an hour before falling back into that odd unconscious state for another second. But at my age I could go without sleep and look as fresh as ever. Our resistance seems amazing to me now.

All London lived feverishly and dangerously. No one knew if he would be alive in the morning, or if his house would be standing. Our first barracks, the Rothschild house, was hit by a bomb, and Minouche, a girl of twenty I thought looked like Lucilla's sister was killed. Because of the atmosphere of tension and loneliness most men and women in the army tried to enjoy every second as much as possible. There was no communication with France except short, anonymous messages through the Red Cross. Most Free French people didn't know English and they were all extremely homesick for their homes, their families, and their country, and because of that were more prone to form emotional ties with young girls as lonesome and homesick as themselves. It was a curious combination of sadness and extreme desire for pleasure. In those war years people were wild and amoral. They knew there would be no disapproval from any family or acquaintance. All ties to home were cut. Everyone was on his own in a foreign land.

Despite easy affairs and wild parties, Chantal, who had a lover, still never undressed in front of any other girl in the dormitory, and blushed at the slightest off-color joke. She and the officer she loved were together during all those years, as faithful to each other as any married couple could be. Jean, the officer, had promised Chantal to take her home to his wife after the war. He told her his wife would understand. I don't know what happened to them, but I heard that after the war Jean did take Chantal home with him.

In our barracks there was a strange mixture of vulgarity and sophistication. The "vulgar" group was headed by a big, dark, coarse woman called Simonot, who was the head cook. She was in charge of a dozen little Brittany girls who had been assigned to our kitchen and she took extreme pleasure in humiliating and nagging any girl she felt was too "delicate" or "snobbish." If one did anything against the rules, like letting her hair grow too long or painting her nails, or being late for roll call, or not shining her shoes properly, she would generally be sent as punishment to the kitchen to help Simonot for a few hours or days. And that could really be a horrible punishment. Simonot saw to it! I remember peeling twenty-five kilos of potatoes there one day because my hair touched the collar of my jacket, while Simonot enjoyed herself tremendously making fun of me.

One great joy of these years was receiving letters from France. I was lucky because I could correspond with Paris through Portugal, and letters from Annie, Monique, or Lucilla were great events. I would read and reread them, then read them aloud to Sophie or Micheline or Odile. The day Annie wrote me that she was going to get married I cried, lying on my bed in the dorm. I felt so far away, so cut off from my friends. I couldn't go to Annie's wedding. The second front hadn't started the spring we had expected it, or the next—the war was going on endlessly, and here Annie was getting married and I would lose her. We could never again have the same friendship: the long conversations after school at *La cour des adieux,* before we parted to go in different directions.

And what I sensed was true. When I did meet Annie again at last we no longer had anything to say to each other after so many years of separation. We had behind us years of such different lives that communication was impossible. I don't know how Annie feels, but after more than twenty years I still regret and mourn our lost friendship.

Another way of keeping a tiny contact with France was to send cans of sardines to people in France through the Red Cross. I must have sent hundreds of those cans. Almost half of my pay went into it and as I was giving the other half to my mother I didn't have much left. I sent sardines to *Mère* Marthe, to Annie, to Monique, and even to Sonia. I had an address for Sonia somewhere in the unoccupied part of France and around 1942 I heard from her once or twice. I heard she was married, but I had no other news.

There were also radio messages through the B.B.C. The B.B.C. was sending messages in code to the Maquis, the underground fighters—messages like "Aunt Bertha is fine and busy with her knitting," which might mean "A plane will parachute arms tonight." Among those coded messages we could insert our own real ones, to confuse, and many times I sent them.

"Tereska sends her love to *Mère* Marthe. She is fine and in the Free French Army in London," and "Tereska wishes a happy birthday to Annie." After the war I asked my friends about it, but very few had ever heard my messages.

Janek was still in London, silent and kind and writing his poetry. He often went to see my mother and I saw him mostly when I went home. My mother had moved from the hotel and had rented a very nice, large room in a boarding house in Kensington. My father came on leave two or three times a year. He had changed, and I was keenly aware of it. He was very sad, which was not like him. He had always been a quiet but happy man. He had always been at peace with himself and with the world around him. But in 1942 I was confronted with a different man—a tormented man.

I think now that his deep unhappiness had several causes. One was the sight of my mother growing sicker while he couldn't be with her and help her. Then there was the absence of his work as an artist which had been his whole life. Last, but perhaps strongest, was the unbearable vulgarity of army life. Being a regular soldier for three years, driving a truck at his age among Polish soldiers who were mostly uneducated peasants must have been very hard for a man who had spent all his adult life in an atmosphere which was totally artistic, intellectual, and mystical. My father never complained, but his eyes looked bruised. Whenever I saw him in London in his heavy khaki uniform, I would hurt all over looking at him. He was such a vulnerable, gentle man.

I had learned all about soldiers. I saw them all day—at work, at army dances, in bars, in pubs—but I didn't have to live with them every minute of my life, and listen to their jokes and limited conversation. Even though I was a soldier too and lived in army barracks, I could escape. There were girls I could really talk to: Odile, Chantal, Sophie, Micheline, Véra, Chartier, there was my life at the Office of Foreign Affairs, and the men I went out with, most of whom were interesting. One had been a well-known publisher in Paris before the war; another was a poet, a Proustian character; another was, in my eyes, a fascinating pervert who always treated me with a marvelous enticing innocence. I knew many exciting people—men and women—in the Free French Forces in London, some of whom have since become quite famous in the French political and art worlds.

But my father had no one to talk to about what interested him; his life was utterly lonely. Only toward the end of 1943 did the Polish army realize that an artist of his age would serve his country better as an artist than as a truck driver. My father and several other Polish artists were given indefinite leaves so that they could paint, sculpt, and write and my father came to live in London with my mother.

For several months he couldn't draw or paint or sculpt at all. Four years in the army had been a traumatic experience for him. He was still terribly sad: he didn't talk and didn't want to go out or see anyone. Then his wonderful good nature slowly came back, and he started joking about his depressed condition, calling it "my Van Gogh period." If he noticed that I was concerned about his mood, he would try to smile and would say, "Don't mind me, my darling, I am only acting my little Van Gogh."

Since being in the army in London, I rarely had time for the talks we used to have when I was younger. There was a sort of shyness between us—I was no longer a little girl—I had grown up, and I had to live my own life and make my own decisions. But I remember we had one talk while walking in Hyde Park one day. My father was on leave, wearing civilian clothes and for once it wasn't I who talked most but he. It was spring and the grass was studded with yellow and mauve crocus. Everywhere couples in uniform were strolling—A.T.S., RAF, nurses, American GIs, WRENS, French sailors, officers from the Colonial Office, ambulance drivers, Scots in kilts. My father spoke to me that day about his youth, his dreams, his religious beliefs, his sculpture, his difficulties in readjusting to civilian life, his worries about my mother's Parkinson's disease. I listened —and discovered a new father. He had always seemed so strong to me, so calm, so happy. But I discovered a vulnerable man, a sensitive man, easily hurt, full of idealism, unprepared for the fights of life, a man who had dreamed a dream of love and unity among all peoples, but who had never had anyone to lean on. He had always been the one others leaned on: my mother, me, his friends.

For the first time he didn't have to listen: he could talk, he could open up and show some weakness. I realized, walking slowly with him along the paths of Hyde Park in that spring of war, how happy he was to talk to me that way, how much he needed it.

He started working again. He found a place to sculpt and a large piece of granite, and began to carve a powerful-looking man emerging from the rough stone with his arms raised above his head. The face was wide and peaceful, the arms had a Maillolesque roundness and smoothness, the trunk was broad and very polished. He called it "Creation," and it stands now in a garden near Paris. From that day my father did, one after another in wood and in stone, his best sculptures.

✿ In the barracks many things were happening in the lives of my friends.

Odile had fallen madly in love with Roland Delorme. Odile was one of those women who couldn't resist seducing an attractive man, particularly if he is unresponsive. Odile knew many officers who were extremely interested in her and were free to marry. If she entered a room every man in it became conscious of her. She was unusually pretty, soft spoken, totally feminine, small, delicately curved, had great style, and was intelligent and charming. There was also an undercurrent of hysteria in her that was attractive to males. Officers old and young fell in love with her right and left. She walked on, picking up their admiration like flowers in a field, but she wasn't seriously interested in more than platonic admiration until a man who refused her came along. That man was Delorme. He was married; he was a very devout Catholic; and he had decided to be faithful to his wife in France, however long the war and the exile lasted.

That this handsome naval officer, who was about sixteen years older than she, would not let himself be seduced, was really intoxicating to Odile. She set about conquering Delorme as someone might train to climb Mount Everest. And she won. Delorme, one night, a few days before he knew he was going to be sent to Africa, yielded and took Odile into his bed. Then he left. A month later Odile found she was pregnant. Odile was pursued by tragedies—if any girl could get pregnant after sleeping once with a man, it was Odile.

Before the war, in France, she had had a stepfather (her father had been killed in an air crash) who fell in love with her.

That was why she had had to leave her home and go to England. Before entering the army she lived with an English couple, and she had already told me that both the husband and the wife had tried to make love to her, which was why she had had to jump off the roof one night to escape them. The army discovered later, after she had fainted a few times, that she had actually broken a rib in that jump. Now she was hopelessly in love with a married man who didn't want her, who had gotten her pregnant, and who was gone.

She had breeding. She never complained, and she never tried to write to Delorme to tell him what had happened. She considered the pregnancy her own responsibility. I admired her, because there was never any self-pity about her. If she got herself into trouble, she didn't run to anyone for help, even to the father of her child. I met Delorme one day when he came back to London. The son he didn't know existed was about a year old then; Delorme had been promoted and was quite a high-level official at headquarters. I knew he had not seen Odile again. I had been sent to his office to bring him some urgent documents, and as I sat waiting for him to read them, I thought with a strange feeling that I could open my mouth and in a few words change that honorable, respectable man's life. I wondered what he would have done if he had been told that he had a son in London. It was a funny feeling to hold his fate in my hands at that moment, though I knew perfectly well that I would never have told him. Of course, his name was not Delorme; I saw his photo not long ago in *Time*. I don't think he knows to this day. That afternoon in London, sitting in his office, I remember that he kept looking at me with a searching, sad look. He knew that I was a friend of Odile's, that we had been in the same unit. He must have known that Odile was no longer in the F. F. L. and that I was probably still in touch with her. He must have wanted to ask me about her—I could feel it—but he didn't. I can still see his eyes, their expression. He signed the documents, gave them back to me, and I saluted and left.

Odile had been discharged from the army during her pregnancy. She got a job, met a famous English actor, and became his mistress. Finally she was happy with a man who loved her and who swore he would take care of her and her baby. He was killed in an air crash over Portugal during a propaganda tour for Britain.

While all this was going on, Chantal was still with the same lover. They dined together every night after work and never saw anyone else.

Micheline had many affairs. She went through all of them gaily and easily. She was the only woman I knew who had not the slightest moral sense. Whatever there was to take she took. It was as simple as that. She was the girl who had never heard about sin, and it is easy never to feel guilty if you have never heard of sin. Even Véra had a sense of sin. Véra would do whatever she chose, but she knew when it was wrong, and sometimes she felt guilty and repentant.

Like Beaulieu and Chartier, Véra was quite religious. She liked to go to mass, she liked religious holidays, and she truly believed in the Trinity and the Holy Virgin. She would light candles and bring flowers to our barracks chapel. Then she would go and participate in an orgy at someone's apartment in town and feel she was wrong, but that she was not strong enough to resist.

After a year or two in the army, another trait started showing in her. She had always liked to drink, but then her drinking became worse and was often out of control. She started seeing enemies all around her and fearing plots against her. She would then intrigue with one group to break up what she thought was another group's plot against her. She was unable to form any real relationship with anyone. She could be mean to her best friends, and would lie about them if it seemed necessary to her at the moment. She had no respect or love for people, only fantasies, desires, and lusts. Her best friend one day would be her worst enemy the next—and every failure would always be explained by plots against her. It was a plot that she was not an officer, it was a plot if she were not assigned a job she wanted, and so on. It was of course easier for her to explain anything that went wrong that way than to face the reality of her own shortcomings. Yet in many ways I liked her. She could be charming when she wanted; she had taste and culture, she was very well educated, and could make any party great, if she were in a good mood—singing, dancing, acting, inventing games.

She had separated from her second husband, the RAF officer, and had had any number of affairs that she would recount for us in great detail. Her tastes were extremely varied and listening to her one got a most esoteric sexual education. Micheline told me in her own typical way, as if she were describing an afternoon in the country picking flowers, about an evening at Véra's which had turned into a small *partouze*. I have the scene in Micheline's own words and rereading them I am struck again by their innocence:

> We started the evening in a very correct way, having dinner in the little dining room, with lighted candles on the table. I was sitting between Véra and Max. After dinner we went to the next room and Max opened a bottle of whiskey, which we emptied little by little, our conversation becoming less and less intelligible. Toward midnight I was in a state of dizziness and vague happiness. We went upstairs to the bedroom. The gas fire had been lit earlier and the room was pleasantly warm. I stretched out before the fire after having quickly taken off all my clothes. It was so nice to relax naked in that warmth and to drink from the glass Véra put in my hand. Then she stretched out next to me, softly caressing my breasts and kissing my

*mouth. When I was excited by her, how wonderful it was
to climb into the soft bed with her near me. Max joined us
and kissed and caressed us both. We three were mixed together
—interlaced. I fell asleep satisfied, happy, in Véra's arms.*

Micheline did tell me that the next day she had a feeling of
depression when she first woke up, but it didn't last. It may have
been from a hangover rather than from any remorse. She kept
telling me how "nice" Véra and Véra's lover had been to her,
although she added, "I should really be ashamed, Tereska.
God gave me a pretty body and here is what I let it do. How sad
I am." But she wasn't very sad, and not for long. I couldn't be
shocked looking at her, listening to her. She really hadn't done
anything "bad." She enjoyed the fire, the warmth, the kisses,
the caresses, without any obscenity in her mind. In many ways
she was much more innocent during a *partouze* than many
people are during a completely normal sex act.

One evening Véra asked me to go out with her to The Little
French Club, a very popular restaurant where all the Free
French gathered. She would often ask one girl or another to go
out with her and, if she didn't start drinking, it was generally
quite pleasant.

We were eating dinner when Véra saw a friend of hers. He
was a man in his late thirties, perhaps older, slim, with very
blue eyes and a high forehead shadowed by rather sparse light
curly hair. When he saw Véra, he got up from where he was
sitting and came over to our table. His name was Alain and he
was a civilian working for the B.B.C., a Frenchman who had
escaped from France but who had not joined De Gaulle's army.
He kissed Véra's hand, sat with us and ordered drinks, then
started talking in an extremely musical voice. He was good-
looking—and intelligent-looking, too. He had extraordinary
charm and I couldn't take my eyes off him.

Very soon Véra tired of us and went away to speak to someone at the bar. Alain and I stayed alone and talked. I had never met anyone, in London or anywhere else, who talked as that man could. He was a master of conversation. Everything he said was fascinating. He was widely read and spoke about art and fashions and politics in that beautiful melodious voice. It got to be one o'clock and I was still hanging on his voice, wishing I could listen all night. Then he said, "Let me take you back to your barracks," and I followed him obediently. At the door of the club we stopped. It was raining hard and pitch dark, as usual in wartime London. Alain said, "We'll get a taxi as soon as we can, but I don't want you to get wet," and he picked me up and started walking in the rain holding me in his arms.

From that evening on I saw him every day. In some ways I was in love with him, in love with his charm, with the poems he wrote, with his voice, with his blue eyes and beautiful forehead. But even when I was most taken by him, I knew that I would never agree to marry him, if he should want to. I felt he would be the best lover in the world, but the worst husband. I couldn't imagine him as the father of my children. I wanted my children to have a real father, not a fairy tale prince.

I enjoyed Alain, knowing very well that it wouldn't last and that it couldn't be serious for me. Meanwhile, he read to me from Proust and Colette, he took me out to dine at Prunier's, and he gave me advice on how to dress when I could wear feminine clothes again. We walked hand in hand through the busy streets of London, among Polish, French, Belgian, Czech, American, Canadian, Norwegian, and Russian army people, everyone saluting everyone else; red double-decker buses passing by; London policemen in tall hats whistling at the traffic; bombed stores carrying signs, BUSINESS AS USUAL; and Alain told me stories and laughed and danced as he walked. He was all grace, all poetry, all charm.

Once he said, "I like you because you don't weigh on me, you don't cling. There is nothing more horrible for a man than to feel trapped by a woman who hangs onto him!" I told him I would never hang on and said, "Alain, please promise me something: If ever, ever you don't want to see me any more, for whatever reason, just tell me and I'll leave at once."

He stopped in the middle of Piccadilly to kiss me, repeating, "Oh, Tereska, I do love you!"

One day he told me that the night before he had met an American girl and had been very taken by her. I asked him if he was serious about her and he said yes, he thought he was. So I said, "Fine, it's all right, Alain, good-bye," and walked away. Going back to the barracks, I tried very hard not to cry. I kept telling myself, "I won't think of him any more. I don't want to be unhappy. It had to end anyway. I will never think of him again."

Twenty years later, I was in Rome with just enough time to change planes. I was in the crowded-to-capacity little airport bus going from the Air France plane to the airport terminal when somewhere behind me in the crowd I heard Alain's voice.

I hadn't heard that voice since 1944. I turned around and saw a man who looked a bit like Alain, as I remembered him, talking in French to a tall, elegant girl. He was wearing a tweed sport hat and carrying a coat on his arm. He was very well dressed in a casual way. The voice was the same: musical, charming, slightly precious. The eyes were the same, and the smile. He didn't see me, and I wondered who the girl was— his daughter? his mistress? a new wife? a secretary? a friend? I wasn't absolutely sure it was he. The hat hid part of his face so I couldn't see his forehead, and I remembered how he used to worry in London about that high forehead, saying he was losing his hair and would be bald very soon.

Was it really Alain?

The bus stopped; everyone got out. The man was walking ahead of me with the girl. The sun came out from behind some clouds and I could see him looking at the sky and smiling. As he started walking up the ramp he reached for his hat and took it off.

As I rushed to catch my plane, I knew it was Alain. He was almost bald.

During most of the war years I spent my leaves in Scotland where my cousins Norek and Lucia were living, in a small town called Lanark, near Glasgow. Their daughter Ryśia, the little girl who had been my chaperone in Portugal, was growing into a nice girl, quite English now. Iza, my friend from the boat and from Gibraltar, who lived nearby, was one of the best students in her class. Both girls had the greatest admiration for my uniform and never tired of hearing my tales—very expurgated—about life in the women's army. Lucia was wonderful to me. She spoiled me, bringing me breakfast in bed and doing everything to make my leave comfortable and restful. Both she and Norek treated me as if I were a war heroine!

On those leaves I really rested.

I took long walks with Ryśia and Iza through the fields and woods, admiring the wild landscape of lakes and hills. I loved to breathe the fresh air and look at trees, grass, and plants again. It reminded me of Héas or Chanteloup, although it looked completely different. As soon as I was in contact with nature, I could feel myself becoming again the girl I had been not so long ago.

Other times, I went on leave with Micheline to Cornwall, to the seashore. Many English people would invite the army girls, especially those in foreign armies, to stay with them. The English were fantastically hospitable and kind. Quite often, in a restaurant in London with another girl, when the time came to pay the bill, the waiter would tell us, "Oh, it's already paid. There were some people sitting here who saw from your uniforms that you were French and who paid for you." They wouldn't even stay to be thanked.

Once I was sent to Newcastle with another girl to run a Free French exhibition; we were to stay during the two weeks of the show with an English family. Daisy, the girl who went with me, had been born and raised in England. But her grandparents were French and she had been to France many times before the war, so she had joined the Free French. Daisy felt that it would be terribly disappointing for the English couple who had offered their home to the poor exiled army girls to find out that one of them was a regular English girl. She made me promise that I wouldn't say a word about her and she invented a whole story, pretending not to speak a word of English. As my English at the time was not very good and the couple's French was even poorer, we passed difficult meals trying to understand each other. Daisy kept saying with a strong, put-on French accent, "Excuse me, madame, I don't understand."

Later in our bedroom we would roar with laughter, our faces buried in our pillows.

In Cornwall, Micheline and I swam and ate mussels and tried to get tanned in the pale English sun. Once we climbed a hill covered with funny little sticks. We tried to pull some out of the ground to see what they were. It was only when we got to the other side of the hill that we saw a large sign reading: KEEP OUT—DANGER—MINES. But we lived so much with danger—during the blitz, and later with the V-1's and V-2's—that we were completely used to it.

Among Véra's tales of her many affairs, there was one which for some reason I remembered particularly. She had met a young man, only twenty years old, who was brilliant, she said —a young genius. She called him her "young wolf" because, she said, "when I look at him at night in a dark room, he smiles and then his white teeth shine like a wolf's." I remembered the image, and that his name was Georges.

One day Véra and I entered the Carlton Gardens headquarters canteen when suddenly she pointed and said, "Look, there near the window, that officer. It is Georges, my young wolf!" I saw a tall, quite dark young man who looked African, although he was white. He had very short, kinky black hair, a very full mouth, a fleshy nose, and dark eyes. He could have been a light-skinned Negro or a Spaniard. He was very good-looking, with a marvelous face, full of personality. He seemed much older than twenty.

"He is French," Véra told me when I asked. "His father is Torres, you know, that famous lawyer." I didn't know who Torres was. I had never heard his name, and as Véra had said "famous," I thought she meant Thorez, the Communist leader. Véra waved to her young wolf and moved toward him. I stayed behind and didn't speak to him or meet him then.

It was around that time—October 1943, I think—that one day when I was at my parents' boarding house I was called to the phone. It was a call for them and they were both away in the country visiting friends.

"This is Meyer Levin," the voice said when I got to the phone. "Do you remember me?" Of course I remembered him, the American who had played those games with me when I was three or four years old, the American who wrote books and who had given me a puppet theater, and whose wife was that very independent woman who had gone to help the Republicans in Spain. I was delighted to hear that he was in London. He had just come over as a war correspondent. He asked if, as my parents were away, he could take me out to dinner.

It was strange, somehow, to go out on a date with someone you had known when you were four years old and who was a friend of your parents. I got dressed and decided not to wear my uniform but a light blue dress, a Schiaparelli model someone had brought to London and had had to sell. I was very proud to own a real *haute couture* dress and I liked to get out of my khaki sometimes.

At the right time the doorbell rang and I looked down from the third floor and watched Levin, in American uniform, climbing up. He must have been remembering me as the little girl he had last seen in Paris, with two braids on her shoulders and wearing a school uniform, because he looked astonished when he saw me—and pleased, too. We went out and had a delightful evening.

The name of the restaurant was the Mirabelle. Couples were dancing. Meyer listened with obvious interest to my army tales: our English training at Bournemouth three years before, the long and murderous blitz, our horrible chief cook, Simonot, who presided in the kitchen. "That one is mean, vulgar, a bootlicker, ready to crawl in front of any officer who can be useful to her. And our officers, I can tell you about them. There is one who is young and not at all good-looking, and scared to death to make enemies among the girl soldiers, but even more scared not to be approved of by our captain. There is another one who is always in a bad mood, and the snobbish one who doesn't condescend to talk to anyone who isn't at least a sergeant." It was fun to explain our barracks life to this man, a writer. I talked my head off, jumping from one thing to another, pleased that he listened and laughed. Then we danced and talked some more. I told him about Véra and painted her beauty and sophistication and strange love affairs in glorious tones. But mostly I spoke of our everyday life.

There were all the injustices of army life, which for years I had somehow accepted as "normal" because that was the way it was; but explaining it all to Meyer without worrying about upsetting him with these tales (as I would have had I been speaking to my parents), I could see more clearly the atmosphere I had been living in for these past years. I began to judge what I had seen. In a way, our barracks was the world in miniature. Our laws were based mostly on the rule of privilege for some and prejudice against others. Those not favored were treated by the rulers with total disregard and cruelty. Small gifts of new pajamas or toothpaste or a musical evening were considered enough to keep the rank and file contented and sufficiently pampered so that they would be quiet and uncomplaining. The rulers were despots. We had to obey rules that the army had made years ago and, as every soldier knew, it was taken for granted that we were ready to die for our country without having anything to say about how we lived.

As I spoke I started asking myself questions: is this the way the world has always been? Is this the way the world will be after this war? Are we fighting this war in order to continue exactly the same way after we win it? What are we building? What are we dying for? Here I was in an elegant London restaurant among a dancing crowd—people laughing, drinking, eating, a nice man listening to me with amusement. He was probably like me once, years ago, when he was twenty. But now he had stopped feeling so strongly about these things. That was the way people became discouraged, little by little, and began to accept things as they found them. Would I also forget and forgive one day?

I remembered when I was eight years old, how I had hoped never to be nine, how when I was twelve, I didn't want to be thirteen, and how when I was seventeen, I had thought that in ten years I would be an old woman. I passionately didn't want to grow old. It was not so much the years that frightened me, but the fear that I would lose hope, lose my desire to change the world, lose my anger at injustice. I tried to tell that man in his

American uniform, a friend of my parents, an older and wiser man, a little of what I felt. Maybe he could give me some answer, some key. I wanted to ask him: did you know more when you got older? Was that why you lost hope?

When Meyer took me back to my parents' room, I felt foolish. Maybe I had bored him? Maybe he thought I was an immature, silly girl? Was there any point in trying to explain one's real feelings? We were so far apart in age, in cultures, in our lives. At the door he asked me to see him again.

It was strange to me, going out with Meyer, having dates with him, because I felt I had always known him. I remembered so well how he had played with me when I was a very little girl. Once we were in the underground in London; Meyer was taking me back to the barracks after dinner. I was acting in what I hoped was a worldly, sophisticated way, telling him about the most unusual sexual happenings in the barracks as if they were all very normal to me. I didn't want him to consider me the baby he had known. I tried to impress him with my great knowledge of human nature as I had experienced it in the army. As we stepped onto the platform, Meyer stopped and showed me a little blond girl sleeping on a blanket on the floor, among the hundreds of people crowded into the underground for shelter at night to escape from the air raids. He said, "This little girl here looks just exactly as you did when you were four years old." I could see that I was still that little girl to him.

Back in London, after a leave, another friend of my parents asked me to dine. Robert was an Irish actor and writer, separated from his wife. He had become quite well known for playing Thomas Becket in *Murder in the Cathedral*. I liked going out with him because he was a great raconteur and a connoisseur of good food and wine. He used to take me out to a famous English actors' club (was it called the Garrick?) and I was very much impressed. One evening I took him to my little French club; as we were early, only a few people were there. However, I glimpsed, sitting at the bar, Véra's "young wolf." I recognized him at once.

Véra had left London a few weeks before and was now stationed with part of the army in Algeria. She had written to me and had enclosed a letter for Georges Torres, because she had lost his address and thought I might see him around London. So I went up to the young officer at the bar and told him I was a friend of Véra's and had a letter for him at the barracks. Where should I send it?

Georges completely ignored Robert, whom I had introduced, and said in a very deep, low voice—which surprised me; I had never before heard a voice so deep—"Why don't you have dinner with me tomorrow night and you can bring the letter with you?" I agreed and made arrangements to meet him and then went with Robert into the other room to have dinner.

A few minutes later Georges came in. Our table was the only one occupied, but Georges sat at the table right next to ours and for the rest of the evening just stared at me and listened openly to every word Robert and I said. I thought he was very rude. But the next night we met and went for dinner to an Italian restaurant in Soho, where we talked as if we had known each other all our lives.

I remember that first night's conversation very well. We talked about things I hadn't discussed for a long time: religion —about Catholicism and Judaism. We sat in that small Italian restaurant, two young people in uniform in wartime London, Georges talking with that extraordinary voice he had inherited from his father, whose voice was so famous that he was called "the lawyer with the bronze voice."

At the age of twenty, Georges Torres was a completely

mature man intellectually and politically. Emotionally, he was as young and romantic as any twenty-year-old. I told him about my parents' conversion and the kind of religious upbringing I had had. I told him about my father, about his hopes and beliefs. I also told him about how I was known and accepted as a Catholic Jew in the convent school and now in the army as well. If anyone ever asked for further explanation I said that my parents had converted to Catholicism and that I was a Catholic Jew. Most people would say, "*Ah! Vraiment.*" Really? And generally that was that.

It was so normal to me that I couldn't understand anyone making a fuss about it. But when I remembered the year that our secret had been discovered and all the commotion it had aroused, I could see that it was not so simple for many people, although I had always known all kinds of Jews: religious, irreligious, assimilated, converted. They were all Jews of one kind of belief or another.

To Georges, too, this seemed uncomplicated and that drew us closer. He told me that evening that before he had arrived in England two years before to join General de Gaulle, he had been taken to Brazil by his father after the fall of France. In Brazil he had met the French writer Bernanos and had become friendly with him. Georges was about sixteen years old then and was already passionately interested in politics, religion, and philosophy. He discussed many things with Bernanos, who was a very religious Catholic, although a nonconformist one.

Georges said that since those discussions he had decided that he would become a Catholic some day, but that he would never convert during the war because of the sufferings of the Jews. His own mother was in Buchenwald with Georges' stepfather, and this was certainly not the time to acquire a new religion. But after the war, he said, he was going to become a Catholic. I didn't approve or disapprove. I listened. I felt that it was not my place to give him any advice. I didn't want to influence him in any way.

From that first evening, I felt a great friendship for Georges. I liked him. I liked him and felt good with him, at ease, accepted. Our thoughts and our hopes were similar. We had the same reactions, the same tastes; we laughed a lot together, we had fun together. After that evening we saw each other two or three times a week for the next five months. We never flirted. We never spoke of love or of marriage.

We walked hand in hand in the blackout, so as not to lose each other under the beams of powerful searchlights sweeping the sky like immense windshield wipers. Our kind of relationship was unheard of in London during the war. Men and women simply did not get together on a platonic basis for any long period of time unless, maybe, they were quite old. You might be friends, but only for a few weeks. Then, if it lasted, you became lovers or you married. Certainly in any case you flirted. Georges and I didn't decide to have a platonic relationship. It just was like that. It was the way we were happy together. With Georges I was my real self, the girl I had been in Héas and in school. Little by little, he told me about his own childhood, about his parents.

His mother and father had been divorced when he was four or five years old and he had gone to live with his mother on rue du Colonel Renard. That name rang a bell—rue du Colonel Renard? I knew that street. I had been there as a child. That was the street where Lucilla had lived before her family moved to Avenue Marceau. At what number on that street had Georges lived? It came out that when we were both ten or eleven years old, Georges had lived exactly opposite Lucilla's house and when I had visited Lucilla there, I must certainly have met him many times in the street. This discovery amused us a lot.

Both Georges's parents had remarried. His father was a famous lawyer—Torres, not Thorez, as I had first understood—but he was also a politician. He had been a deputy and Georges had known French politicians all his life. All conversation at meals had revolved around politics, and Georges wanted to go into politics too after the war.

Georges loved his mother and spoke of her a great deal. He called her "Janot" (a nickname, her real name was Jeanne), instead of "Mother."

After marrying a second time, she had fallen in love again. A year or so before the war, she had fallen in love with the French Premier, Léon Blum, a distant cousin of hers. When Léon Blum was arrested by the Vichy government in 1940, Janot had left her second husband to stay near Blum and visit him every day in jail. While Georges had been taken out of France to stay for a while with his father in Brazil, Georges' mother had remained in Riom near Léon Blum's jail. Her second husband died—he committed suicide in New York— and when Léon Blum was delivered to the Germans and sent to Buchenwald, Janot had begged Laval, then Premier, who had once been a friend of Torres, to allow her to join Léon Blum in Buchenwald. Laval had agreed to help her to be sent to Buchenwald and the Germans had agreed. All Georges knew was that his mother had been sent to the concentration camp and that she had officially married Léon Blum there. It was the only marriage ever performed in a concentration camp between two Jews.

I could understand why Georges loved and admired such a woman.

Now Georges' father was in New York, where he was the editor-in-chief of a Franco-American newspaper. Georges' stepmother Suzanne was also in the Free French Forces, a captain in the Ambulance Corps with the army of General Leclerc in Algeria.

On Christmas Eve of 1943 my parents had a small party in their room at the boarding house. Janek was there, Georges was there, Meyer Levin was there. I cannot remember any parties given by my parents at home, in Paris, during my whole childhood and adolescence. We had guests all the time, but people just dropped in. We had no telephone, but our friends knew that my parents were generally at home around five o'clock, and almost every day someone came; stayed for tea; stayed for dinner. My mother didn't prepare any special food. Whoever was there ate what we were eating.

On the rare occasions when my mother cooked a meal herself, it was almost inedible—she was a totally helpless cook. That Christmas Eve in London is the only occasion I can remember when people were officially invited to a "party" and I have no memory of what my mother served them. I can see Meyer Levin talking to my father all evening. They had known each other for almost twenty years and Meyer was one of the very few friends who had been told of my father's conversion from the beginning. Meyer had been very nice to me, taking me out to the best London restaurants, telling me about his work and his life. He had a son who was four or five and lived in the United States with his mother. Meyer was considering divorcing his wife, he told me, but he loved his son and was very lonesome for him.

That night Meyer talked mostly to my father—about art, I think, and perhaps about Hasidism, as well. Those were their usual subjects. Meyer admired my father's sculptures very much and my father was working well and talked to Meyer about a large stone he was working on. As for Hasidism, my father had been, years before, the first person to awaken Meyer's interest in the subject. He knew hundreds of Hasidic stories and was a great admirer of that sect. He loved what he called the Hasidic joy of God and I remembered how, when I was a child, he would often dance Hasidic dances, accompanying himself with the songs he had heard in his own childhood in Zgierz.

Janek sat quietly, as always, looking around with his big dark eyes—a small, plump boy in Polish uniform, his round face so serious, looking at me sadly. And Georges whispered to me that evening: "Your mother has the face of a Roman empress." Georges talked the most. He was always a great talker, and it was easy to imagine him as the political leader I thought he would certainly become. But when my mother, that night, asked him what his idea of a perfect life was, he said: "The life of a poor country school teacher."

It was a week before the New Year of 1944 and the second front had still not opened. For years, every spring we had hoped and hoped that the Allies would launch the second front. But then we stopped hoping. It seemed as if the war would last forever.

It was always around Christmastime that we all got particularly homesick. In the army we told one another, "Next spring we'll be in Paris, next spring we'll be in France." It had become our "next year in Jerusalem," but each Christmas we were still in London. It rained, the "pea soup" blanketed the whole city in fog, and our memories from the past would come surging in on us from all sides.

I missed Paris and my friends and *Mère* Marthe. Whenever I met General de Gaulle in a corridor of Carlton Gardens, I remembered Annie's face. Everything reminded me of my past. One day I had managed, as I often did, to be on the staircase around two thirty, as I knew that the General came back from lunch around that time. He walked up toward the landing, alone, and saw me there again, a girl in the uniform of his women's army, a girl whose name he didn't know but whose face he often saw at that hour, on that landing, so obviously waiting for him. I stood at attention, looking so eager that the General smiled at me. I had never seen him smile before. Maybe that day Churchill had been less unpleasant at lunch, maybe the General had received some good news. He looked at me and smiled. I went back to the office, my heart pounding—the General had smiled at me—the General had smiled at me! He had inspected our unit a few times, but never smiling. Once we had a parade under arms in Wellington Barracks, with units from the Navy and the RAF, with the "commandos" and units from the Allied Forces. After the review, we had marched along the streets to French marching songs, *Sambre et Meuse, La Marseillaise, La Lorraine.* We marched before an enormous crowd of enthusiastic Londoners. Children were shaking small tricolor streamers, windows were decked with French flags, the crowd was yelling, "*Vive la France,*" "*Vive le Général de Gaulle.*"

I had walked with tears in my eyes. Who wouldn't? We were all terribly moved and felt excited, proud, and patriotic. And I really loved London. I wrote:

I love London with a deep, a strong affection. I am attached to this heavy and dark city. We have suffered together during the terrible blitz. I only know this city in darkness. I have never seen lights in London. For me London is fighting and war. But it is also adventure and discovery. I know a blacked-out London. I know each puddle where one shouldn't walk in the darkness, every pole, every step. I know every little yellow lantern, every landmark telling me where to turn. I know each ruin, I have seen new ones every morning. I have seen the house just off the park fall down in the winter, and another, next to it, burn in the spring. I love London, with its red buses, its hurrying crowds, everyone in uniform saluting every other uniform. I know London, its squares and its parks, the Soho restaurants, the cinemas, the streets in the Strand and the streets

in the West End, around St. Paul's Cathedral—the forest of
charred beams, these stretches of ruins proclaiming London's
resistance.

Each morning I get off the army truck and walk toward
Headquarters in Carlton Gardens. The flag so blue, so white,
so red. On every street familiar faces appear. Major Kieff, who
walks in such a funny way because of his flat feet, Maurice
Schumann, who speaks every night on the B.B.C. in the name
of the Free French Forces, Maurice Dejean, head of the Committee of Foreign Affairs, small, round, and smiling—everyone
says hello as if they were in France: *"Bonjour! Ça va ce matin?
Toujours du vent dans ce sale pays."*

We were all lonesome, homesick. The French officers who
took us out were always complaining about the terrible English
food, the terrible English women. They dreamed, the way I
dreamed, counting hours, days, weeks, months, years. Those
were the years of our youth.

The years of my youth included also those months when
Georges and I walked hand in hand in the blackout, sat in
Soho restaurants, laughing so much and looking so happy that
at all the other tables people watched us and smiled.

Georges was great at imitations. He would improvise dis-
courses "in the manner of." His best was a "discourse on the
death of the Pope" as delivered by Bossuet or Victor Hugo or
Lenin or Sacha Guitry or Léon Blum. He would launch into
these improvisations at once when asked.

We played games. We would walk in the streets for hours,
pick someone passing by and invent for him a life, a personality,
each of us adding more details. Whenever Georges passed in
front of a fancy hotel where a doorman stood in resplendent
regalia, gold buttons and stripes and visored hat, Georges would

stand at attention and salute smartly as if he had seen a general. We were still so childish in some ways that this joke amused us no end. Then Georges adopted a lost puppy, a product of mixed breed, whom we named "Médor" because it was the most banal French name for dogs. Médor went everywhere with us.

Georges had a room in a boarding house in Hampstead and worked during the day at some army job. When he heard that the famous French First Division of General Leclerc was going to arrive from Africa and would have room for only common soldiers to join it, he decided to give up his rank of first lieutenant and become a common soldier instead in order to be eligible to join that armored division. His stepmother Suzanne, who belonged to that division, was coming with them.

I had been transferred away from London to a camp at Camberly for my officer's training. I was learning to shoot a rifle and a machine gun, to command drills, to jump high walls, to find my way with only a compass, to march all night. I also had theoretical courses about my unit's work in case of an invasion of France. It was interesting and I had a wonderful time, the best I ever had in the army.

In the spring the English countryside was beautiful. Our camp was set in the middle of woods. There were a few thousand men there and about fifty women. Most of the men and women were interesting people and the atmosphere was stimulating. Each weekend I took the train back to London and spent evenings with Georges, or sometimes with Meyer, and of course I saw my parents, Janek, and the girls from the barracks. Micheline had recently married a French officer, Odile was raising her baby and was more determined than ever to find a suitable husband to be the baby's father. Chantal was still with the same man. Sophie was in love, I had been told, with an older officer whose brother was in Camberly too.

On May fourth or fifth, 1944, I was sitting on the floor of

Georges' room in Hampstead among piles of his army shirts and underwear, marking each piece of clothing with his name in indelible ink. The army had requested it and Georges had seemed so nonplussed at the idea of doing it that I had offered to help him. Médor was jumping around, pulling at socks and ties, barking joyfully, wagging his ridiculously long black tail. It was late and getting dark in the room. Georges didn't put on the lights. He just sat near me and watched me work, quite silent, a rare thing with him. There had been rumors that his unit might be sent to Italy and I felt very sad at the idea that he might leave. I had gotten so used to him, to his low, deep voice, to his great laugh, to our long walks in the blackout and our jokes and talks. I had never had a brother and he had never had a sister; our relationship must have been, I think, what we had both missed in our lives. It was the purity of this relationship which, from the first day, had been so precious to me, because there was so little purity around us in London. There was courage and excitement and danger and reality, but no in-nocence. For five months Georges and I, without discussing it, but with a common desire, it seemed, had established between us something totally unusual in wartime London—an abso-lutely pure friendship. That is why I had been astonished at a dream I had had a few nights before. In the dream Georges was kissing me—he was holding me very tightly against him and kissing me with such force that I awoke and lay wondering what it had meant. Was I in love with him? I chased the thought away. Of course not. What we felt for each other was something else. It wasn't physical love; we had something else, something very rare and beautiful, but not love.

I was thinking about that dream, which of course I hadn't told Georges, sitting there in near darkness. I could no longer see what I was writing and looked up at Georges, questioning his silence. Médor had fallen asleep on a pile of shirts, and through the open window I saw a corner of blue-gray sky turning navy blue. Suddenly Georges spoke. He said, "Tereska, let's get married." When he said it, I knew immediately. There was not a second's hesitation. I knew he was not my brother, I was not his sister. I said, "Let's," and still we didn't move toward each other. We had both kissed others before, but this was so different. We approached each other slowly. It had taken us five months, and even now that we knew we were going to get married, we didn't want to change the incredibly precious gentleness we had established in a time of frenzy. When he did come nearer and took me in his arms, it was exactly as it had been in that dream a few nights ago—the same kiss. And I was back in that dream.

I wrote my new name on a piece of paper: "Tereska Torres." I still have that piece of paper. And Georges wrote an official request to his commanding officer asking to be allowed to marry me.

My parents, when I told them the news, were delighted. They liked Georges very much. It was characteristic of my father that he didn't ask anything about our plans for a religious ceremony, or in what religion we would raise our children. He knew that Georges was Jewish, and he never gave the slightest hint that he would have liked me to marry a Catholic.

As for Georges and me, at first we only tried to get rid of all the army red tape connected with weddings. We hoped that if we got all the papers ready we could get married that same month. In the meantime, I still had to pass my officer's exam. I came back to London and we went out together every night.

Once we were walking in Hampstead when Georges saw the gate of a large estate standing open. He said, "Let's go in and look." I was rather scared of walking into private property, but

Georges was never bothered about such things. We went in. It was almost evening. We saw a very large garden behind a small mansion. There were trees and grass and surprisingly fresh country air. The garden was more like some abandoned field in Normandy than a London estate. All was silent. The house looked closed and there was no one around. Georges and I sat on a stone bench, and for a while we didn't speak. It was so beautiful. It was like the park found by the Grand Meaulnes in Alain Fournier's novel *The Wanderer,* which we both loved so much.

It was a magical place, a place in a fairy tale. Georges said that it reminded him of the large country estate his mother owned near Paris. It was called *Le clos des Metz* and Georges had spent the last years before the war there. It had three houses on the grounds and a house reserved for the children: Georges, his brother Jean, and his stepbrother. Their house was called *La maison des enfants.* When Georges spoke, I could feel his love for the place and how homesick he was for *Le clos des Metz.* Then Georges said, "I want you to be very, very happy." He told me about his father's wives and numerous mistresses and how unhappy they had always been, how many lies and intrigues he had always seen around him because of these unions. Then he said: "In our marriage, there will never be anything sordid." And I felt we were two children lost in the war, lost in the world. Nothing belonged to us, only the army clothes on our backs. We had no house, only barracks. Our country was closed to us. Georges had no family, no one but me, in London, and I had only my parents and Georges. It felt good to be without ties, without possessions, rootless, unburdened. I wished we could sit forever on that bench in that unknown garden, with no problems and no allegiances except to each other.

When we finally left, we passed a Catholic church and Georges said, "Let's go in and find out about being married."

We went in and found a young priest. Georges said with his strong French accent, "Father, we want to know if it is possible to get married."

The priest started laughing and answered, "I have never heard that the church forbids marriage." Then he asked us questions and told us to go to my parents' neighborhood church and to the army chaplain. The next day we saw the chaplain and Georges explained that only I was Catholic. The chaplain said that was no problem if Georges would agree to have our future children raised in the Catholic religion, and Georges agreed. So there was nothing more to do but to fix a date and make the arrangements.

I didn't want a big wedding. I didn't want a bridal gown or a reception. I really didn't care to invite anyone, not even my parents. Georges' parents couldn't be there, so it seemed fairer not to have mine either. The whole hullabaloo of weddings didn't appeal to me. But after we discussed it, Georges decided that it would be too sad for my parents not to come to their only child's wedding, so we decided to invite them. Once they were invited, we really had to invite my cousins Norek and Lucia and their daughter. Then I had to ask my army friends and Georges knew a lot of people in London, mostly friends of his father and stepfather, so he had to ask them too. By the end of the day we had enough names to fill the whole church.

The date was fixed for May twenty-fourth, first at the English registrar's office, then at a church in Kensington. All was going well. We had obtained and filled out piles of documents: birth certificates, army licenses, all requiring photos. Then on May twenty-third the English authorities suddenly discovered that Georges was not yet twenty-one and had to have his father's consent. Georges's father didn't even know of my existence and was in New York. During the war it took several days to send a cable to the United States and receive an answer. I thought we would have to postpone the wedding, but once Georges had decided something, he never gave up easily. As we came out of the registrar's office Georges said, "It's very simple. Only Churchill can send a cable to New York quickly, so let's go and see him." I looked at him in disbelief, but he was perfectly serious. I said. "How can we go to see Churchill?" And he replied, "By taxi." He hailed one and we got in. Georges said to the driver, "Ten Downing Street."

When we got there Georges went to the door and rang the bell. The door opened and he told the guard, "I am President Léon Blum's stepson and we are getting married tomorrow, but we have an urgent problem and I would be very grateful if we could speak to the Prime Minister." The guard didn't look particularly surprised. He asked us to come in and told us to sit down. After a few minutes a secretary came and asked us to wait in the living room. He took Georges's name, asked a few questions, and left.

Only a short time later the door opened and Mrs. Churchill came into the room. All I could think was that she looked exactly like her photos. She was very kind and explained that her husband was not in London that day and asked what she could do to help. Then she told us not to worry, that someone would get in touch with the registrar's office so that we could be married the next day as planned, and that she would have a cable sent to New York anyway. We thanked her and left.

The next day I put on a fresh white army shirt and a new officer's uniform (I was a second lieutenant now, while Georges was back to private), and at eleven o'clock I went with my parents to the registrar's office where Georges was to meet us; we would go from there to the church. The guests were already at the church. When we arrived we just walked in, Georges and I, in our army uniforms, and went up the aisle to the sacristy to wait there for the chaplain.

In the sacristy, as we were signing some more papers, Georges had been talking to me, saying "*vous*." We still addressed each other that way, having used the "*vous*" form all those five months. One of our witnesses, a friend of Georges's mother, who was in the Free French Forces, started laughing at us, and had said, "My God, you'll be married in a few minutes, you can start saying '*tu*' to each other." I didn't feel as if I were really getting married, maybe because I was dressed as I was every day. And I didn't care who the guests were, and we were not going to have any reception. In a way I had felt married to Georges since the moment he had said, "Let's get married." What was going on was just not very important, rather a nuisance.

Finally the chaplain arrived, late, as he had gone by mistake to another church. We walked to the prie-dieu and knelt while the priest married us. After that there was a line of people whose hands we had to shake. Many guests had come. Meyer Levin was there, and Janek and all our own friends, but some people had refused to come, mostly people I didn't know from the Jewish-English Establishment, important Socialists with whom Georges had been in contact because of Léon Blum, who objected to his getting married in church. Georges said he couldn't care less. He was the most sure-of-himself person I had ever met.

After the congratulations and handshaking and kissing, an official-looking car drove up to the church. One of our witnesses was a minister in General de Gaulle's Free French Government. He was Micheline's boss and had always been very friendly to us. He had offered his car to take us to the place where we were going to spend the three days the army had generously granted us for a honeymoon. The place was near Oxford and belonged to Admiral Muselier, whom Georges knew. Admiral Muselier had had a falling out with General de Gaulle and lived on an estate near Oxford in a sort of exile. He had told Georges that we could have a little house on the estate to ourselves.

My parents didn't cry or act up the way parents sometimes do at a daughter's wedding. I had never felt that they gave much thought to my marrying or not marrying, maybe because I was still young and there was no hurry. But mostly I think that their minds didn't work that way. They certainly wanted my happiness, above all, but they knew that I could be happy in many ways which they never tried to influence. Since I had fallen in love with Georges they were very pleased, but if I had not gotten married that day, they would have been just as pleased—so long as I was happy. The ones who were really beaming were my cousins Norek and Lucia, who felt that I had "honored the family" with a very distinguished choice. Their little daughter, Ryśia, a teenager now, was in tears.

So we gave our last kisses, took Médor's leash—he was coming along on our honeymoon—and got into the chauffeured black limousine. Our small suitcase had already been placed in the trunk. As the car left, we sighed in relief and started at last to laugh again.

We got to the estate in the late afternoon. The admiral and his mistress, to whom the estate belonged, were waiting for us with champagne and a festive dinner table, all set up with lighted candelabra and flowers.

Muselier impressed me. He had an air like Napoléon's at St. Helena, I remember thinking. He was writing his memoirs and looked quite sorrowful and melancholy, but the arrival of a pair of young newlyweds cheered him up considerably. Dinner was in the main house and it lasted a long time. We had to eat many courses and listen to the admiral's tales of plots and woes, trying to keep interested expressions on our faces. Finally it ended and the admiral's mistress showed us the way to our house, which she told us was called "The Little Red Farm."

It was dark by this time; the air smelled of grass. We walked, with Médor running ahead, along the narrow path leading to "our house." It was a small, one-story, red-roofed house. When we went in, we stood in silence, and I was ready to cry. The rooms had been buried in white lilacs. There were vases and vases of them everywhere, and old-fashioned paraffin lamps were lit on tables and *guéridons*.

It was so beautiful. It was as if the adult world, which had led our generation into war, was trying to make amends by turning our honeymoon into a fairy tale. We got out of our uniforms, put on pajamas, and decided to go out and walk in the wonderful-smelling fields, in the grass, under the trees. We were so happy. We felt that we had all the time in the world.

We went out. It was a warm night, but the grass was wet so Georges hoisted me onto his back. With me perched on his back, barefooted and in pajamas, and Médor barking and jumping around us, Georges ran around under the starry sky. I laughed, my mouth against his kinky hair, and he ran until he was out of breath. Only then did we go back to our house full of flowers and soft lamplight.

When we got back to London on May twenty-eighth, 1944, I went straight to my new job. I was now a liaison officer and was to work with the American OWI. The first person I ran into at the American Information Services was Meyer Levin, who was also working there as a war correspondent.

I had moved into Georges's room at his boarding house in Hampstead and there, too, when we came back from our honeymoon, the landlady had decorated our room with white flowers and had hung a crown of mistletoe above the door.

A week after we got back, I arrived at my office early one morning. My boss rushed in, his face very red. He was holding

a paper and he was yelling, "They've landed! The second front
—it has started!" I can't explain how we all felt. We had been
waiting four years for that moment. People cried and screamed
and kissed each other.

I called Georges. He said he would probably be leaving to
join the Leclerc Division at any moment. He did leave, that day
or the next, but only for an army camp near York. We all read
the newspapers feverishly. We were glued to the radio. Soon we
could see the newsreels of the first Allied troops rolling along
the French roads and the people, hysterical with joy, throwing
flowers at the tanks. I didn't see Georges for about two weeks.
He wrote almost every day from Yorkshire, and I wrote back.
He was with his unit, the First Regiment of the Tchad. His stepmother Suzanne, whom he hadn't seen in several years, was a
captain, an ambulance driver, in that regiment, and was stationed in the same village. She had only known of Georges's
marriage through the cable sent to New York. Henri Torres,
Georges's father, had written to her telling her that he was worried. Who on earth was this Tereska Georges had married?

During those two weeks my parents heard that Janek had
decamped with a Polish regiment for Normandy. Then very
soon the news came that he had been killed. He had gone to the
rescue of a wounded soldier, and while dragging him back to
his unit had fallen under sixteen shots. A few weeks later my
parents received a letter. It had been addressed to them with
Janek's instruction that it be delivered only if he were killed.
It said that Janek loved me and had wanted to marry me, but
that he had never said anything because he felt he had nothing
to offer me, "no home, no security, no future." This news sad-
dened me dreadfully.

About twelve years later I was at a party in New York. A
small, plump lady with a Polish accent was sitting near me.
She heard me called by name and asked me if I had ever lived in

London. I said yes, during the war, that I had been in the Free French Forces there. The lady got up, very pale, and asked me to follow her to another room. She started crying when we were alone and told me she was Janek's mother. Janek had written home during the war, to South Africa where his parents were then, and apparently all his letters had mentioned a Tereska with whom he was in love. It was very sad. I had never been in love with Janek, although I had respected and liked him, but to this poor mother I was the sweetheart of her lost child, and the idea was a kind of consolation. The idea that her son had loved before he was killed, that life hadn't totally passed him by, that he had had some happiness, comforted her. I tried to explain how much I had liked Janek, how wonderfully gifted he had been, but I could see that she didn't want to hear about that. I had not been in love with her boy, but she treated me like a daughter-in-law. I saw her after that a few times. She was very lonely, a widow, a very sad woman. Then we left the United States and I never saw her again.

During the weeks following D-Day, many boys I knew were killed. Bernanos' son, Michel, a close friend of Georges, was killed, as was the son of a well-known French movie director. I had seen him just before he left for the front in Normandy, and I had told him how I envied him. He had answered, his face lighting up with happiness, "I am so happy, I envy myself!"

Georges was still in Yorkshire. The Allies were in no hurry to send the French Armored Division to France, preferring to be the sole liberators, and I could understand why General de Gaulle was furious. Two weeks after D-Day, I received permission to spend a few days with Georges in Yorkshire. I took a train and traveled to a small village, Cottingham. Georges had given me complicated instructions about how to get there and had told me to ask for the Ambulance Drivers' housing unit, where my stepmother-in-law Suzanne would be waiting for me and would drive me to see him.

I arrived a few hours late, as I had had to change trains several times. When I got to the house where the ambulance drivers' were billeted it was after dinner. A young woman in uniform told me that Suzanne was not there and wouldn't be back until late that night. When I explained who I was, all the women gathered around me. They were extremely nice. I could see that they all loved Suzanne, who was their captain, and they had met Georges when he had come to see Suzanne. We sat and talked, but they couldn't take me to Georges. I had to wait for Suzanne. Finally, when it was quite late, they opened up a folding cot for me in an empty room, and I went to sleep. That night they played a trick on their captain.

Suzanne had told them many times how worried she was about the unknown "Tereska" who had married her young stepson. Georges had offered absolutely no explanation. To all her questions he had answered, "You'll see her when she comes here." So Suzanne told "her girls" that with such a name I was most probably some Russian adventuress, certainly an older woman, who had gotten Georges to marry her, realizing what a catch he was.

When I arrived at Cottingham and the girls saw me, they remembered this and decided to play a joke on Suzanne. When she came back late that night, her three or four best friends among the drivers were still sitting in the lounge. They looked very sadly at Suzanne, shook their heads, and told her that Georges's wife had arrived. "How is she? What sort of woman?" Suzanne asked with trepidation. "Terrible," said Suzanne's friends. "My poor Suzanne, she is a real adventuress, a woman at least forty years old, a red-head, heavily made-up—vamp type." Suzanne sat down and kept repeating, "That bad? My goodness. What can we do? Poor Henri, how will I ever break such news to him? I didn't think it would be that bad. Georges is young, but I never thought he would let himself be led into such a trap—not as bad as that."

Suzanne didn't sleep all night. In the morning she braced herself, put on her uniform, and went to the room where I was sleeping. I heard a knock at the door, said, "Come in," and sat up in bed. I was wearing my army pajamas and my short hair was falling all over my face. I saw a blond woman who stood in the doorway a second, then ran toward me and hugged me against her, laughing and repeating, "My little girl! Oh! How happy I am. Oh, it's too funny, Tereska. I can't tell you how relieved I am. But tell me—how old are you, fifteen?" I didn't know what was the matter with her, but I liked her at first glance and since then she has been a woman I have loved and admired deeply. Suzanne explained the joke her friends had played, and I laughed too. But I wasn't feeling too well and was pale and nauseated. My period was a week late and when I told Suzanne, she said she hoped I wasn't pregnant. I said that, on the contrary, Georges and I wanted a child right away, and that I hoped it might be that, but it was much too early to know. Suzanne gave me breakfast and then we drove in her ambulance to Georges's camp.

When we arrived there and I saw Georges, I felt sick again and almost threw up. So instead of kissing him, I had to lie down, and Suzanne looked at Georges accusingly and told him that he was crazy to start a child in such times. But Georges was overjoyed, as I had known he would be. We still didn't know for sure, but we hoped very much. I spent about five days in Cottingham, sleeping in the ambulance drivers' quarters with Georges. It was all very illegal, I think. Georges went back to camp at dawn every morning and sneaked into his tent. Then late in the afternoon he came back to Cottingham and we spent the evenings together. The ambulance drivers were delighted and everyone fed us extra rations and brought us small gifts. On Georges's day off Suzanne took us to a famous restaurant in Hull—The White Horse. When Georges was away at camp, she told me long stories about when Georges was a child and had been the terror of his family. She spoke of Georges's father, to whom she was still married but whom she was thinking of divorcing, and of Georges's mother Janot, who was in Buchenwald. Even then no one really knew what was going on in the camps in Germany. We were sure that they must be terrible places, but how terrible we had no idea. My parents always talked about my uncles, aunts, cousins—all our large Polish family—and wondered where they were, what had happened to them; worrying about their fate during the war. But we couldn't ever have guessed. It was impossible to conceive that after the war, of all that large family in Poland, there would remain only half a dozen survivors. Buchenwald was just the name of a camp to which Georges had tried many times to send letters and packages through the Red Cross, but from which he had never received any news.

After five days I had to go back to London, and then I went to see the army doctor, who examined me and had tests made at a laboratory. A few days later he confirmed the news. I was pregnant. The baby would be born, he said, at the end of February. Now I was allowed a one-week maternity leave, so I took the train again and went back to Yorkshire, but to another village, to a place nearer where Georges's unit had been moved. This time Georges received an official permit to spend the nights with me all that week, and he rented a room for us in a farmer's cottage.

It was July. I remember small thatched-roofed houses and gardens overflowing with zinnias and petunias, snapdragons and sweet peas. Everywhere the trees and grass were of that special English green, greener than any other green, almost translucent. There was a fairyland quality to that countryside—all those flowers, colors, bees, sun, cottages, peaceful fields. It seemed impossible to believe that at that very time the greatest battles of the war were being fought in Normandy, not very far away, and that similar villages there were burning, that bombs were exploding, killing small children, destroying all life, and that any day Georges, his division, Suzanne and her girls would all be there.

All day I walked alone around the countryside, and every evening Georges came back from camp. We had dinner with the farmers and then went out and walked and talked. We talked of the baby. We chose names—Catherine if it were a girl and Dominique if it were a boy. But Georges was certain it would be a boy and he talked of Dominique as of an absolute reality. We never gave a thought to any material considerations. What would we do with a baby in the midst of a war? Where would we live? How would I raise a baby while I was in the army? Even if the war ended by the time Dominique was born, where would we be then? We had no house, no profession, Georges was not twenty-one years old yet. He hadn't finished his studies. But those problems simply didn't exist for us.

The way we saw things, I would remain in the army until Dominique arrived and then we would just keep him with us in some barracks and the army would provide for the three of us, as it had provided everything we had needed for years now.

At night we came back to the cottage. The farmers were asleep upstairs. There was no bathroom, so we washed in the dark kitchen, where a big log fire was always burning. It was very quiet. The fire gave the only light and we sat next to it, and talked some more, and dreamed. Georges put his head on my lap and said, "My child is here," and looked so happy, so at peace.

One night there was a big army dance held under two huge

tents. Suzanne drove us there, but we didn't dance. Georges didn't know how, and he asked me not to dance with anyone else. So we went outside and sat on a fallen tree trunk in a field, listening to the music and the voices. In the darkness Georges's bronze voice sounded even deeper. He put his arm around me and said: "Every day I love my little wife more."

When the last day arrived, Suzanne arranged for a jeep to pick me up and drive me to the station. Georges could only take me as far as the jeep, then he had to return at once to camp. He put my bag in the jeep and I climbed in next to the driver. He stood very erect near the jeep and I looked at him, so tall and serious, in his khaki uniform. The jeep moved forward and I thought very clearly: "This is the last time I shall see him."

A few days later General Leclerc's First Armored Division disembarked in Normandy and started on the road to Paris. I continued working as a liaison officer, but it wasn't easy because I was constantly nauseated. I moved back with my parents and rented a room in their boarding house. It was better than living alone in Hampstead. I didn't have to sleep in our barracks any longer because I was an officer and married.

Micheline was married too and her husband was away with the army. Odile had married an Englishman who had adopted her child. Then I heard that Sophie was pregnant and that the father of her baby was in Normandy with the Armored Division. I saw Sophie once when I went to the barracks on payday. She seemed happy, although she wasn't married because of some complication. Maybe the father of her child was already married, I didn't know. But Sophie didn't talk about it and one couldn't see that she was pregnant, it was in such a very early stage.

I was in my office at the OWI one day later on, when Micheline called me. She sounded very agitated. She said, "Tereska, did you hear what has happened?" I said, "No, what happened?" And Micheline said, "Sophie Kropotkin killed herself." I said, "What? Sophie? I can't believe it." Micheline told me that the father of Sophie's baby had been killed in Normandy and when Sophie heard the news, she had somehow gotten some sleeping pills from the barracks infirmary and had committed suicide. The funeral was going to be the next day.

Sophie—I remembered her that first day in Waterloo station: the shy little girl who had passed herself off as almost eighteen so she would be accepted. Sophie had never really adjusted to army life—Sophie with her sad eyes, her small pale face with the childlike expression, her passionate love for Véra and her tales to me about it—Sophie, who was so easily hurt, so vulnerable. I had seen her very little in the last two years and I hadn't known how she had met the man she fell in love with. What had happened to her? All I knew was that she was dead.

I remembered something else that had happened to Sophie. We had had a gas-mask drill. It was during the first year, in the winter of 1941, at the time when Sophie was so much in love with Véra and so unhappy because of it. We were all sitting on benches in a room in our old barracks, which later had been bombed. We had our gas masks on and an officer was explaining how to use them. We looked so strange, so awful: a bunch of young girls nodding to one another like outer-space monsters with dreadful black rubber snouts. Sophie was sitting near me and I noticed that she seemed crushed. I could see it even without seeing her face. She didn't move, her shoulders were hunched and her hands were clenched in a tight knot in her lap. I looked around and I saw Véra sitting not far away, her arm around Micheline's shoulders, her mask nosing Micheline's mask in a comical kiss. They were obviously having a great time together. Suddenly Sophie slipped down from the bench and lay stretched out on the floor. In a second everyone was crushing around her, the officer shouting, "Move away, move away." I tried to undo the clasps on the mask. I was afraid she might suffocate in it. Véra had run toward Sophie and put her arm under Sophie's head. Finally we got the mask off and Sophie opened her eyes. She saw Véra bent down over her and smiled, a childish, wonderful smile. We carried her to the dormitory and put her on her bed. After a while everyone left, but Chartier allowed me to stay with Sophie and make sure she was feeling better.

Sophie closed her eyes and sighed, and in a very small voice said, "Listen, Tereska, I must tell you the truth. I didn't really faint. I only made believe, because, because. . . ." She turned her face against the wall so I couldn't look at her and said, in a whisper, "It was because of Véra. I wanted her to pay attention to me. I know it is silly, childish, I know, but you saw her, Tereska, she came back to me when she thought I had fainted, and she was worried about me. You saw that, didn't you?" But when Sophie had taken the dose of pills, she wasn't making believe any more. This time it was no longer a game, and now there was no more Sophie.

I received a few letters and cards from Georges, but not many. Mail got lost or was delayed. He didn't receive all my letters either. Our women's army was preparing to leave England altogether. All the offices at headquarters were packing documents. In our barracks, preparations had started for the move out. The Allies were advancing on the roads toward Paris. It was the end of July. It was early August, it was August twenty-first. They were near Paris. Paris was fighting the Germans. It was August twenty-fourth, August twenty-fifth. Paris was liberated. Georges's Armored Division under General Leclerc had liberated Paris, together with the F.F.I. and the resistance movements.

I sat for hours in dark cinemas, watching newsreels of the uprising in Paris and the victory, looking desperately at all those unshaven, dirty, grinning French soldiers, trying to find Georges's face among them atop a tank in a street in Paris. There had been no letters from him for weeks now, but suddenly letters started arriving from *Mère* Marthe, from Annie and Monique. They had seen Georges. He had gone to every address I had given him in Paris. He had gone to my school; he had been shown my desk; he had told *Mère* Marthe that we were going to have a baby. The news poured in. Annie had a baby, a son, who had been born in France on the same day that I had married Georges in London.

Then Meyer Levin wrote from Paris. He said to tell my parents that he had been to our house and ". . . everything is as they left it. No one has lived in the place since you left. The concierge was very nice about the whole thing. She said the Germans never came around. So you can move right back in when you get to Paris." He added: "You know I keep on being in love with you. Perhaps that is why I've never been more moved by Paris." I knew.

Mère Marthe wrote: "My Tereska darling!

"What a surprise for us, last Monday, when one of our dear French soldiers appeared, saying he was 'Tereska's husband.'"

A very long letter followed—the first long letter since 1940 —with so much news. It was a wonderful feeling to be able to write freely. It was the extraordinary feeling of being together, in one world again.

Now the *Division Leclerc* was on its way toward Germany. I received my military papers for transfer to France. No one in the women's army knew that I was pregnant and I had no intention of telling them. They might have decided not to take me along. I was lucky; the baby didn't show at all.

I was still working in the same office and writing a special diary for our baby at night. I called it "A Message for Dominique." It was a notebook in which I told the baby about his great-grandparents in Poland and the great-grandparents who were now in Canada, about my father's childhood and my mother's, and how I had met Georges, and all my hopes for the future, for a world when war would never, never exist again, when men would be *real* brothers, whatever their color, race, or religion.

One day I met an officer who told me, "This is not a time to bring children into the world." I laughed at him. I wasn't afraid to have children now. If times were troubled, my children would only grow up stronger, like iron that has passed through fire. It was mid-October. I was still writing the same novel. Georges had read the first part and liked it very much.

I thought sometimes of that sentence I had written in my diary when I was ten or eleven, that prayer to God in which I had asked Him to let me marry one day a Catholic Jew, so my children would be Jews of Catholic religion and I would become the mother of a new tribe of Jews. Now I was carrying the first such child. I had married a Jew who wanted one day to become a Catholic too, and it all seemed to be an answer to that wish. I had done nothing to make it come true. I hadn't tried to convert Georges. He had had the idea before he met me. I had not even encouraged him in that direction. I had never told him about that prayer in my diary. I had not even asked him to get married in church. It had come entirely from him, and now our baby would be a third generation Jewish-Catholic child.

I didn't feel that this was an important proselytizing achievement. It was not because of any missionary zeal that I wanted to continue in my father's path. I felt about it rather the way I did about intermarriages. I wanted more than ever that people mix together as completely as possible, whites and blacks, Christians,

Jews, Arabs, Chinese. I wanted bridges, more and more bridges between them, more and more ties. I had gone through one war and hated all wars, all divisions, barriers, prisons. For me, being Catholic and Jewish at the same time was like being black and white at the same time. The less arbitrary categorization, the more mixing, and maybe we could finally achieve brotherhood. I realized that I had been lucky because I had been raised not one thing, but so many things. I hoped that more and more children would have not one, but dozens of identities.

In my free time I went out with my parents to concerts and to art exhibits. There were several Polish painters and writers and poets in London. My father had also met a few English artists. Slowly a little group was gathering around him, as it had in the Paris days. I wanted Dominique, our baby, to be artistic, so I went conscientiously to all those concerts and art exhibits, thinking I was influencing the baby in my womb. I thought of the baby all the time and talked to him, but Dominique still didn't show at all under my army uniform.

Then one morning late in October the letter came. It was from Suzanne, Georges's stepmother.

My poor dear child:

I have waited and waited before writing to you because I could not find it in my heart to give you this worst possible blow. But I am afraid that in spite of all my efforts and the promises made me, you have been informed officially of the disappearance of our poor little Georges. I had not left him all these days since our departure from Paris. He ate all his meals with me, washed up in my place, then went on patrol. One evening the Commandant came to tell me that he and one of his comrades had not come back. It is impossible to go to the spot itself. I have questioned everyone, all those who were present, his comrades who adored him, his officers. Alas, nothing very hopeful. He was so brave. He was considered one of the heroes

of the regiment. He left on the patrol as leader, of course. I
cannot tell you anything more, my poor darling. My thoughts
are ever with you. Though I have no absolutely certain knowl-
edge yet, neither have I any hope to give you that we'll ever
see him again. I am telling you this frankly because I think
it would be monstrous for you to keep a great hope, only to have
it all collapse in the end.

The place where it happened has not yet been taken by our
army, so it is impossible to go there. I am nearby, less than
two kilometers from it. It is terrible not to be able to go there.
I live horrible days, but I am thinking only of you, then of my
poor Henri, of Georges' mother, of his poor grandmother. My
child, you must be brave for the sake of little Dominique
whom you carry. Think only of this baby. His life, his health,
will depend on your courage. For his sake you have to be
strong, not let yourself go. Eat, sleep . . . all the things that
seem impossible for one who suffers what you are suffering.
I wish I could be with you, cry with you, speak with you of
him. I have all his possessions, his wallet which he gave to one
of his comrades just before he left, to be handed to me in case
of accident. I have two snapshots of him and me taken a few
days before and which I will have developed.

My little one, I beg of you, don't let go. I love you so much.
We spoke of you all the time. He worshipped you. I cannot go
on. It is too terrible for me to think of you reading this. I live
among his comrades in continuous remembrance of him. Write
to me. I'll do everything to get the whole truth and will write
you without delay.

I embrace you with infinite tenderness, my poor little girl.

Suzanne

From the Diary:

November 11, 1944
I don't want to believe that he is dead. I won't until the last
second of hope. Tuesday morning. I got my orders from the

army. I am flying to Paris. There I shall try to see Suzanne and to get more news. I don't stop asking God for a miracle.

Paris, November 17, 1944

I am in Paris, which I have waited for four years to see again, and I don't see anything, I don't feel anything—I walk as though in a dream, deep in such despair that it seems to me I shall never again be able to feel any joy. I have been everywhere to learn something about Georges. This afternoon at the Ministry of War, they confirmed officially that Georges had been listed as missing on October 8th. I have asked that Suzanne be brought back from the front and it was promised me. I don't know anything, I don't understand anything. I can only repeat "God make a miracle," "God save Georges" ... "God make a miracle." ... I have been to my convent school where I wept and cried for hours. The mothers put me in a big bed, dressed me in a long white nun's nightdress, brought my dinner to bed, and this morning my breakfast. They were all extremely kind, as everybody has been—the Fumets, the Hillerets, the captain at the Ministry of War, the Millots, all those I have seen and who told me to continue to hope. . . .

❦ I lived in Paris in the hotel requisitioned for my unit. It was the Château Frontenac on rue Pierre Charron. I had a room of my own. Every night, night after night, I cried and cried.

In the daytime, I never showed anything. I still believed that Georges was only missing, that he was not dead. I had a plan. I had been waiting for Suzanne to come back to Paris from the front, and as she wasn't coming, and it was impossible for me to write to her or to communicate with her in any way, I decided that I would get myself to the front lines and see her and find out the truth. That was why I had gone to the War Ministry. No one was allowed inside without a pass, but I had entered enough army headquarters by now to know that in uniform I could enter without a pass, if I looked sure of myself.

That was how I had gotten in; I was even saluted by the sentinel at the door. Once inside I had no idea where to go. I saw corridor after corridor, stairs and more stairs. I think I took them all. I just kept on walking, looking for a door with a sign that would seem helpful. In that way I came upon a door with the name of a Captain Mayer and something about the *Division Leclerc*. I knocked and walked in. The captain was very nice, very helpful. When I explained why I was there and gave him my name and Georges's name, I found out that he had known Henri Torres very well before the war. He said he would help me get an Order of Mission to go to the front where Suzanne was and that I should wait at the Château Frontenac for his phone call.

I had another thing to do. Georges had told me that his grandmother lived in Paris—his mother's mother. I had her name but no address. As she was an elderly Jewish lady, with her daughter married to Léon Blum and in Buchenwald, Georges had had little hope of ever finding her alive. I had no idea if Georges had found her, as no letters at all from him had reached me in London since the *Division Leclerc*'s entry into Paris.

I got a phone book in a café and started looking at all the "Humbers" listed. There were a few. The first one was a Mme Charles Humber who lived on rue de Constantine, on the Esplanade des Invalides. I decided to try her first. I walked over to the rue de Constantine and took the elevator to the floor where the concierge had told me she lived. A young maid opened the door and I asked if I could speak to Mme Humber. I heard a voice saying, "Who is it, Madeleine?" and a small, delicately built, elderly white-haired woman appeared. Before I had time to say one word, the old lady ran toward me, hugged me against her, crying and repeating, "You are Tereska, you must be Tereska! Oh, my child, my child! I am your *bonne maman,*" which was Georges' name for her. I followed her into a large, beautiful living room. She sat next to me holding my hands and looking at me. She said, "You look exactly like the picture Georges showed me." I told her I was going to the front to meet Suzanne. *Bonne Maman* had had no news at all from Georges either and she didn't know that he was missing. Sitting there, holding hands and talking as if we had known each other all our lives, we convinced ourselves that Georges was certainly not dead. He had told me many times in London that if he were ever near enough to the German lines, he would do all he could to pass through and somehow get to Buchenwald to save his mother. It never occurred to us that it was an impossible plan. When I told *Bonne Maman* this, she at once believed as I did that this must have happened and that was why he was "missing."

Bonne Maman was in her seventies then and about the same size as I was. I am sure we could have worn each other's clothes. She had snow-white hair and wore a narrow black dress, dark-gray silk stockings, and very narrow hand-sewn shoes with high heels. She was the image of elegance. Around her neck was a black ribbon. Her face was soft and beautifully lined and her eyes were Dresden blue. She was very nearsighted, which gave her a charming puzzled expression. She wouldn't hear of my staying at the army hotel, so I moved my things to her apartment that same day. She had a folding cot which, she said, Georges had always used when as a young boy he came to sleep at his grandmother's; she had her maid open up that cot for me in her bedroom. *Bonne Maman's* apartment was extremely elegant. Everything in it was antique. There were rows and rows of leather-bound books, tall Chinese vases, thick Persian carpets, ancient engravings. It was the most beautiful apartment of that kind I had ever seen. That she had been left alone by the Germans and that they hadn't touched her during the entire war was a miracle. This fragile, aristocratic-looking elderly widow had lived all alone in Paris during the four years of occupation, while her daughter was in a concentration camp, her grandson was in London with De Gaulle, and another grandson, Georges's brother, was in Brazil. Most of her friends had been deported; others had fled. She had been left alone and she had survived, selling, little by little, her furs, jewels, and carpets.

That evening after dinner we talked for hours, late into the night. She described to me Georges's arrival at her apartment the day after Paris had been liberated. About two weeks before the liberation, *Bonne Maman* had moved out of the apartment where I had found her, because she was afraid the Germans would come and arrest her. She had somehow gotten into another house not far away, in a furnished apartment on the ground floor. But the concierge of her own apartment, whom *Bonne Maman* trusted, knew where she was hiding.

One afternoon during the days when Paris was liberated—August twenty-fourth or twenty-fifth—*Bonne Maman* was sitting in the living room of the ground-floor apartment when she heard a loud noise in the street outside her open windows. Suddenly a young soldier in the uniform of the Free French climbed onto the window sill and then jumped into the living room. A cheering crowd was following him so closely that it had been impossible for him to reach the entrance door. *Bonne Maman* looked at the soldier. He was wearing a beard and she didn't recognize him until she heard the famous Torres voice, "*Bonne Maman,* it's me, Georges!" She had last seen him when he was a fifteen-year-old boy; now he was a tall, strong, bearded man who lifted her off her feet and hugged and kissed her. He put *Bonne Maman* in the jeep that was waiting outside and drove her back to her own apartment, where they sat and talked and where Georges showed her the photo of his wife and listened to the story of how *Bonne Maman* had survived the war. Then he decided to show her the streets of liberated Paris, so he sat her in his jeep again and drove her through the boulevards and avenues and along the Champs Elysées. I could imagine little *Bonne Maman,* dressed all in black, with her snow-white hair, the black ribbon around her neck, sitting very upright and proud in a *Division Leclerc* jeep, while her grandson, in uniform, an arm around her shoulder, drove her through the delirious crowds who cheered and waved wherever they passed.

Later *Bonne Maman* told me her whole life story, and it had been a very agitated, eventful life; but that day with Georges certainly had been the most extraordinary. I stayed with *Bonne Maman* while I waited to hear from Captain Mayer. We encouraged each other to hope and believe that we would see Georges again.

I had a surprise at that time. One day *Bonne Maman* told me that nobody knew about it but that she had converted to Catholicism. She didn't want it known and she told me in secret. I was touched by her secret, so similar to mine—one an old lady's, one a little girl's. My baby then was going to be not third but fourth generation Jewish-Catholic.

I went to see Monique and Lucilla and Sonia, and Annie came especially to Paris from the small town where she lived to see me. Most of these meetings were sad. Beyond the fact that I was in a great state of distress, I could no longer find any contact with all these friends I had missed so for more than four years.

With Monique, the main problem was that she and her family had been supporters of Maréchal Pétain during the war. That created such a gulf between us that it never was bridged, although outwardly we remained quite friendly.

With Annie I felt that she had become "a married lady." I

was married too but I hadn't become a "lady." I thought of myself as inexperienced and young and free. Annie was mistress of a large provincial house. She had responsibilities, a son, a husband who was a notary—a maid, a very bourgeois life. It seemed horrible to me. She acted and talked like an older woman, not like a twenty-two-year-old girl. During the war she had helped the resistance as much as she could and her husband had been arrested by the Germans and almost shot. So politically we were close to each other, but still there was this awful feeling of having lost the girl with whom I had had those long talks at the *Cour des adieux*—big Annie, with her loud laughter and logical mind and her admiration for what she thought of as my Crazy Bohemian Life.

Sonia, when I met her again, was a widow, but she only found it out a few months later. Her husband had been deported. She was told that when the Russians were approaching to liberate the camp in Poland where he was a prisoner, he had run out toward the entrance of the camp toward the approaching armies of liberators, and had been shot at by a German sentinel. Sonia had a little girl about four years old who had been hidden in a convent since the day of her birth and was still there. Sonia's father and uncle and grandmother had been deported and had never come back. But Sonia's mother had suddenly reappeared. She was in the United States with a new husband. She had written to Sonia and Sonia was going to send her little girl to her mother. Later Sonia herself went to the United States, but she never raised her daughter. Just as Sonia's own mother had never raised her, Sonia's daughter was raised by her grandmother.

When I saw Lucilla I got a shock. Lucilla had changed entirely. The gay, carefree, mischievous Lucie had become a deeply neurasthenic girl. She was still young and beautiful, but her face was deadly pale and she hardly talked at all. Her sister told me that Lucilla stayed for days in her room, refusing to leave it, refusing to eat. She had spent the war years in Paris. Only when I came to see her would her face light up a little. I had no knowledge of psychiatry or of mental diseases, and I thought it was just a passing depression brought on by the war and that she would get over it. She didn't. Four years later, when Lucilla was still in the same state, her family finally sent her to a psychoanalyst who didn't help her at all. For a short while she was interned in a mental home. Then she seemed to improve and they let her out. She went home to the apartment on the Avenue Marceau and threw herself from a window on the sixth floor.

The last time I saw her, she was lying in a coffin covered with white flowers. She didn't look dead at all. She looked eleven years old again—her small face had that pixie look and there was a sort of mischievous smile around her lips.

And *Mère* Marthe. I went to see her several times, but with her too the contact was gone. I tried to tell her about my life in the army but it was all incomprehensible to her. All the freedom, the license we had, the bars, the parties, girls living like soldiers or young bachelors. She tried to hide her shock, to be open-minded and modern, but, poor nun, she couldn't say the words I needed at that time. She only knew how to talk to protected, virginal girls. I still loved her very much. She was my mother, warm and full of affection, but we couldn't talk, as we had before, about everything.

After the war I saw her very little. One day about three years later I was passing through the flower market in Paris when I remembered that Monique had told me *Mère* Marthe had been sick. She liked flowers very much so I decided to buy some and bring her a bouquet. I told the flower vendor to arrange an especially nice bouquet for a nun who was sick. I chose flowers I knew she liked, then took them to the convent school. When I got there, the sister-nun at the entrance door was crying. She told me *Mère* Marthe, in her room, was dying at that moment, and she hurried to the bedside with my flowers. I was not allowed to go, as only the nuns could enter what was called "the community." I know that she was given my flowers and told that I had brought them for her. She died a few moments later.

❦ Finally, my Order of Mission from Captain Meyer's office arrived, and I left for the front.

From the Diary:

Paris, December 6, 1944

Last night I got back from the Front. Now I know there is no hope. I had left Paris in a small convoy, with three commando cars. We slept in a slummy hotel in Nancy, traveled for two days in bitter cold, passed Sarrebourg and Savern, and finally on the second night arrived in Strasbourg which had just been liberated and was bombed out and deserted. We went first to look for rooms, in the pitch-black streets. Sentries stopped us every few steps, demanding the password. It was "Fifi mast." From time to time a lighted rocket brightened the sky. We could hear the sound of cannon all around us, and in all the windows flags were flapping in the cold wind. Wherever we walked we stumbled on ruins, broken glass, half burned logs. I had never before seen a city after a battle, only London as it was during the blitz and all the other bombings we had suffered there, but this was even worse.

Next morning I had to find a jeep to take me to Suzanne's unit. An officer, seeing my Mission Order, promised me one for 10:30. It arrived and we went at full speed through destroyed villages, army camps, convoys of tanks. In the distance I could see the Vosges Mountains covered with snow and beyond them Germany, the Black Forest. The jeep left me with an ambulance which finally brought me to the headquarters of Major Putz, Georges' chief. Suzanne was there too. She couldn't believe it when she saw me. She took me to her room in the village, a cold little room with broken windows in an evacuated vicarage. There she told me she could not have come to Paris, it had been impossible. The fighting was still going on and she couldn't leave her unit. She had sent me two letters to London, explaining everything. One of her girls had just gone to Paris with Georges' wedding ring and his identity bracelet, and must have passed me on my way to the front.

There in that room, a kilometer or so from the German lines, she told me how Georges and two other soldiers had volunteered for a patrol on Sunday, October 8th. Before leaving, Georges had given his wallet to one of Suzanne's ambulance drivers and had said: "Keep it. I have a bad premonition." He went, calmly smoking his pipe. The girl said he hadn't been wearing his helmet and that he was reciting a poem as he walked away with his comrades. There was a castle near where the unit was stationed and the army wanted to know if any German S.S. were hiding inside. The name of the castle was the Château de Villers. It was a very dangerous mission, the ground was flat and there was nowhere to hide. There were three men—Dahan, D'Ornano, and Georges. There was one small elevation to cross. D'Ornano, who was the last in line, saw Georges and Dahan climb the elevation and disappear down the other side. From the castle he heard machine-gun fire. He stopped, unable to see anything or to follow his comrades, and came back. The other two never returned.

On October 26th, the unit captured a German prisoner who said there were two bodies lying in front of the castle. One had a beard and a name like Torres on his identity bracelet. That was when Suzanne had written me her first letter. All of Georges's comrades asked to go as volunteers to look for the bodies. The major refused because the prisoner had said that the grounds there were mined. Four men left one night, without permission, to go and look for their comrades' bodies, but couldn't reach the place. Finally, on November 8th, Major Putz himself went. He found the bodies, came back, and sent some men to bring back Georges and Dahan. Suzanne saw Georges. She swore to me he was intact except for a small bullet hole behind one ear. On his face was no sign of suffering. It had been a beautiful, calm, peaceful face, she said. The unit chaplain slipped off his wedding ring and took his identity bracelet and his division insignia. I will keep them for you, Dominique. The father buried him with the medals I had given him around his neck. He was covered by the tricolor; the unit formed a guard of honor. It was a burial he would have liked. Suzanne was there—poor Suzanne, the only one from the whole family. She took care of everything; she was admirable.

I slept in Suzanne's room. For long hours, in this room, lit only by a candle, she talked to me about Georges: of his family, of the way he had been brought up and of the love he had for you, Dominique, and for his wife, and of all the projects he had had for after the war.

The next day I visited Major Sarazac, who had been one of the last to see Georges. I spoke with the soldiers and officers of his regiment. All of them told me Georges was a "crack," an outstanding man, a leader. At Sarazac's I copied Georges's citation. He has been proposed for the Cross of the Liberation and for the Military Medal, France's two top decorations.

During those days I took all my meals with the men from the Division and with Suzanne, with all those young boys who knew death was waiting for them every second. Suzanne leads a heroic life in terrible physical conditions. I have such admiration for her. She goes looking for the wounded on the battlefields; she sleeps on the ground or in her ambulance; sometimes for days she doesn't wash or undress. She told me that during a bombardment she had gone to pick up a wounded soldier. He was delirious and didn't recognize her. He thought she was a priest and begged her to give him absolution. Suzanne, who is Jewish, said to me, "I wanted him to die in peace, so I said to him, 'In the name of the Father, of the Son, and of the Holy Ghost I absolve you,' and then he relaxed and lost consciousness." When Suzanne came back to the unit she told the chaplain, Father Fouquet, who had buried Georges, what had happened, and Father Fouquet told her it was a valid absolution even though she was a woman, and Jewish, and an unbeliever in any religion! The soldier's intention had been pure, as had what she had done.

Georges and his comrade Dahan: Citation to the "Order of the Army"
Doncières
Elite fighters, during a very dangerous patrol, approached very near enemy lines, showing great bravery. They found death in action.
2e. D.B.
3/R.MT.

🌷 I was back with *Bonne Maman*. One rainy day she took me to see the place in the country near Paris where Georges's mother had a country house called *Le clos des Metz* in which Georges had lived before the war. He had often described it to me, promising to take me there after the war.

Now I was there. It was raining and the lanes were full of yellowish mud. It was winter and the bungalow and the "children's house" were empty, abandoned, desolate. A shell had entered one room, breaking through the wall; all the windows were broken, spider webs covered the ceilings; the floors were strewn with empty wine bottles left by the Germans. But I looked out the little window in Georges's bedroom. The same weeping willow he had seen in his childhood was leaning there before my eyes, the fields were the same, as were the grass, the trees, the bushes. From the earth came the same smell of rain and soil which Georges had breathed as a child. I had found the marvelous house where he had wanted to take me. I had found Georges's shadow in the lanes and I felt him there, guiding me through his past.

🌱 The girl from Suzanne's unit did come to Paris and she brought me two photos taken by the army captain about a week before Georges died. She also brought me his identity bracelet and his wallet. The photos were a shock. I hadn't seen Georges since the previous July. He had left for the Normandy front a young man who had never seen war—real war. He had seen the bombardments in London, but that was not war.

I had pictures of Georges taken on our wedding day—a tall, dark, serious-looking boy. He was still a boy, not yet twenty-one. He was innocent with the innocence of youth and the eyes of a twenty-year-old. Now I had the photos taken at the front: Georges after only two months of fighting. If anyone wanted to see in a man's face what war did to men, he had only to look at these pictures. They were clear pictures, in focus, sharp. The soldier, photographed a week before his death, had aged in two months the way a man ages in ten hard years. He had grown a beard and looked very tired. His eyes had become the eyes of a man who had to kill and who had seen death every day. They were tragic eyes—imploring eyes, begging for an end to killing.

My husband, my young and carefree husband. Even if Georges had come back, he would never have been the Georges I had known. Never again—the war had killed him even before he died in battle.

Right after the war I had a stone placed at the head of Georges's grave. On it I had carved a poem by Charles Péguy. It

was one of Georges's favorite verses and he had written it over
and over again on many pages of his notebooks:

> Heureux ceux qui sont morts
> Dans les grandes batailles
> Couchés dessus le sol
> A la face de Dieu.

Part VI 🌷

After the War

In January 1945 I was still in Paris. Meyer Levin came to see me at *Bonne Maman's*. He had been in Paris when I was at the Château Frontenac and I had asked him then to try to go to the front as a war correspondent and see Suzanne and tell her I was in Paris. But as it turned out, I found Suzanne before Meyer got to her. It was not easy to find anyone at the front. I was then preparing to leave Paris and go back to London. Dominique was to be born at the end of February and I did not have much time left to arrange for a nursing home. My parents were in London and I wanted to be near them; besides, it was much more convenient to have a baby in London than in Paris, where all the hospitals were full of wounded soldiers.

On January thirteenth, *Bonne Maman* had a heart attack. I was alone with her. In a second the lively, young-hearted woman was a slim motionless body on the floor. I thought she was dying. I called a doctor, and until he came I sat on the floor next to her, afraid to move her. Her face was colorless, and she started moaning. There was red foam on her lips. The doctor arrived and gave her injections. With her maid, the doctor and I undressed her and put her to bed. I remember her body. It was like a young girl's. She was still—at seventy—slim, small-breasted, and narrow-hipped, with delicate shoulders. The next morning she was very weak, but better. The doctor said it was serious and I was afraid that if I left for London I might never see her again. I loved her more than I loved my own grandmothers. But on January twenty-third, I couldn't wait any longer—I had to catch an army plane for London. In London, it was very hard seeing the sorrow on my parents' faces. I couldn't bear to think that my unhappiness was making them suffer so and I tried to be as cheerful as I could.

From the Diary:

February 12, 1945

Your little bed, Dominique, has arrived today and is waiting for you, next to mine. I have a room in the same boarding house as my parents, but a flight above theirs. I look at your bed without being able to realize that our child will be lying in it in so short a time. I spend my days knitting for you, or taking walks. I can't read, can't concentrate on any book. But I found my diary in Paris and reread it recently. It was the diary I had written in Normandy during that splendid summer of 1938 in the house we had rented right on the beach. It was one of the most beautiful summers I remember.

It is strange to be back in London. I became accustomed, so quickly, so immediately, to being in Paris again—a strange, empty Paris, without any civilian cars, a hungry, sleepy Paris but still luxurious in many ways, and it had become my Paris again at once. I recognized it, I rediscovered it in one day. I adjusted to it without transition after all the years of exile. I didn't even mind the frightful subways, packed to improbable capacity, the shortages of electricity, the cold water, the lack of food, the exorbitant prices, the freezing-cold apartments, the empty streets, or even the horrible war fashions: high-piled hair, thick wooden-soled shoes. I didn't mind anything. I accepted that new Paris—marvelous, severe, and more beautiful than ever. The worst part was the estrangement from so many friends who, during the war, had stayed in France and had taken such different roads—so many friends who had become strangers, incomprehensible, lost forever.

It rains in London all the time. But London is full of memories for me . . . Hampstead: the district where you are going to be born. That is where Georges' room was. It was there that, nine months ago, one evening, he said to me, "Let's get married." We were sitting on the floor, it was the beginning of May, and we were so happy. It is in Hampstead that we bicycled, in the evenings, after work. It is there that we discovered the mysterious garden that looked like *Le clos des Metz*. It is also there that we came back to Georges' room after the three-day honeymoon near Oxford. And when we came back we found a crown of mistletoe hanging above our door. It is in Hampstead that Georges kissed me for the first time.

Piccadilly: How many times did we walk along here, Georges telling me about a book he wanted to write which he was going to call *The Tyrant,* or about his childhood, and about his mother whom he loved so much. Or we just looked at the passers-by, imagining who they might be, and we laughed, laughed, all the time.

Soho: We went for lunches or dinners to Celeste, to Rose, to Santi Romano, or Perlemont. The morning of May 6th I met Georges in front of 3 St. James's Square, where my office was then. I think that neither of us could believe yet that since the night before an astonishing thing had happened: we were engaged. We went to eat in Soho and in Old Compton Street. Georges bought me a bunch of May-lilies at the stand of an old flower-seller.

In Charing Cross Road there is a little street with a Negro club where we went sometimes, and some other clubs where we had once found a poor, lost Polish girl who couldn't speak a word of English. She had pale-yellow hair and was wearing a combination of the military uniforms of three or four countries all at once. She was dead drunk, and no one paid her any attention. She kept repeating the words "Siu Siu" in Polish and I was the only one who understod what she needed. Poor "Siu Siu," I had seen so many lost girls wearing military uniforms during those years of war, but she was the most miserable.

I have so many memories in London. Everywhere I go I find

Georges—Georges wearing his large khaki overcoat and smoking his pipe, Georges sitting in front of me in a Chinese restaurant, Georges holding my hand in his coat pocket, Georges in the elevator in St. James's Square Headquarters when I told him I had been accepted as an officer and he was so pleased, Georges at Camberley after we were married, coming to get my things with me, Georges in Surrey visiting friends a few days before our wedding, and saying to me, "I want you to be very, very happy." He also said: "In our marriage there will never be anything sordid." . . . I don't want to let myself think what it would have been like if he had not died, if, on this morning, writing this diary, I could write that he was going to arrive soon, on leave, for your birth, Dominique; that he was going to see you in this little bed and take you in his arms. . . . I don't want to let myself think of all that happiness that died with him.

February 18, 1945

Maybe two more weeks, maybe ten days, and I will know who you are and I will have a child, the son or the daughter of Georges. In ten days . . . and I have waited so long for this happiness. When I was fifteen, I looked at all the babies in the streets and I was thinking of you, I was already waiting for you, I already loved you. . . . All these years and now in ten days you will be here—my child, our child, for whom I must replace a father and at the same time make real that father who gave life to you. Ten more days. The future? I don't know anything. It is not possible to know less. I only know that I am going to take you to France as soon as possible, to Paris. This is all I know. How I will manage to bring you up, where we will live, what will happen later, I don't know. I don't know anything and I would rather not think about it now. I am afraid to be afraid.

At the four corners of the world, people are thinking of your arrival, Dominique. People await you, hope for you: your grandfather in New York, your uncle in Brazil, your great-grandparents in Canada, your grandmother in prison in Germany, your great-grandmother in Paris, my parents in London, Suzanne at the front—so many people are waiting for you.

February 21, 1945

A beautiful spring, Hyde Park and the little square facing our boarding house full of crocuses—wonderful weather for the arrival of our child. Already the earth smells good, the buds on the trees show little, green, fresh tongues.

I put a vase of small blooming branches on either side of Georges' picture. Every day I look at the blossoming of these delicate marvels. Each branch is different. Some are covered with yellow petals, another has put out a kind of red tuft, another has thick leaves, almost blue. There are pointed buds which become so green, and others, round ones, which burst open suddenly. I don't know the names of any of these flowers, but they would have become trees.

I had a doctor in London who was Polish and had been specializing, on the side, in illegal abortions. He was my doctor because my parents knew him well and he had offered to take care of me without payment. When I was nine months' pregnant, I finally acquired a regular belly and got out of uniform and into a real maternity smock. Whenever I went to see Dr. B. at his office I would sit in the waiting room with his other patients, all young women who hid behind dark glasses and wide-brimmed hats and who looked at me with indignation. It was one thing, their looks said, to get rid of an unwanted baby in the first few weeks, as they were going to do, but for a woman in such advanced stage as mine, it was criminal.

As for Dr. B., he loved every minute of taking care of me. I soon understood that there was nothing that could make him happier than to be able to help a baby to be born instead of helping to kill one. I was his justification, his compensation, and I couldn't have had a kinder, more considerate doctor.

From the Diary.

February 26, 1945
4 o'clock in the morning.

You are beginning to be born. In five minutes the ambulance will be here. My darling child, now I have only a few hours to wait. You are hurting me very much.

Dominique, I am happy.

Dominique was a girl—a lovely little baby with a funny, very wide-awake expression. All night long, the night she was being born, I heard, whenever I stopped screaming long enough, the distinctive drone made by the V-2's, Hitler's last weapon. Dominique was born at noon and my room at the nursing home quickly became buried in spring flowers. There were daffodils and tulips everywhere. The nurse couldn't find enough space to spread her bandages, cotton, and scissors. A log fire burned in the fireplace and my daughter slept in a bassinet next to my bed. My parents were allowed to come whenever they wanted, as were all my friends, to look at the baby and admire her.

I had wanted a son so much during those long months since Georges' death. Yet as soon as the nurse said "It's a girl," I was happy and I didn't for a second miss the little boy I had been waiting for.

The nurse only took Dominique away from me at night to let me sleep. All day I had her with me to cuddle, to wonder at, to enjoy. Two days after she was born, the head nurse started to come to my room to make me do exercises. During the hours before she was born, the same head nurse had come to my room and repeated smilingly while I screamed my head off, "Nice little pains, nice little pains."

In the clinic I learned to bathe my baby, to change her, to dress her, to give her a bottle. By the time I went back to my

parents' boarding house, I knew perfectly how to take care of
my child. It was March then, a beautiful spring. Every day I
took Dominique out to the garden in front of the house. The
tenants from all the houses surrounding that garden had keys to
the gate. I was on maternity leave from the army, but in June
I had to report back. Most of my friends were already stationed
in France. France was completely liberated. The armies were
now fighting in Germany.

In May I heard from Georges's mother. She and her husband
had been saved. She sent a telegram to me in London. She had
found out all at once that her son Georges had been killed, that
he had been married, and that he had a child. She was back in
Paris and the French government had put at her and her husband's disposal an apartment in the Palace of the Sénat, at the
back of the Luxembourg Gardens.

Meyer Levin came to London again, on his way to the United
States. He told us about the horrors of the concentration camps,
which he had been among the first to enter. The names Dachau,
Auschwitz, Ravensbrück, Buchenwald had come out of an in-
ferno worse than Dante's, and would never be forgotten.

We had no news at all from Poland but my grandparents in
Canada were fine and very happy to have a great-granddaugh-
ter. My uncle in Portugal wrote an indignant letter because I
had named the baby Dominique. He said that the Dominican
Order had been in charge of the Inquisition, and that I should
have called the baby Georgette, in memory of her father. I
thought Georgette was a hideous name and I would never have
given it to my beautiful little girl. But as I was certain that I
would never have any more children, being a widow, I gave
Dominique four first names to make up for all the children I
thought I would never have. She was called on her birth certifi-
cate "Dominique Marie Raphaelle Georges Torres." Raphaelle
was her Jewish name. Meyer admired her and held her in his

arms. She was two months old and she looked around at everything with an expression of intense curiosity.

I was in a great hurry to go back to France as soon as possible. The war seemed almost finished. Mussolini had been killed and Hitler was said to be hidden in a shelter in Berlin.

My mother-in-law, Janot, had sent a friend of hers to London to see me and he said that she would obtain permits for my parents to come back to Paris with me. Janot had also asked him to tell me that she would have an apartment for me, and a job. It all looked perfect. But beyond those material advantages, what I wanted most of all was to meet and love Georges's mother. I had heard so much about her from Georges, who had had total admiration for her. Suzanne, who knew her husband's first wife very well, was less enthusiastic.

April thirtieth, I thought, might be the last day of the war. Peace was expected any minute. Goering had run away and newspapers wrote that Himmler had asked for a cease fire.

In London the blackout was lifted. For the first time in five years blinding lights burst out all over the city. For the first time I saw London illuminated at night. I had forgotten how a city looked at night with all the windows lighted, with neon signs and street lamps. I stood and looked around. I couldn't believe it.

On May sixth, peace had not yet been declared, although we were being told that the fighting had stopped except for the Russians who were still fighting in Czechoslovakia. Peace arrived too late for anyone to be excited; no one yelled for joy. There were no parades in London; nobody understood what was going on. The Allies were quarreling among themselves. In San Francisco, Molotov had left the conference. Japan was still at war with the United States.

In 1939 I thought that the war was going to last only a few months. In 1940, when I arrived in England and joined the

Free French, my friends and I all dreamed of a glorious victory parade down the Champs Elysées. In 1941 and 1942, I thought of what happiness it would be to live without blackouts, without coupons or rations. In 1943 and 1944, we stopped dreaming and hoping. We weren't sure any more the war would ever end. In 1945 we were so used to a state of war that the idea of peace seemed impossible, unbelievable. War had become our permanent way of life. Finally it came—May eighth, V-E Day!

A few days later, I wrote:

I have packed your little dresses, Dominique, your tiny shirts and gowns, in a trunk with your father's clothes. His khaki uniforms, his shirts, his books and papers are now close to your rompers and pink coats and little shoes. It is like a caress from him to you, from what has touched his body to what will cover yours.

On May 23, 1945:

Tomorrow is our first wedding anniversary and tonight, a year later, I have a daughter, a big daughter almost three months old. A daughter who smiles, who moves, who is even starting to lift her head on her own, when a year ago today she didn't exist.

Tomorrow is our first wedding anniversary and you have already left me. Do you remember that day? Do you remember "I want you to be very, very happy," and "In our marriage there will never be anything sordid"?

We had only those few days, but even if I had known that we would have only one hour, I would have married you. So what more can I want? We had a month and I love you.

At the beginning of June 1945 all of us finally got on a boat. I was back in uniform and was carrying three-month-old Dominique in a sort of portable crib. My parents had packed a trunk with powdered milk and baby food, as there was nothing of the sort in Paris yet, as well as the accumulation of things they had gathered during the five years in England. The war was over but I wasn't officially demobilized yet. That would happen when I got to my headquarters in Paris.

Janot was awaiting us when the train arrived in Paris. She was forty-five years old, a tall, extremely good-looking woman, strong and majestic. But her hair was gray and her face was tense and sad. She hugged me for a long time and looked at the little baby who was all that was left of her son. I adored her instantly. Later I learned that Janot had the gift of awakening in people, men and women alike, such an instant feeling of adoration.

A car was waiting for us, and the chauffeur, a policeman hired by the French government to protect Léon Blum, helped with the luggage. We drove to my parents' house and it was like coming home after just a few days, even though it had really been five years. Nothing at all had changed. The same flowers and bushes were growing in the garden. A bush I had planted five years before had grown into a small tree. Inside the house the Teddy bear given to me by my uncle Samuel when I was a year old was still sitting on my bed, very badly moth-eaten. All my father's works and tools were still in the studio.

After my parents got over their emotion at being home again, I left Dominique with them and Janot took me with her to the Senat to meet her husband. This began a new aspect of my life.

Léon Blum, that first day I met him, impressed me immediately with his aristocratic manners. The chief of the French Socialist Party, once considered a dangerous revolutionary, looked like Nordic royalty. He was about seventy years old then, tall, slim, and white-haired, with a sensitive, intellectual

face and beautiful, elegant hands. That day he was wearing a
short brown woolen smoking jacket with a silk collar. He kissed
my hand and then my cheeks, and there were tears in his eyes.
His voice was gentle, melodious.

The apartment in the Sénat was rather small but very well
furnished. We sat there and talked for hours. Janot told me then
and many times later about her life with Léon Blum in the small
house in the Buchenwald compound. That day we also decided
what I should call my stepfather-in-law. I couldn't call him
"sir," and I couldn't call him by his first name, as I called Janot.
So we chose "Grappy" as a suitable name for Dominique and
me to use. I made it up on the spur of the moment, a sort of
masculine version of Granny.

I telephoned *Bonne Maman* from the Sénat and as I talked
with her I could hear how happy she was that I was back.

Janot, Grappy, and I had lunch, the first of many such
lunches, in the small dining room. Grappy spoke of literature,
art, friends—rarely of politics. He had the most astounding
memory. That man, who had never been out alone in the streets
of Paris for fifteen or twenty years, who was driven
everywhere in chauffeured cars, could remember every turn of
every street in Paris, every short cut, every twisting lane. Once
at the table we were talking about children's books and I told
him that when I was six or seven years old I had read a story
I loved and remembered well, although I had forgotten the
author's name. I said, "I wish I could remember where it was
published, Grappy, because I would so much like Dominique to
read it one day."

Grappy said: "What was the name of the book?"

I remembered that it had been called *Monsieur Le Vent et
Madame La Pluie.*

"Oh, yes, I remember that book," Grappy said. "I read it myself when I was about five years old. It was published by —

and written by —." I have forgotten again who it was, but Grappy, who had last seen that book at the age of five, could tell me, sixty-five years later, the name of the author and the publisher. He told me that he had taught himself to read when he was four years old. His older brothers studied near him and he learned by listening to them and looking at the books they were reading.

In the next few days Dominique was introduced to Grappy and of course to *Bonne Maman*. Grappy and *Bonne Maman* were about the same age and it was strange to see Janot with them, because her mother certainly looked more likely to be Grappy's wife than she. Janot, as a distant cousin of Grappy's had known him all her life and had known his first two wives. She told me that she had loved him as long as she could remember, but it had only been after both had been married twice that they had gotten together. Their relationship was a wonderful thing to watch. They were like my parents, romantically and youthfully in love. But their marriage had a more formal structure than my parents'. They said *vous* to each other and in general used an old-fashioned politeness. Janot listened to every word of Grappy's as if it were God talking, and Grappy looked upon her as the most beautiful, clever woman in the world.

Henri Torres, my real father-in-law, who had a very sharp tongue, once said to me, when he returned to France from New York, "Janot and Léon are by themselves a complete Mutual Admiration Society." Another time he said of his ex-wife, "Janot has entered into her legend in her lifetime." And it was true. Janot at forty-five was a legendary figure. She was the woman who had abandoned her two sons and her husband to be with the man she loved. She had lived next to his prison in Riom in 1940. She had organized his escape—although unsuccessfully—and when he was deported, she had had herself sent to the concentration camp to be near him. There she had saved his life several times. She had watched over his health, kept up his spirits and his courage, and finally had supported him with her own strength until their liberation by the American Army. Now Léon Blum was a hero in post-war France, and Janot was a hero's wife.

I was living with Dominique at my parents' apartment. She slept with me in my childhood bedroom. The apartment Janot had written me about had not been practical for me to move into. It was only two rooms in somebody else's apartment, and I felt that if I had to live with another family, it would be more pleasant to be with my own. Also, I couldn't afford to pay rent, having no job and no money at all. My father was having a very difficult time selling his sculptures. Right after the war people were not in a mood to buy art. And he had not only mother and me to support but a grandchild as well. But somehow we managed.

Almost everything in the apartment was as we had left it except for some books, paper, and paintings which were missing. What had happened was that a Frenchwoman, a friend of my parents, knowing that the Germans might come any day and empty the apartment, came every week or so for months, on her bicycle—her only means of transportation—and as the concierge knew her, Marie-Thérèse would quickly take out things she thought might be precious to us and carry them away to her own apartment to hide for us. One winter day, as she was bicycling in the snow, her little luggage rack full of our books, she fell off and broke her arm. But as soon as she was well again, she returned to rescue more of our things. The concierge too had certainly saved our things by never mentioning our apartment to the Germans when they came to inquire about the building.

. . .

✿ At about that time my godmother, Mya, died at Lectoure. I hadn't had the time or means to go to Lectoure since we had returned, so I never saw her again after the war, never saw her round, always freshly scrubbed face, her red cheeks; never again heard her voice with the Gascony accent calling her chickens, cats, and dogs to come and get fed. Romeck was still in a monastery.

Summer was coming.

On August twenty-fifth, the anniversary of the liberation of Paris, Dominique was baptized in a Dominican chapel near my parents' house. By now *Bonne Maman* had told everyone of her own conversion, which had taken place in 1939. Around Dominique were her great-grandmother, her grandmothers, and her mother, as well as my father, Léon Blum and many friends. Dominique wore a long white lace dress that had belonged to Georges when he was a baby.

Some admirer offered Grappy the use of a house in Auvergne, not far from the town of Riom, where he had been imprisoned and tried for treason in 1941. Janot asked Dominique and me to come with them for a month in the country. Only one guard, the chauffeur, was coming along. It was a peaceful and pleasant month. I took care of my baby, but had no other worries of any kind. Once more everything was provided for me, as it had been in the army. I was grateful, because I found that five years of this treatment had made me unused to fighting for myself.

Dominique was six months old and she still slept a lot or played in her crib. Grappy was writing articles and Janot and I would talk for hours. I loved to listen to her. She spoke of Georges and of her first husband Henri, whom I still hadn't met because he was in New York. She spoke of her life in Buchenwald, of her present husband, of their love, of her ideas. She had many ideas. She was the purest Utopian that ever existed. I could never quite follow her. She would explain the most improbable, impossible scheme, going into such complicated reasoning that I always lost her before she was half way through.

She was very affectionate with me. She would sit me on her knees as if I were a little girl and then start talking about one of her unbelievable projects, such as a plan for bringing socialism to the world by having the proletariat concentrate more on their leisure time, or some such idea. She would explain it all very minutely and intimately. She spoke to everyone as if she were imparting to him innermost thoughts that no one but the listener could understand. As for socialism, she had never in her life had any contact with any workers other than maids and chauffeurs. She had had the childhood and adolescence of a very rich girl. She had first married a famous lawyer and then a Swiss millionaire. It was not her fault if she was utterly impractical. On the other hand, she had extremely good taste, a high sense of decoration, and a very intuitive, brilliant mind.

In the late afternoon we went for walks, leaving Dominique asleep in the guard's care. Grappy loved those walks. He said it was the first time in many long years that he could walk by himself without being surrounded by policemen. Whenever we met country people passing on the road, they smiled and raised their berets, and Grappy would stop, shake hands, and ask questions about their lives and work. There were many socialists in the village and once they came in a group to talk to him. He received them with his natural grace, his aristocratic gestures, his respectful air. He had great respect for every human being. But many people who didn't know him hated him. There was still a sign written long before the war on the wall of our house in Paris which said, "Death to Léon Blum."

Once I remember being in a car with Janot and Grappy when they came back to Paris after a mission to Washington. We were

speeding from Orly Airport and policemen on motorcycles were ahead of us, their sirens screaming. On the side of
the road some people had gathered and were looking at Grappy
in the car. At one turn a fat woman thumbed her nose at him. I
was very shocked, but he didn't seem disturbed.

It was in that country house that Grappy told me that if he
could relive his life, he would like to spend it studying St.
Francis of Assisi's philosophy. He said he admired him greatly.

One evening Janot was sitting on my bed. She always came
in to kiss me good night. Suddenly she asked me, very seriously,
"Tereska, tell me, do you think that Grappy and I should have
a child?" I was amazed. Grappy was over seventy years old.

But the event I remember best about that month was a visit
we made to nearby Riom. Janot had told me that when Grappy
was in jail in Riom, she had looked desperately for a way to
arrange an escape. The escape itself could be planned, but the
big problem was to find someplace to hide Grappy for a few
hours until he could be safely driven away. A very poor peasant
couple had offered their house, but the escape had been unsuc-
cessful. Janot got in touch with the woman and her husband
and we were invited to visit them. They lived in a small half-
barn, half-house: two rooms and a kitchen. They were very
simple people who had prepared a fabulous meal, and when
we arrived they were standing in their doorway in their best
clothes, very shy and uneasy. Grappy put them at ease at once.
He sat down and, with chickens running between his feet,
started discussing problems of farm life as if he had been a poor
farmer all his life. The husband brought out a bottle of wine and
we all clicked glasses and drank. Then we ate that wonderful
meal. Outside the car was waiting and the whole village had
gathered around it, gaping in wonder.

When we came back to Paris, my problems began again. The
main one was money. I had no profession and a baby to support,

and my parents had no money either. It was going to take my father quite some time before his name would be back in art circles and collectors or museums would start buying again. In the meantime, I felt terrible about his having to support me and Dominique. I looked everywhere for some work that I would be able to do satisfactorily. Then Janot got one of her ideas.

As I said, Janot's ideas were never simple or practical. What she now decided was that it would be excellent for the Socialist Party if I had a radio program on which I could indirectly explain socialist principles to listeners in various ways. There was nothing wrong with that, except that I had never run a radio program, I had not the slightest idea how it was done, and besides, no one at the radio station wanted me or such a program. But Léon Blum was so popular then that any wish of his wife's had to be satisfied. So I was given an office, but no budget whatsoever, no information of any kind, no help at all. Janot was delighted. She telephoned all kinds of people to arrange radio interviews for me and planned programs for years ahead, while I sat in that empty office desperately trying to figure out what to do.

During that summer of 1945, my parents had the surprise of seeing Jacques. He appeared at their apartment one day in his white robe, straight from his Trappist monastery. He was the same Jacques, with his round head and red-rimmed eyes, except that he looked haunted. He was in a state of shock over what had happened to the Jews of Europe while he had been living in peace, undisturbed and unknowing, in his retreat. He had two sisters whom he loved and a large family in Poland. Like my parents, he had no idea what had happened to any of them. There had been only a vast silence from there since the end of the war. Jacques's superior had allowed him to leave the monastery temporarily to go to Poland and search for his family. He was just passing through Paris and had stopped only long enough to see my parents. Then he changed into civilian clothes and left for Poland.

Since our return to Paris we had begun to find out about our friends and relatives who had spent the war years in France. One day there was a knock at my parents' door and a young, very attractive girl came in. My parents' didn't recognize her. She was Ianka, my cousin, whom they had last seen when she was about nine years old, the one I played those "sexy" games with. Ianka had survived Auschwitz, but she was absolutely alone in the world except for my parents. After being liberated from the camp she had gone back to Poland to search for her family. She had found no one. Then she had remembered my parents. All she knew about them was that there had been some cousins in Paris, years ago, who had converted to Catholicism— a scandal in her childhood. Who knew, maybe they had survived. Not knowing what to do or where to go, Ianka had gotten into one army truck after another and had hitchhiked across bombed-out Europe until she arrived in Paris. There she started looking for my father. She had only his name and the information that he had been a well-known artist. She found him.

My parents asked her to stay with them, and when I came back from Auvergne Ianka had been added to my parents' household. She slept on a sofa in our living-dining-study room. She was an unusually good-looking girl, except for her legs. Years of hunger had provoked some sickness called—I think—elephantiasis. Her legs were terribly swollen and nothing seemed to help to get them back to normal. Every night at dinner Ianka told us stories about camp life. She had been in several different camps and was the only survivor I ever met who could make one laugh about life in a concentration camp. Somehow she remembered unbelievably funny details. She had a way of describing how she had looked with her head shaved, in her camp clothes, which sounded ridiculous rather than tragic. She was also the only survivor I know who told me about romances in camp, girls flirting, and spring at Auschwitz. Even there Ianka had noticed grass and trees and had felt the summer sun. She was always cheerful, and determined to make a new life for herself.

Except for Ianka and, a few months later, a nephew of my father's who also arrived from Poland and stayed with my parents for a while, no one else appeared. My grandmother's sister, Aunt Jadja, who had lived across the street and who used to wave so gaily to me; her daughter and granddaughter, a seven-year-old whose photo I had in my album feeding pigeons in Warsaw's Old Town; my uncles and other aunts and cousins; Pietrek, the cousin to whom I had been "engaged" when I was four or five; Hela, my uncle Henio's fiancée; and so many others, had all disappeared in smoke.

Later, two more members of the family were heard from. A first cousin of my father's, a very extravagant woman who had had five or six husbands, was still living in Warsaw and had become a well-known journalist; and a cousin of my mother's, a doctor who had been a fighter in the Warsaw ghetto uprising, was still there. Our large Polish family was reduced to fewer than half a dozen people.

Then my grandfather, died in Canada and my parents started taking steps to bring my grandmother back to France. It was about that time that Janot dumped me on the radio station, and I was becoming deeply depressed. Paris after the war was still a difficult place to live. There was little food, hardly any hot water or heat, and it was impossible to find housing. Every day another report would come about someone else we knew who had been murdered during the war. My father had great difficulty feeding all of us, and I couldn't get even essential foods such as eggs or orange juice for Dominique.

One day a woman appeared at the apartment. She was a friend of a friend of a friend of some friends of my grandparents in Canada. She came with greetings and saw Dominique and came back the next day with eggs. Hala was the wife of a doctor and they had a house with a garden a few kilometers from Paris. Hala grew lettuce, tomatoes, and raspberries, and raised chickens. From that day on, and for two years after, she came every week with a basket on her arm and brought me fresh food from her garden.

Dominique could stand up. She was almost nine months old. Her *Bonne Maman* adored her but thought her too energetic. *Bonne Maman,* who still dressed like Queen Mary, was used to very quiet little children raised by nannies. She was amazed at my daughter's early energy. She used to look at Dominique with her nearsighted eyes and shake her white head, saying, "Tereska, this child is a force of nature." She meant the way a cyclone is, or a hurricane. Sometimes, when the car came to fetch me, I would take Dominique to the Sénat. She sat on Grappy's and Janot's bed and one day I found her happily playing with telegrams and papers stamped SECRET and CONFIDENTIAL. Grappy saw her, smiled, and said to her: "Dominique, you are holding in your hands the fate of France!"

My mother-in-law and Grappy had two friends called Bill and Junius. They were the same size as Janot's two little fingers. As a matter of fact they were her two little fingers. She had given them names and referred very seriously to them in front of strangers as a private joke. Junius used to express her opinions and Bill expressed Grappy's. Once, making a speech at a Socialist meeting, Grappy said very gravely, "A friend of mine, Professor Junius, always used to say. . . ." Janot had to bite her lip to keep a straight face. When there were people my parents-in-law had to see who were bores or snobs, Janot would say, "Léon, don't forget you have an appointment with Professor Junius," or "Léon, Bill just phoned. He has to speak to you," giving an excuse for Grappy to get up and get rid of his visitors. Nobody ever asked who this professor and this Bill were.

Several times when Grappy was speaking at a Socialist meeting, I would be late and arrive at the door without any pass or ticket. When that happened I always said to the guard, "Excuse me, I am Mrs. Léon Blum's daughter-in-law. Mrs. Blum is waiting for me in the front row." It never once happened that the guard asked me to wait or went and checked. Each time he just waved me in and I walked up to the speaker's platform. It always seemed incredible, because several times before the war people had tried to assassinate Grappy. I thought how easy it would be to murder a political figure if one wanted to.

I saw Suzanne whenever she returned from Indochina. She was still officially Henri's wife, but she didn't live with him anymore. During the war she had fallen in love with a colonel in the Leclerc Division and was going to divorce Henri. The colonel, whom she later married, was Jacques Massu, who was to become the famous General Massu, head of the paratroopers in Algeria. He was the man portrayed in the film *Battle of Algiers* as Colonel Mathieu.

At that time, I met many famous people through my in-laws, but it only depressed me. There was too strong a contrast between that glittering public life: the car driven by a policeman, the official dinners, the Socialist meetings where Grappy was treated like a king, the conversations with famous writers, politicians, artists—all the bowing and the formalities—and my real situation, to which I always had to return: my parents' small house, very crowded by then, my father's financial difficulties, my child who had to be fed, and the job at the radio station, which was too much for me and which I felt no one except Janot wanted me to do.

I have always hated to impose on anyone. I would rather die

than force myself on a person or an institution. But there I was, clearly being imposed on the radio people, who didn't need me or my program, but who couldn't say so to my famous mother-in-law. All those things made me terribly depressed, although of course I tried to hide it. I didn't want my parents to suffer on my account. My mother was getting sicker and sicker with Parkinson's disease, so my father was sculpting and at the same time taking complete care of the house and of my two surviving cousins, my sick mother, and my baby. And he had the extraordinary ability to do it all with a happy smile and to produce during that time the best sculptures of his whole life. At night I lay in my bed listening to my baby's breathing and thought about how I had no father for her, no husband, and no work for myself.

I wrote:

> . . . Each time a man smiles at Dominique, takes her in his arms with that awkward gesture men have, my heart breaks at the thought that Georges will never hold her so.

After becoming convinced of Georges' death, I had thought a few times of committing suicide, but had always pushed back the idea. For one thing, I couldn't have killed the child I was carrying. But the idea began to return more and more frequently. What was I good for? I wasn't helping anyone; I was only making things worse. If I were gone, Janot would have to face her responsibilities as a grandmother. She had the means to bring Dominique up easily and in comfort. She had a big house and estate at Jouy: *Le clos des Metz,* where *Bonne Maman* and I had visited during the war. There were three houses on the estate, and hundreds of fruit trees and a large vegetable garden. Janot was in the process of renovating and redecorating the place. There would certainly be enough room for one small baby.

My parents would have two people less to worry about. Of course they would be unhappy at first if I died, but after a while wouldn't it be better for them too? My reasoning wasn't very logical, but I was too depressed to think logically. Still, although such ideas came to me, I was frightened of them. One day I told a doctor friend of my parents', a very kind Russian woman called Raya, that I was feeling very depressed, and she insisted that I see a psychoanalyst. She arranged for an interview and took me there herself.

I sat in front of the psychoanalyst's desk and answered his questions. I remember that he told me to hold something in my raised hand and he looked inside my eyeballs or some such thing. Then he told Raya that I was fine and only needed calcium.

The next day I got hold of some sleeping pills. I don't remember how many of the small white pills I swallowed. It was in early December and cold and rainy. I stood there in my parents' house after swallowing the pills and waited to drop dead. But nothing happened. I felt fine. That day I was supposed to take some papers about the radio program to a friend of Janot's. She didn't live far away, so I thought that I could just as well go and take the papers. Maybe I hadn't taken enough pills and it wasn't going to have any effect after all. I took my bicycle and pedaled over to the woman's apartment. She lived near the Luxembourg Gardens. Her husband had been one of Léon Blum's lawyers during the Riom trial, and her daughter was supposed to help me with the radio venture.

Once I got there I began to feel terribly sleepy, so sleepy I could hardly open my eyes, or my mouth. The daughter asked me what was wrong. I said I didn't feel well, that I must have caught the flu. Then I guess I fell asleep right there. A little later she shook me awake. I was in bed in her room. She asked me if I wanted to eat something and I mumbled "No," I only wanted to sleep. I later heard that I slept there all day and that finally toward evening Janot's friends called her and asked what they should do. Janot sent her car, the chauffeur wrapped me in a blanket and carried me downstairs to the car and drove me to Janot at the Sénat. I awoke in bed at the Sénat and Janot asked me how I felt. I told her I was very sleepy but that I would be all right, she shouldn't worry, only let me sleep. Janot and Grappy had a dinner at the American Embassy that night and they had to go. They left me in bed after deciding that the best thing for me was rest.

I awoke again. I was all alone in the Sénat apartment. My mind was very fuzzy. I thought: I am not dead. I didn't take enough pills. I must get some more. I remembered that Janot had a bottle of sleeping pills in her bathroom for use when she had insomnia, so with great difficulty I got up. I could hardly walk. I held onto furniture and stumbled toward the bathroom. I found the pills and filled a glass of water. Carrying the glass full of water back to my bed reminded me of the usefulness of my early Montessori education. They really think of everything, those children's educators. I didn't spill a drop. Back in bed I swallowed the pills, drank the whole glassful down and went back to sleep.

At the Embassy dinner Janot became increasingly uneasy. She kept thinking about me and wondering why I had slept so much and what the matter was with me. She decided she ought to have had a doctor look at me before leaving for the dinner. When the dinner finally ended, she whispered to Grappy that she wanted to rush home. She was very worried. They explained that I was sick and alone, and left. When they got home I was still sleeping. There was an empty glass near the bed with some white powder still in the bottom. Janot took one look and called Grappy, and he called a doctor, who rushed over.

I awoke because someone was hurting me. Someone was sticking a needle into my arm. I heard a voice say, "I can't find her vein." They stuck the needle in all over both my arms. It hurt and I moaned. I wanted to tell them to stop hurting me.

Three days later I awoke. I was in bed at the Sénat. I looked at Janot sitting beside my bed, but I saw two faces. Grappy and the doctor in a white coat also had two faces. Everyone and everything was double. I couldn't focus my eyes. I could hear them talking. They were saying that I was out of the coma. At some point my father was there, with Dominique in his arms. He stood her next to my bed, her head level with mine. She had such curly hair, kinky like Georges's, but a lighter color, like mine.

Suddenly I thought of how it had been when I was still almost a baby and my mother had slept for six months. I could vaguely remember standing at the side of her bed, my head not quite reaching the top, tugging at her blankets and calling her. Many years later in New York I dreamed that I was standing next to a dark room. My mother was in that dark room. I could only see her head behind a small window and in the dream I was calling, "*Maman, Maman, Maman,*" in a terribly anguished voice. But she would not answer me and I kept calling, "*Maman, Maman.*" Finally she said in a very sleepy faraway voice "*Oui*" and I cried out, "Why don't you answer me?" but she didn't say anything. So I repeated "*Maman, Maman, Maman.*" When I awoke I could still hear my frightened voice, a baby's voice, calling "*Maman, Maman.*"

The doctor when he came was very jovial. He said I was a silly, very silly, girl. He said he had given me strychnine and that I was lucky to be alive. I didn't think I was lucky. I told him I would take a drug again as soon as I could find some. The inside of my arms hurt me badly and I couldn't bend them. Then the psychoanalyst came, the one who had said I needed calcium. He asked me many questions again, but I was too weak to answer much. I heard later that he went home and killed himself. It still makes me sad today. Anyone can be mistaken and he was a very nice man. Janot was very nice to me also, but as I was getting less fuzzy and starting to be able to focus my eyes again, I felt that deep inside she was angry with me. It had been difficult to avoid publicity, and Léon Blum should never have had any scandal around him. I had endangered Léon Blum. No one knows what the papers would have invented if they had gotten hold of such a story. Thank God it was a carefully kept secret among close friends.

As I lay in bed I realized that in my heart I had really asked too much of Janot. She had enough on her hands, being the wife of a famous man. She couldn't take care of me. I had wanted her to do everything for me, to replace Georges, to take care of Dominique, and to provide entirely for me. It was high time, if I were going to go on living, for me to begin taking care of myself and of my child, by myself.

So that was it.

I was in my early twenties and was lying half dead in bed, trying to reconstruct my life, trying to grow up and become a woman, a mother. Until that moment I had been a child. I had married and had given birth to a baby, but I had remained a child. Now I had to make the choice of going back to death or to start to live.

I wasn't sure I could do either.

❦ *Epilogue*

My Lodz grandmother had arrived from Canada at about that time. I hadn't seen her since we had left Portugal. My last image of her was a small, round figure standing with my tall, white-bearded grandfather, waving as the *Neuralia* slowly pulled away from the last free shores of Europe.

Now she was back with us. She had buried the tall grandfather in a cemetery in Montreal. She was all alone, a little old woman, a survivor from another world, the world of middleclass Polish Jews, where people owned fine stores, read Yiddish literature, the ladies played mah-jongg and lived in large apartments, complaining about their peasant maids, secure in their tight community, isolated in their own state within a state. How many millions had there been before that September in 1939?

There she was in my parents' house, admiring her greatgranddaughter. She was back from the wars, back from halfway around the world, still alive—the only one left from her own family in Poland. She had aged a great deal. She was in her seventies by this time and had lost her plumpness and was now a small, skinny woman, her hair as gray as her face, her voice very different. It was her voice that I couldn't get over. She had some fancy Canadian false teeth and they had changed her speech. The sounds seemed to stick against the false enamel denture before coming out of her mouth in strange, cavernous tones.

My parents had prepared my childhood bedroom for her, upstairs—the room where Dominique slept too. It was the room where I had spent years doing homework, reading Alexandre Dumas, then Paul Claudel, the room where I had sat giggling with Annie and Monique, the room where I had refused Emile's marriage proposal on the grounds that I was going to become a nun.

My grandmother and my daughter had their beds there now. My father had four generations of women under his roof and he took charge of them with as much warmth and patience as ever.

For several years "Baba" lived with my parents. Each Jewish holiday my father took Baba to the synagogue, and every year at Passover my father made a Seder for her at our house. Baba prepared all the ritual food and my father read the Haggadah in Hebrew. Baba loved my father, I think, more than she had ever loved anyone in her life. With my Catholic parents she lived a life that was becoming more and more religiously Jewish each year. She, who had never been more than a once-a-year observant, was now an old Jewish woman, reading religious stories in Yiddish as her own grandmother had read them, sitting in an armchair, a shawl over her now-skinny shoulders, an image from the past. She had always been tyrannical, but now she became more so with age. Yet she seemed extraordinarily well adjusted to life in an artist's studio, among French intellectuals. She enjoyed my parents' Christmas trees as they enjoyed her Seders. It was a refreshing and hopeful sight to see a Jew like my father and a Jew like my grandmother together. They were so tolerant, so eager to please each other. She often quarreled with my mother when her pride in her cooking was insulted by my mother's total ignorance of that art, or when a sheet was displaced in the neat piles she made in the cupboard. She complained a lot when it was too hot or too cold, or if the Italian *femme de ménage* who had worked for my parents since 1945 had not dusted her many mementos properly. But when it came to religion, she had a wonderful tolerance—more than tolerance. She had completely accepted my father's conversion;

for her, he could do no wrong. It was something she didn't understand but which she never criticized. She gave him the same respect and liberty that he gave her and, one day when she was very old she died peacefully in his arms and was buried with a Jewish ceremony in my parents' burial plot at Bagnolet.

During the next two years I traveled extensively with Meyer Levin in connection with two films he made in Palestine and in Europe. That is how, one rainy day in October 1947, I was sitting in our American station wagon as it drove slowly through Lodz's main street. How strange it was. I was back in Poland. The last time I had been there I had been ten years old and my father had said to me, "Don't cry, darling, you'll be back soon."

Now I was back. It was gray everywhere, rain was falling, and the city looked poor. Of course it didn't look at all the way I remembered it. But I had the address and when we got there and I looked up, I recognized the building and my grandparents' apartment with the balconies, only before there had been a signboard about the fur store on the balcony. Now the sign was gone. Meyer stopped the car and said, "Let's go in." We asked the others in the car to wait and entered the building. We started climbing the stairs, but I stopped halfway up. I said, "No, I don't want to," and walked back downstairs. Meyer couldn't understand it. Didn't I want to see my grandparents' apartment? I had told him so much about my childhood there, about the fur store, the tall porcelain stoves, the big kitchen. Didn't I want to have a look, to see how it was now? But when I had started up the stairs and had seen the peeling walls and dirty landings, I knew that I didn't want to replace the images in my memory with new images that would destroy the others.

We walked out onto the street again. I looked up and saw my aunt's windows directly opposite. But no one waved.

In the fall of 1948, a young American arrived in Paris. He had been a pilot during World War II and had flown many times over Germany.

One day he walked into the U.S. Embassy in Paris and handed over his passport. He told the astonished consul that he didn't wish to be a U.S. citizen anymore. He was fed up with any form of nationalism or patriotism: he wished to become a world citizen.

His name was Gary Davis, and a few days later I was in the public gallery of the United Nations Assembly when Gary Davis interrupted a speech going on downstairs, stood in the gallery, and shouted his opposition to the Assembly's useless and bureaucratic ways. He said that the people of the world had had enough of wars and frontiers. He was speaking for the people who wanted to be citizens of a united world.

Paris was electrified. Three years after a horrible war, thousands of people responded emotionally to this appeal. Every newspaper carried stories about him, every radio station tried to interview him. When he made a public appearance at the Salle Pleyel, the hall was jammed and people stood outside in a pouring rain, for blocks, trying to get in. Not only French people, but also Belgians, Swiss, English, Germans, and Italians responded enthusiastically. Something new was awakening, which could replace individual patriotism by a larger concept.

In Paris French intellectuals as well as the man in the street came to Gary Davis, Jean-Paul Sartre, Camus, *l'Abbé* Pierre, and others, poets and painters and musicians.

For me, he represented hopes and ideas which had been planted in me since I was born. We had come to a period in history in which we had to transcend our individual patriotic loyalties to a race or a nation; we would have to become world citizens and world brothers not only if we wanted the world to survive, but also if we wanted to grow up as human beings. To be a member of one nation was to stand on one step. We all had stood on that step. But the steps were part of a flight of stairs. We had to climb those stairs to reach the platform at the top.

That platform was world citizenship. Total world unity.

✿ In 1958 we were spending the year in Israel, Meyer and I, and we had been married for ten years. We were planning to bring my mother and father to Israel where they would stay with our children—Dominique, Gabriel, and Mikael—while we traveled around the world.

My father was so happy. He would see Israel. This had always been his dream. Since childhood, when Bialik and Ushiskin had come to my father's house, Marek had wanted to go to the Holy Land one day. Now I was making that dream possible. We wrote letters and made plans.

About a month before my parents were to come to Israel, my father had to undergo a simple operation. He thought it would be better for him to have it done before going to Israel, so he would be in good shape to stay with his grandchildren and visit the country. He was operated on successfully in a Paris hospital. The day before he was to leave the hospital, three weeks after the operation, on December twenty-seventh, 1958, Meyer arrived in Paris from New York. When he heard that my father was still in the hospital, he went to see him there on a Saturday evening. Meyer was leaving for Israel the next day. He sat next to my father's bed and they talked of the approaching trip and of my father's last sculpture. My father told Meyer that he felt it wasn't quite finished yet and that he wanted to work on it some more after he came home. It was a large piece of olive wood which he had worked into an elongated figure with raised arms. The arms had been formed from the roots of the tree. My father's name for the sculpture was *Libera Me*. Meyer left him and went back to his hotel.

Early the next morning, Sunday, the hospital priest brought communion to my father. He looked well, but as the nurse was helping him to dress, he had a heart attack. He started choking and the nurses rushed to him with oxygen. He was very much loved by them all and they rushed around and fussed over him, and called the doctor.

My father started breathing again and his face once more took on a peaceful expression. He looked around at the nurses and said, "I feel better. I thank everybody. *Remerciez tout le monde.*" Then he died, like Moses, before seeing the Promised Land.

A Note on the Type

This book is set in Granjon, a type named in compliment to
ROBERT GRANJON, *type cutter and printer—in*
Antwerp, Lyons, Rome, Paris—active from 1523 to 1590.
The boldest and most original designer of his time,
he was one of the first to practice the trade of type founder
apart from that of printer. This type face was designed by
GEORGE W. JONES, *who based his drawings on a type used by*
CLAUDE GARAMOND (1510–61) *in his beautiful French books,*
and more closely resembles Garamond's own type than do
any of the various modern types that bear his name.